EARS

FROM

HARVESTED SHEAVES

OR

DAILY PORTIONS

SELECTED FROM THE WORKS OF

J. C. PHILPOT
BY HIS DAUGHTERS

The words of the wise are as goads, and as nails fastened by the masters of assemblies, which are given from one shepherd. – Ecclesiastes 12. 11.

A word spoken in due season, how good is it! – Proverbs 15. 23.

Fifth Edition
2015
Gospel Standard Trust Publications
12(b) Roundwood Lane,
Harpenden, Herts. AL5 3BZ. England

First Edition 1884
Second edition 1896
Reprinted about 1927 and 1940
Reprinted 1962
Reprinted 1977
Reprinted 1990
Third Edition Re-set and Reprinted 2003
Fourth Edition 2005
Fifth Edition 2015

ISBN 978-0-903556-23-1

Managed and Manufactured by
Jellyfish Solutions Ltd.

PREFACE

It is nearly 120 years since J. C. Philpot's daughters, following the death of their father, made this selection from his sermons, and arranged them as daily readings. How apt was the title they chose *Ears from Harvested Sheaves;* for we believe that many a gleaner in the gospel field has found day by day in these pages a few "handfuls of purpose" (Ruth 2. 16)!

Over the years there have been several reprints and there is still a steady demand for the book, both in England and in other countries. So, the last edition being completely sold out, we are pleased once more to present *Ears from Harvested Sheaves* to the Christian reader.

Times have changed; but how J. C. Philpot would have been gratified to know that, even in the 21st century his writings are still loved by (to use his oft-repeated words) "the living family of God"!

B. A. Ramsbottom
December 2004

"The soul's best, truest safeguard is love. Men fall into error because they never really loved the truth which they profess. Once love the truth, and error never more can have a place in your heart."

EARS FROM HARVESTED SHEAVES;

or

DAILY PORTIONS

January 1

"So teach us to number our days, that we may apply our hearts unto wisdom." – Psalm 90. 12.

Casting our eyes back upon the year now past and gone, are there no mercies which claim a note of thankful praise? It is sweet to see the Lord's kind hand in providence, but sweeter far to view his outstretched hand in grace. Are we then so unwatchful or so unmindful of the Lord's gracious hand in his various dealings with our soul as to view the whole past twelve months as a dead blank in which we have never seen his face, nor heard his voice, nor felt his power? "Have I been a wilderness unto Israel? a land of darkness?" (Jer. 2. 31,) the Lord tenderly asks. Has he been such to us also for twelve long and weary months? What! No help by the way, no tokens for good, no liftings-up of the light of his countenance, no visitations of his presence and power, no breakings-in of his goodness for all that long and dreary time – for dreary it must indeed have been for a living soul to have been left and abandoned of the Lord so long! If not blessed with any peculiar manifestations of Christ, with any signal revelations of his Person and work, blood and love, grace and glory, for such special seasons are not of frequent occurrence, have we not still found him the Way, the Truth, and the Life? If we have indeed a personal and spiritual union with the Son of God, as our living Head, there will be communications out of his fulness, a supplying of all our need, a drawing forth of faith, hope, and love, a support under trials, a deliverance from temptations, a deepening of his fear in the heart, and that continued work of grace whereby we are enabled to live a life of faith on the Son of God.

January 2

"Set thee up waymarks, make thee high heaps; set thine heart toward the highway, even the way which thou wentest." – Jeremiah 31. 21.

To look at the past is often a blessed encouragement for the future. If we are travellers in the way Zionward, we shall have our various waymarks. A conspicuous call, or a signal deliverance, or a gracious manifestation of Christ; a promise applied here, or a marked answer to prayer there; a special blessing under the preached word; a soft and unexpected assurance of an interest in the blood of the Lamb; a breaking in of divine light when walking in great darkness; a sweet sip of consolation in a season of sorrow and trouble; a calming down of the winds and waves without and within by, "It is I, be not afraid" (Matt. 14. 27) – such and similar waymarks it is most blessed to be able to set up as evidences that we are in the road. And if many who really fear God cannot set up these conspicuous waymarks, yet they are not without their testimonies equally sure, if not equally satisfying. The fear of God in a tender conscience, the spirit of grace and of supplications in their breast, their cleaving to the people of God in warm affection, their love for the truth in its purity and power, their earnest desires, their budding hopes, their anxious fears, their honesty and simplicity making them jealous over themselves lest they be deceived or deluded, their separation from the world, their humility, meekness, quietness, and general consistency often putting to shame louder profession and higher pretensions – these and similar evidences mark many as children of God who cannot read their title clear to such a privilege and such a blessing. But whether the waymarks be high or low, shining in the sun or obscure in the dawn, the virgin of Israel is still bidden to "set them up," and to "set also her heart toward the highway, even the way by which she came."

January 3

"And I, if I be lifted up from the earth, will draw all men unto me." – John 12. 32.

Wherever Jesus is graciously and experimentally manifested to the soul, and made known by any sweet revelation of his glorious Person, atoning blood, and finished work, a secret yet sacred power is put forth, whereby we are drawn unto him, and every grace of the Spirit flows toward him as towards its attractive centre. Thus Jeremiah speaks of the saints of God as coming and singing in the height of Zion, and *flowing* together to the goodness of the Lord (cf Jer. 31. 12). And thus Isaiah speaks to the church of God, "Then thou shall see, and *flow* together, and thine heart shall fear [or as the word rather means, shall 'palpitate' with love and joy], and be enlarged" (Isaiah 60. 5). This view of Christ by faith is what the apostle speaks of to the Galatians, as Jesus evidently set forth before their eyes (cf Gal.3. 1). As thus set before our eyes, he becomes the object of our faith to look at, ("Look unto me and be ye saved, all the ends of the earth" Isaiah 45. 22); "the altogether lovely, (Song of Solomon 5. 16)" to whom love flows; and the Intercessor within the veil in whom hope effectually anchors. As, then, the blessed Lord is revealed to the soul by the power of God, his glorious Person held up before the eyes of the spiritual understanding, his blood and righteousness discovered to the conscience, and his suitability to all our wants and woes experimentally manifested, the blessed Spirit raises up a living faith whereby he is looked unto and laid hold of, and thus he becomes precious to all that believe in his name.

January 4

"Wilt thou shew wonders to the dead? shall the dead arise and praise thee? Shall thy lovingkindness be declared in the grave? or thy faithfulness in destruction?" – Psalm 88. 10, 11.

This is not the language of a soul dead in trespasses and sins, but it is the breathing of a living soul struggling and grappling with death. What a difference there is, where there is life working in and under death, and where death reigns absolutely! between the quickened soul and that in which there is nothing but death, death without one spark of spiritual life, death without one ray of heavenly teaching. There is no groan, no sigh, no lamentation, no piteous inquiry, no pouring out of the heart before God, where the soul is utterly dead, any more than there is life and breath in a corpse in the tomb. But wherever life is implanted in the soul from the Fountain of life, that life groans under death. It sighs from out of the grave; it gasps for breath, under the corpse which overlies it; and seeks to heave itself up from that dead weight, from that superincumbent mass of carnality which clasps it in its rigid and chilling embrace; it endeavours to uplift and extricate itself from that body of sin and death which spreads its cold and torpid mass all round it so that it is unable to arise. Do you know the workings of life in this way? the heavings, the gaspings, the uprisings of the life of God in your soul, pressed, overlain, overwhelmed, and all but suffocated by that carnal, dead, barren, earthly, devilish nature, which lies as a weight upon you? Depend upon it if you have never known what it is to gasp and pant and groan and sigh under the weight of a body of sin and death, you know nothing of the vital operations of the Holy Ghost in your conscience.

January 5

"Give strong drink unto him that is ready to perish, and wine unto those that be of heavy hearts." – Proverbs 31. 6.

The wise mother of king Lemuel gave her son gracious directions when she spake these words. It is when we begin to feel the misery into which we have been cast by sin, and thus become ready to perish, and of heavy hearts, that the pure wine of gospel grace is suitable to our lost condition. As the holiness and justice of God are discovered to the conscience, and we are made to see and feel the depths of the Adam fall, we look out of ourselves for a salvation which we could not find in our fallen nature or in our deeply corrupt and unbelieving heart. When, then, we obtain by living faith a view of the Son of God as a Mediator between God and men, when we see by the eye of faith the blood of the cross, and the full and complete atonement which he, as the Lamb of God, made for sin, then we heartily embrace him "who of God is made unto us wisdom, and righteousness, and sanctification, and redemption" (1 Cor.1. 30). We see and feel that there is salvation in him and in no other (cf Acts 4. 12); and as this salvation is seen to be worthy of God and suitable to us, as it answers all the demands of God's holy law, and glorifies it by rendering it an obedience as far excelling ours as heaven excels earth, and God surpasses man, we embrace it as our justifying righteousness and covering robe, from the eyes of him who, out of Christ, is a consuming fire (cf Heb. 12. 29).

January 6

"That ye be not slothful, but followers of them who through faith and patience inherit the promises." – Hebrews 6. 12.

Patience is necessary in order to prove the genuineness and reality of faith. The Lord generally – I may say invariably – does not accomplish his purposes at once. He usually – I might say almost invariably – works by gradations. Is not this the case in creation? Do we see the oak starting up in all its gigantic proportions in one day? Is not a tiny acorn committed to the ground; and is not the giant oak, whose huge limbs we admire, the growth of a century? Men and women are years growing up to their full stature. So spiritually. "He that believeth shall not make haste" (Isaiah 28. 16). Faith in the soul is of slow growth for the most part; for the Lord takes care that every step in the path shall be tried by the perplexities and difficulties that surround it. And he has appointed this that it may be a means of distinguishing the faith of God's elect from the faith of those who have a name to live while dead. They apostatize and turn away from the faith. Like the stony-ground hearers, they believe for a time, but in temptation fall away. The various hindrances of nature, sense and reason, sin, the devil, and the world get the better of them; thus they turn back, often give up all profession of religion, and die in their sins. But the Lord's people cannot so die. Their faith is of a lasting nature, because what God doth he doth for ever. Thus their faith stands every storm and endures for ever.

January 7

"To be carnally minded is death; but to be spiritually minded is life and peace." – Romans 8. 6.

Just in proportion as our heart and affections are engaged on heavenly objects, shall we feel a sweet savour of heaven resting upon our spirit; and as we can only give back what we receive, every going forth of divine life from the soul below is but the fruit and effect of the incoming of that life from above. Christ is our life above (cf Col. 3. 4); and as he by his Spirit and grace maintains the life of faith in the soul, it manifests itself in gracious actings upon himself. Without this spirituality of mind, religion is but a mere name, an empty mask, a delusion, and a snare. God does not take into heaven, into the fulness of his own eternal bliss, those whom he does not love, and who do not love him. It is a prepared people for prepared mansions. And this preparedness for heaven, as an inward grace, much consists in that sweet spirituality of mind whereby heavenly things become our only happiness, and an inward delight is felt in them which enlarges the heart, ennobles the mind, softens the spirit, and lifts the whole soul, as it were, up into a holy atmosphere in which it bathes as its choice element. This is "life", not the cold, dead profession of those poor carnal creatures who have only a natural faith in the Lord Jesus Christ and the truths of his gospel; but that blessed life which shall never die, but live in the eternal presence of God when earth and all it holds shall be wrapped in the devouring flames. And it is "peace" – the Redeemer's dying legacy – whereby, as he himself fulfils it, he calms the troubled waves of the soul, stills every rebellious movement, and enthrones himself in the heart as The Prince of Peace.

January 8

"I cried unto thee; save me, and I shall keep thy testimonies." – Psalm 119. 146.

If you know anything for yourself inwardly and experimentally of the evils of your heart, the power of sin, the strength of temptation, the subtlety of your unwearied foe, and that daily conflict betwixt nature and grace, the flesh and the spirit, which is the peculiar mark of the living family of heaven, you will find and feel your need of salvation as a daily reality. Think not that the only salvation to be felt and known is salvation past - salvation accomplished by the blood-shedding and death of the Son of God. There is salvation present - an inward, experimental, and continual salvation communicated out of the fulness of Christ as a risen Mediator. Don't you want to be daily and almost hourly saved? But from what? Why, from everything in you that fights against the will and Word of God. Sin is not dead in you. If you are reconciled and brought near to God; if you have an interest in the precious blood of Christ; if your name is written in the Lamb's book of life, and heaven be your eternal home, that does not deliver you from the indwelling of sin, nor from the power of sin either, except as grace gives you present deliverance from it. Sin still works in your carnal mind, and will work in it till your dying hour. What then you want to be saved from is the guilt, filth, power, love, and practice of indwelling sin.

January 9

"Then said Jesus to those Jews which believed on him, If ye continue in my word, then are ye my disciples indeed; and ye shall know the truth, and the truth shall make you free."
– John 8. 31, 32.

The truth is not known at first in all its sweetness, liberty, and power. We have "to continue in the Word"; it may be at times in very great darkness, distress, exercise, temptation, and trouble; and yet, such has been the power of the Word upon the heart, it cannot, will not let us go. We see and feel the misery of departing from the truth, the wretchedness of getting back into the world, and being entangled in the spirit of it; and what must be the consequence if we leave those things we profess to know and believe, and embrace error or fall into the arms of sin! There is, therefore, a continuance in the Word, – it may be often, as I have said, in much darkness, much exercise, many trials, many temptations: but still we are brought to this point, never to give up the Word which has been made life and spirit to the soul. And though the Lord sometimes may very much hide his face, and we seem to be very poor, dull scholars, and to be much condemned for our unfruitfulness, to know so little of the spirit of the Master, and walk so little in his blessed ways; yet there is a looking unto him, a longing after him, a cleaving to him; and this manifests genuine discipleship. Now, as we still cling, cleave, hang, trust, and hope, we begin to know the truth; it is opened up to the mind, it is made exactly suitable to our state and case; and the wonderful way in which it addresses and adapts itself to our various and pressing wants and necessities becomes more and more manifest.

January 10

"We have an advocate with the Father, Jesus Christ the righteous." – 1 John 2. 1.

This advocacy is here called, as elsewhere, "pleading the cause" of the believer, and is connected with deliverance, for such an advocate can never fail: "O Lord, thou hast pleaded the causes of my soul; thou hast redeemed my life" (Lam. 3. 58). The figure is taken from a lawyer pleading the cause of a criminal, and using his best endeavours to bring him off uninjured. But such advocacy may fail for two reasons: 1. the incompetency of the advocate; or 2. the badness of the cause. But there are no such hindrances to the success of the advocacy of Christ. How he can plead his own sufferings, blood, and obedience. His very Person as the Son of God, and yet son of man, gives unspeakable value and validity to every plea of the great Intercessor. What validity, then, has his intercession in the court of heaven!

It is true that he cannot deny the truth of the charge brought by the accuser of the brethren against his client; but he can present his own meritorious sufferings, and the sorrows he endured for the culprit. On this ground he can stand up as his surety and representative, and plead with the Father that he has suffered in his place and stead. On the firm, solid ground, then, of justice and equity, he can plead on his behalf, "Let him go, for I endured the penalty due to him".

January 11

"Watch and pray." – Mark 13. 33.

There is no keeping up faith except *by prayer and watchfulness.* As prayer declines in the bosom, so does the strength of faith. You may go on neglecting prayer and supplication until every grain of faith seems lost out of your bosom, and may come at last to think you never knew anything of a work of God upon your heart, and have been deceived in believing there was any grace there. By watchfulness also is the love of God maintained. Unless you watch against your besetting sins, against the snares spread for your feet, against the temptations that daily and hourly beset your path, against being overcome by the strength or subtlety of your unwearied foe, you are sure to fall; and if you fall you will bring guilt and bondage, darkness and distress into your mind, and cut off for a time all friendly intercourse with God. Therefore you must pray and watch; for without watchfulness, prayer is of little efficacy. And if we neglect the Scriptures, or read them carelessly, unbelievingly, they will do us little good. They must be read with believing eyes and heart, received as the revelation of God, and must be mixed with faith, or assuredly they will not profit us (cf Heb. 4. 2). The life of God is a very deep, secret, and sacred thing in the soul. God, it is true, will maintain it; he will not leave his work unaccomplished; but unless we read and pray, watch and meditate, wage war against besetting sins, and seek the Lord's face continually, we shall find the strength and power of faith very sensibly decline; and if so, there is no comfortable walking with God.

January 12

"I am the door; by me if any man enter in, he shall be saved, and shall go in and out, and find pasture." – John 10. 9.

There is a finding pasture in providence. A sweet and healthy pasture indeed this is to watch the Lord's providential dealings with us spread through a long series of years. It is seeing the Lord's providential hand which makes the commonest temporal mercies sweet. Every nibble of grass or lock of hay which we can believe to be specially provided for us by the hand of that good Shepherd becomes thereby doubly sweet. But O what pastures in grace has God provided for his hungry sheep! Look at the promises and declarations, the sacred truths and heavenly consolations scattered up and down the Scriptures of truth. But of all spiritual pasture thus provided for the flock, the chiefest is the flesh and blood of the Lord Jesus. This is his own divine declaration: "For my flesh is meat indeed, and my blood is drink indeed" (John 6. 55). And every communication of grace to the soul out of the fulness of Christ, every promise applied with a divine power to the heart, every truth which drops with heavenly savour, every season of encouragement; in a word, every part of God's word which the soul can eat and feed upon is spiritual pasture. Thus the prophet found it of old: "Thy words were found, and I did eat them; and thy word was unto me the joy and rejoicing of mine heart; for I am called by thy name, O Lord God of hosts" (Jeremiah 15. 16).

January 13

"Beloved, think it not strange concerning the fiery trial which is to try you, as though some strange thing happened unto you." – 1 Peter 4. 12.

The "fiery trial", then, is not a strange thing which happens only to a few of the Lord's family, but is more or less the appointed lot of all. Do we not hear the Lord saying to his Zion, "I have chosen thee in the furnace of affliction"? (Isaiah 48. 10) All then that are chosen must pass through the furnace of affliction, and all know experimentally the fiery trial, for by it they are made partakers of Christ's sufferings. But this is indispensable in order to be partakers of his glory. "If so be that we suffer with him, that we may be also glorified together". (Romans 8. 17) Thus they suffer with him, "that, when his glory shall be revealed, ye may be glad also with exceeding joy". (1 Peter 4. 13) And this suffering with and for Christ in the furnace of affliction salts the soul, preserves it from corruption, communicates health, gives it savour and flavour, is a token of interest in the everlasting covenant, and is a seal of friendship and peace with God.

January 14

"Come out from among them, and be ye separate, saith the Lord, and touch not the unclean thing; and I will receive you." – 2 Corinthians 6. 17.

If we are entangled in the love of the world, or fast bound and fettered with worldly anxieties, and the spirit of the world is rife in our bosom, all our profession will be vapid, if not worthless. We may use the language of prayer, but the heart is not in earnest; we may still manage to hold our head high in a profession of the truth, but its power and blessedness are neither known nor felt. To enjoy any measure of communion with the Lord, whether on the cross or on the throne, we must go forth from a world which is at enmity against him. We must also go forth out of self, for to deny it, renounce it, and go forth out of it lies at the very foundation of vital godliness. There must be a mortifying, through the Spirit, of the deeds of the body (cf Romans 8. 13);" a being "alway delivered unto death for Jesus' sake, that the life also of Jesus might be made manifest in our mortal flesh" (2 Corinthians 4. 11); and unless there is a going forth out of self by this self-crucifixion, there is no walking in hand with Christ, no manifest union, no heavenly communion with him; for there can no more be a partnership between Christ, the soul, and self than there can be a partnership between Christ, the soul, and sin.

January 15

"But we have this treasure in earthen vessels, that the excellency of the power may be of God, and not of us." – 2 Corinthians 4. 7.

Be not surprised if you feel that in yourself you are but an earthen vessel; if you are made deeply and daily sensible unto what a frail body God has communicated light and life. Be not surprised if your clay house is often tottering; if sickness sometimes assails your mortal tabernacle; if in your flesh there dwelleth no good thing; if your soul often cleaves to the dust; and if you are unable to retain a sweet sense of God's goodness and love. Be not surprised nor startled at the corruptions of your depraved nature; at the depth of sin in your carnal mind; at the vile abominations which lurk and work in your deceitful and desperately wicked heart. Bear in mind that it is the will of God that this heavenly treasure which makes you rich for eternity should be lodged in an earthen vessel. We are to carry about a daily sense of our base original to hide pride from our eyes. We are to be despised by others; and by none so much as by our own selves. We have ever to feel our native weakness, and that without Christ we can do nothing; that we may be clothed with humility, and feel ourselves the chief of sinners, and less than the least of all saints. We thus learn to prize the heights, breadths, lengths, and depths of the love of Christ, who stooped so low to raise us up so high.

January 16

"Jesus Christ himself being the chief corner stone; in whom all the building fitly framed together, groweth unto an holy temple in the Lord." – Ephesians 2. 20, 21.

Christ is the Head of every member individually, as he is the Head of the whole body collectively. Growth of the body, from babyhood to manhood, is the growth of individual members in the body. If, then, I am a member of the mystical body of Christ Jesus, I shall grow. My growth may be so slow and gradual as to be scarcely perceptible; but it will be growth still. If I have union with Christ, I shall be supplied, at least in some measure, out of his fulness. He is my life, and he has promised, because he lives, I shall live also; and if I live by him, I shall live upon and unto him. Paul could say, "The life which I now live in the flesh I live by the faith of the Son of God" (Galatians 2. 20); and also, "And that he died for all, that they which live should not henceforth live unto themselves, but unto him which died for them, and rose again" (2 Cor. 5. 15). By a sound gospel ministry our souls are fed. Christ is set before us in all the glories of his divine Person, in his Deity and Sonship, and in all the graces of his suffering humanity. His covenant characters and gracious relationships, his blood and righteousness, his death and resurrection, his ascension and glorification at the right hand of the Father, his present mediation and intercession, his sympathy as a once suffering but now exalted high Priest, and his ability to save to the uttermost all that come to God by him, are brought before us as the food of our faith; and as we taste that he is gracious, and feed upon him as the bread of life, there is a growth into him.

January 17

"Love is of God; and every one that loveth is born of God, and knoweth God. He that loveth not knoweth not God; for God is love." – 1 John 4. 7, 8.

If ever you have loved Jesus with a pure affection; if ever you have felt him near, dear, and precious to your soul, that love can never be lost out of your heart. It may lie dormant; it does lie dormant. It may not be sweetly felt in exercise; but there it is. "If any man love not the Lord Jesus Christ, let him be Anathema Maranatha" (1 Cor.16. 22). You would be under this curse if the love of the Lord Jesus Christ were to die out of your heart. But this love is often sleeping. When the mother sometimes watches over the cradle and looks upon her sleeping babe with unutterable affection, the infant knows not that the mother is watching its slumbers; but when it awakes, it is able to feel and return its mother's caresses. It is so with the soul sometimes when love in the heart is like a babe slumbering in the cradle. But as the babe opens its eyes, and sees the mother smiling upon it, it returns the smiles, and stretches forth its arms to embrace the bending cheek; so when the eyes of the soul are opened to see the smiling face of Jesus stooping to imprint a kiss of love, or drop some sweet word into the heart, and there is a flowing forth toward him of love and affection – this is the power of love.

January 18

"For we are his workmanship." – Ephesians 2. 10.

Consider what is here declared of those who are saved by grace through faith – that they are God's *"workmanship"* – the fruit and product of his creative hand. All, then, that we are and all that we have that is spiritual, and as such acceptable to God, we owe to the special operation of his power. There is not a thought of our heart, word of our lips, or work of our hands, which is truly holy and heavenly, simple and sincere, glorifying to God or profitable to man, of which he is not by his Spirit and grace the divine and immediate Author. How beautifully is this expressed by the church of old, and what an echo do her accents find in every gracious heart: "But now, O Lord, thou art our Father; we are the clay, and thou our potter; and we all are the work of thy hand" (Isa. 64. 8). How suitable, how expressive is the figure of the clay and the potter. Look at the moist clay under the potter's hand. How soft, how tender, how passive is the clay; how strong, how skilful are the hands which mould it into shape. As the wheel revolves, how every motion of the potter's fingers shapes the yielding clay, and with what exquisite skill does every gentle pressure, every imperceptible movement impress upon it the exact form which it was in his mind to make it assume. How sovereign was the hand which first took the clay, and as divine sovereignty first took it, so divine sovereignty shapes it when taken into form.

January 19

"For they that are after the flesh do mind the things of the flesh; but they that are after the Spirit the things of the Spirit." – Romans 8. 5.

None but those who are partakers of a heavenly birth feel heavenly realities to be their choice element, holy things their sweetest meditation, and the solemn worship of God their supreme delight. Look at this mark as a touchstone of divine life; for to be spiritually-minded a man must be spiritual, and to be spiritual he must have received the Spirit and been made a partaker of that "kingdom of God which is righteousness, and peace, and joy in the Holy Ghost" (Rom. 14. 17). Have you never found in reading the Scriptures a sweet peace distil over your soul, as the glorious promises came forth one after another as the stars in the evening sky, each one brighter and clearer, and you felt a blessed persuasion of your interest in them? When at the throne of grace, favoured with liberty of spirit and access to your heavenly Friend, have you never felt the peace of God to drop into your heart, and like oil upon the waves, to allay every rising of rebellion within? Have you never found, in conversing with the saints of God, a sweet flowing of heart to heart and soul to soul, and felt that such conversation left behind a blessed fragrance upon your spirit? Have you never in the house of prayer had your heart and affections drawn up to the things of God; and as you sat and heard Christ, his Person and work, his grace and glory set forth, faith was drawn out to believe, hope to cast forth its anchor, and love and affection to flow, so that you experienced a spirituality of mind, a heavenly calm, and a holy peace that touched every spring of your soul, and watered it as the river that went out of Eden to water the garden?

January 20

"Then shall we know, if we follow on to know the Lord." – Hosea 6. 3.

To know the Lord is to know experimentally and spiritually the power of Jesus' blood and righteousness; to know our eternal union with him; to know him so as to be led by the Spirit into soul communion with him, that we may talk with him as a man talketh with his friend; to know him so that the secrets of his heart should be revealed to us, and we enter by faith into the length and breadth and depth and height of the love of Christ which passeth knowledge; to know him so as to drink into his spirit, and to have his image stamped by the Holy Ghost upon our souls; to know him as coming down into our hearts out of his glorious sanctuary, filling our souls with his presence and his love; to know him as formed in us the hope of glory, making our bodies his temple, dwelling in us, breathing himself into us, speaking in us, moving as it were every affection of our heart and every faculty of our soul. Thus to know the Lord is the sum and substance of vital godliness. And, as "to know the Lord", implies, as well as comprehends, the knowledge of Jehovah in his Trinity of Persons and Unity of Essence, well may we say that, to know Jehovah the Father in his eternal love, to know Jehovah the Son in his redeeming blood, and to know Jehovah the Spirit in his divine operations and blessed teaching, is the foretaste of bliss below; and to know and see God as he is, is the consummation of bliss above.

January 21

"Behold, we count them happy which endure. Ye have heard of the patience of Job, and have seen the end of the Lord; that the Lord is very pitiful, and of tender mercy." – James 5. 11.

The words translated "endure" and "patience" are the same in the original; and in fact, the example of Job is given as an instance of the happiness of those who endure. The same word is also used by our blessed Lord, where he says, "He that *endureth* to the end shall be saved" (Matt. 10. 22). We have need then of endurance. As he that runs a race needs not so much swiftness as enduring strength to hold out to the end, never to give up as long as he can drag one limb before another; as the British soldier must never suffer himself to be beaten; so it is in the Christian race: we must never give up; we must never say "die"; we must never allow ourselves to be beaten by sin or Satan. If God himself seem to thrust us away from his throne, we must still plead and not take "No" for an answer, like the widow with the unjust judge. O what need we have of patience or endurance still to fight, though the battle be against us; still to run, though we may almost fear to lose the race; and still press forward, in spite of every discouraging circumstance! But if in this way we do the will of God, as he would have us and patience is given to us of which we have such deep need, let us not fear but that we shall receive the promise. "Let us not be weary in well doing; for in due season we shall reap, if we faint not" (Gal. 6. 9). We are bidden therefore to be "steadfast, unmovable, always abounding in the work of the Lord, forasmuch as ye know that your labour is not in vain in the Lord" (1 Cor.15. 58).

January 22

"I the Lord do keep it; I will water it every moment: lest any hurt it, I will keep it night and day." – Isaiah 27. 3.

The Lord Jesus Christ, who lives at God's right hand, has to send down supplies of his grace continually to keep your soul alive unto himself. Without this life being kept up and maintained by these continual supplies of his grace, you cannot pray, or read, or hear the word, or meditate with any feeling or profit. You cannot love the Lord and his blessed ways; you cannot submit to his righteous dealings; or hear the rod and him who appointed it. You may approach his throne but your heart is cold, clouded, and unfeeling; your spirit sinks under the weight and burden of the trials and difficulties that are spread in your path; nor are you able to do anything that satisfies yourself, or that you think can satisfy God. By these painful but profitable lessons, you are experimentally taught that you want the life of Christ as well as the death of Christ, the resurrection of Christ as much as the crucifixion of Christ; Christ as an ever-living, ever-gracious, ever-glorious Mediator, to send down supplies of his love and power into your soul, as much as you needed him to die upon the cross for your redemption.

January 23

"Man's goings are of the Lord; how can a man then understand his own way?" – Proverbs 20. 24.

Does not your heart sometimes quake with fear lest you have nothing but a nominal profession, lest the god of this world be blinding you, and lest your conscience be hardened through the deceitfulness of sin? It is good to have such fears. He who feareth not, who has no solemn apprehensions, no anxious inquiries, who is never exercised with some internal trepidation of soul, it is much to be feared has never known what it is to have "the candle of the Lord searching the inward parts of the belly". (Proverbs 20.27) But if God has quickened your soul into spiritual life, and you have ears to hear, I would just put two questions to you: Have you obtained righteousness by a manifestation of Christ's righteousness? pardon by the application of Christ's blood? love by a shedding abroad of love? deliverance by a discovery of God's outstretched hand? My other question is this – If you have not, and let conscience bear its honest testimony – if you have never experienced righteousness, pardon, love, and deliverance, is there a cry in your soul after them? Is there anything like fervent supplication that God would bestow them? Is there anything of a groan in the depth of your spirit that the Lord would reveal them? These are marks of life; and he that has these marks will have the blessing, because God has quickened him into spiritual life. It may be long delayed, but it will come at last; it will surely come, it will not tarry. (cf Hebrews 10. 37) It may be withheld for wise purposes, and you may have to travel through many a dark season and many an anxious hour, but deliverance is sure; it is reserved for you in Christ, and you are reserved for it, kept by God himself "unto salvation, ready to be revealed in the last time". (1 Peter 1. 5)

January 24

"Hold thou me up, and I shall be safe." – Psalm 119. 117.

We are surrounded with snares; temptations lie spread every moment in our path. These snares and temptations are so suitable to the lusts of our flesh, that we shall infallibly fall into them, and be overcome by them but for the restraining providence or the preserving grace of God. The Christian sees this; the Christian feels this. He has had, it may be, a bitter experience of the past. He has seen how, from want of walking in godly fear, for want of circumspection and standing upon his watchtower, he has been entangled in times past in the snares of death. He has rued the consequences, felt the misery of having slipped and fallen; the iron has entered into his soul; he has been in the prison house, in bondage, in darkness, and death; in consequence of his transgressions he has been "the fool" described in Psalm 107, as "afflicted because of his iniquity," and can re-echo Hart's mournful description of his own miserable folly:

> "That mariner's mad part I played,
> Who sees, yet strikes the shelf."

As, then, a burnt child dreads the fire, so he dreads the consequence of being left for a moment to himself; and the higher his assurance rises and the clearer his views become of the grace of God which bringeth salvation, and of his own interest in it, the more is he afraid that he shall fall. If his eyes are more widely opened to see the purity of God, the blessedness of Christ, and the efficacy of atoning blood, the more also does he see of the evil of sin, and his own weakness and inability to stand against temptation in his own strength. And all these feelings combine to raise up the earnest cry, "Hold thou me up, and I shall be safe".

January 25

"Turn thou us unto thee, O Lord, and we shall be turned; renew our days as of old." – Lamentations 5. 21.

Are you not often destitute of the power to repent, and confess your sins before God? Does not conscience often bring to view a melancholy retrospect of carnal thoughts, wicked desires, vain imaginations, foolish words, frivolous speeches, and all that catalogue of evils, that huge bill which godly fear sometimes files in the court within, as seen in all our departures from the life of God? But are you able to repent? are you able to feel cut to the very heart? are you able to mourn and sigh because conscience brings against you this long indictment? Can you always feel your soul melted down with sorrow on account of it? Are you always able to feel contrition because you are proud, worldly, covetous, everything that is evil, everything that is hateful in God's sight? But, then, there are times and seasons when the Lord is pleased to work upon the conscience, to move and stir the soul, to touch the heart with his gracious finger – then repentance and godly sorrow flow forth. It is with us as with the rock that Moses struck. There was water in the rock; but it required to be struck with the rod before the waters flowed out. So we may have the grace of repentance in our souls; but it requires the divine hand to strike the rock, to cause the waters of godly sorrow to gush forth.

January 26

"And he taught them many things by parables." – Mark 4. 2.

The Scripture employs two beautiful figures to illustrate the reception of the divine testimony.

One is the committing of the seed to the ground, as in the parable of the sower. The husbandman scatters the seed in the bosom of the earth, and the ground having been previously ploughed and reduced to a beautiful tilth, opens its bosom to receive the grain. After a little time the seed begins to germinate, to strike a root downward, and shoot a germ upward; as the Lord speaks, "First the blade, then the ear, after that the full corn in the ear". (Mark 4. 28) This emblem beautifully represents how the testimony of Jesus Christ finds an entrance to the soul, takes root downward and carries a shoot upward. The root downward is into the depths of a tender conscience, and the shoot upward is the aspiration, breathing, and longing of the soul for the living God. The other figure is that of grafting. "Receive," says James, "with meekness the ingrafted word, which is able to save your souls". (James 1. 21) Now when a scion is first put into the stock, after a little time sap begins to flow out of the stock into the scion, and this sap unites the two together. So it is spiritually when the soul receives the testimony of Christ. The testimony of Christ is received into a broken heart, as the scion is inserted into and received by the stock. As, then, life flows out of the stock into the scion, it creates and cements a sweet and blessed union with God's word and him of whom the word testifies. Thus it grows up into a living bough, which brings forth blossoms of hope, leaves of a consistent profession, and fruit of a godly life.

January 27

"And you hath he quickened, who were dead in trespasses and sins." – Ephesians 2. 1.

Death in sin is of course a figure, and must be interpreted as such; for moral death is its meaning, and by moral death we understand the utter absence of everything holy, heavenly, spiritual, and divine; the entire want of participation in, and conformity to the life which God lives as essentially and eternally holy, pure, wise, and good, and for ever dwelling in the glorious light of his own infinite perfections. To be dead, then, is to have no present part or lot with God; no knowledge of him, no faith, no trust, no hope in him; no sense of his presence, no reverence of his terrible Majesty; no desire after him or inclination toward him; no trembling at his word, no reliance on his promise, no longing for his grace, no care or concern for his glory. It is to be as a beast before him, intent like a brute on satisfying the cravings of lust, or the movements of mere animal passion, without any thought or concern what shall be the issue, and to be bent upon carrying out into action every natural purpose, as if we were self-creators, and were our own judge, our own lord, and our own god. O what a terrible state is it to be thus dead in sin, and not to know it, not to feel it, to be in no way sensible of its present danger and certain end, unless delivered from it by a mighty act of sovereign power! It is this want of all sense and feeling which makes the death of the soul to be but a representation of, as it is the prelude to, that second death which stretches through a boundless eternity.

January 28

"And hath raised us up together, and made us sit together in heavenly places in Christ Jesus." – Ephesians 2. 6.

There is a distinction between being quickened together with Christ and being raised up together with him. Is not this true in the experience of God's people? To be quickened into divine life, to be convinced of sin, to have the fear of God planted deeply in the soul, is the commencement of a work of grace. But this is not a deliverance, not a being raised up out of darkness, bondage, doubt, guilt, and fear. This is not a knowledge of Christ, and the power of his resurrection; this is not a full coming out of the dark and silent tomb into the glorious light and warmth of day. But here is the great blessedness of a mystical union with the Lord Jesus Christ that, as by virtue of interest in him there is a partaking of the benefit and power of his having been quickened, so there is a partaking in the benefit and power of his having been raised up. God does not quicken a soul into divine life to let it remain in the dark tomb of doubt, fear, guilt, and bondage. In raising up Christ there was not only a pledge of the spiritual, but a virtual resurrection of the members of his body. Liberty, then, the liberty of the gospel, deliverance from all doubt and fear, the manifestation of pardon and peace, the shedding abroad of the love of God in the heart, are blessings as much assured to the members of Christ's mystical body as their first quickening into spiritual life, and both are equally assured them in Christ their covenant Head.

January 29

"A wise man feareth, and departeth from evil: but the fool rageth, and is confident." – Proverbs 14. 16.

I believe no living soul can be satisfied with a notional religion: though a miserable backslider, and driven into the fields to feed swine, he cannot feed on their husks, but sighs after the bread of his Father's house. The eyes being enlightened to see the nature of sin, the justice and holiness of God, and the miserable filthiness of self, the quickened soul can find no rest in anything short of a precious discovery of the Lamb of God; and the more that the soul is exercised with trials, difficulties, temptations, doubts, and besetments of various kinds, the more does it feel its need of that blood of sprinkling that speaketh better things than that of Abel. What is a Christian worth without inward trials and exercises? How dead and lifeless are our prayers; how cold and formal when the soul is not kept alive by inward exercises! Where are the sighs, cries, groanings, wrestlings, and breathings of a soul that is at ease in Zion? The world is everything and Christ nothing, when we become settled on our lees, and are not emptied from vessel to vessel; but inward exercises, fears, straits, and temptations stir up the soul to cry, and pray, and beg for mercy. The certainty, the power, the reality of eternal things are then felt, when guilt, and wrath, and fear, and disquietude lay hold of the soul. Mere notions alone of Christ, false hope, a dead faith, a presumptuous confidence, a rotten assurance, are all swept away as so many refuges of lies, when the soul is made to feel its nakedness and nothingness, its guilt and helplessness before God. And thus all these inward exercises pave the way for discoveries of Christ – those views of his blood and righteousness, that experimental acquaintance with his Person, love, grace, and work, which is life and peace.

January 30

"The King's daughter is all glorious within; her clothing is of wrought gold. She shall be brought unto the king in raiment of needlework." – Psalm 45. 13, 14.

This is a beautiful description of the bridal garments of the church as the queen. The gold was to be wrought into her clothing, the raiment to be of needlework, intimating that her robe of justifying righteousness was wrought, as it were, as in needlework, stitch by stitch; yet that every thread was embroidered with gold. Here we have the thread of the humanity in union with the gold of Deity, and yet each in such close union that the thread is but one. In gold thread the beauty, the value is in the gold; yet how close the union. Gold by itself could not be made into embroidery. So Deity cannot suffer, bleed, or die; but humanity can in union with it. Thus, as our blessed Lord went through the whole work which the Father gave him to do, his Deity, being in union with his obeying, suffering humanity, stamped each successive movement, as he went through it, with all the value and validity of Godhead. It is this union of Deity with humanity which made the work of redeeming love so unspeakably glorious, and so meritoriously efficacious. As Hart says:

> "Almighty God sighed human breath."

It is indeed a mystery; but "great is the mystery of godliness: God was manifest in the flesh" (1 Timothy 3. 16). O glorious mystery!

> "The highest heavens are short of this;
> 'Tis deeper than the vast abyss;
> 'Tis more than thought can e'er conceive,
> Or hope expect, or faith believe."

January 31

"Who worketh all things after the counsel of his own will."
– Ephesians 1. 11.

By these words the apostle brings before our eyes God's omnipotent power as carrying into effectual performance the counsel of his own will towards the objects of his distinguishing favour. An especial blessing is couched in this. Next to a believing view of the purposes of God's grace, and a sweet persuasion of our interest in them, nothing is more strengthening and encouraging than a realising apprehension of the power of God to carry them into full execution. Feeling, as we do, our own miserable helplessness, sinking under the pressure of our daily weakness, mourning over continual failures, and grieving on account of perpetual backslidings, encompassed by foes, and distressed by fears, how strengthening it is to our faith, thus tried to the utmost, to believe that he who has purposed has power to perform. This persuasion of the almighty power of God was the support and strength of Abraham's faith, which bore him up in the face of seeming impossibilities, and whereby he gave glory to God (cf Rom. 4. 18-21). When, then, as walking in the steps of the faith of Abraham, we can look up believingly to the God and Father of the Lord Jesus Christ, as we behold sovereign grace in his heart, and infinite wisdom in his mind, so we see almighty strength in his arm, and thus become sweetly persuaded that all which his loving heart feels, his infinite wisdom directs, and his omnipotent power can execute.

February 1

"They shall come with weeping, and with supplications will I lead them." – Jeremiah 31. 9.

Until God is pleased to pour out upon us the spirit of grace and of supplications, we cannot worship him aright; for God is a Spirit, and those who worship him must worship him in spirit and in truth; nor can we without this spirit offer up that spiritual sacrifice which is acceptable to him through Jesus Christ. When this spirit has been once given and kindled in a believer's breast, it never dies out. It is like the fire upon the brazen altar, which was first given by the Lord himself from heaven, and concerning which God gave this command: "The fire shall ever be burning upon the altar; it shall never go out" (Lev. 6. 13). This fire might sink low; it might be covered with the ashes of sacrifice, but it never was suffered to go out for want of supply of fuel. So at times it may seem to you as if there were scarcely any spirit of prayer alive in your bosom; and you may feel as destitute of a spirit of grace and of supplications as if you had never known its lively movements and actings. But you will find it drawn out from time to time by circumstances. You will be placed under peculiar trials, under which you will find no relief but at a throne of grace; or God will in tender mercy breathe again upon your soul with his own gracious Spirit, and by his quickening breath will revive, I will not say kindle, for it is not gone out, that holy fire which seemed to be buried under the ashes of corruption, that inward spirit of prayer which he gave you at regeneration, and which will never cease till it issue in everlasting praise.

February 2

"But the anointing which ye have received of him abideth in you, and ye need not that any man teach you: but as the same anointing teacheth you of all things, and is truth, and is no lie, and even as it hath taught you, ye shall abide in him." – 1 John 2. 27.

Have you ever had a solitary drop of this holy anointing oil fall upon your heart? One drop, if it be but a drop, will sanctify you for ever to the service of God. There was not much of the holy anointing oil used for the service of the tabernacle, when we consider the size and quantity of what had to be consecrated, for Moses had to anoint therewith the whole of the tabernacle of the congregation, as well as all the vessels, with all their various appurtenances. When he went through the sacred work, he touched one vessel after another with a drop of oil; for one drop sanctified the vessel to the service of the tabernacle. There was no repetition of the consecration wanted; it abode. So if you ever had a drop of God's love shed abroad in your heart, – a drop of the anointing to teach you the truth as it is in Jesus; a drop to penetrate, to soften, to heal, to feed and give light, life, and power to your soul – you have the unction from the Holy One; you know all things which are for your salvation, and by that same holy oil you have been sanctified and made meet for an eternal inheritance.

February 3

"If ye then be risen with Christ, seek those things which are above, where Christ sitteth on the right hand of God." – Colossians 3. 1.

How many there are even of those who desire to fear God who are kept down by the world, and to whom it has not lost its attractive power; who are held fast, at least for a time, by worldly business, or entangled by worldly persons or worldly engagements. Their partners in business or their partners in life; their carnal relatives or their worldly children; their numerous connections or their social habits; their strong passions or their deep-rooted prejudices, all bind and fetter them down to earth. There they grovel and lie amid, what Milton terms,

> "The smoke and stir of this dim spot
> Which men call earth;"

and so bound are they with the cords of their sins that they scarcely seek deliverance from them, or even desire to rise beyond the mists and fogs of this dim spot into a purer air, so as to breathe a heavenly atmosphere, and rise up with Jesus from the grave of their corruptions. But if, as members of his mystical body, they are already risen with Christ, as it was not possible for the Head to be holden of death when God loosed the pains thereof (cf Acts 2. 24), so neither shall they ever be buried in the grave of carnality and worldliness. They must rise spiritually if they rose mystically. If interested in the *reality* of Christ's resurrection, they must know the *power* of Christ's resurrection.

February 4

"Let us be glad and rejoice, and give honour to him: for the marriage of the Lamb is come, and his wife hath made herself ready." – Revelation 19. 7.

We want two things to take us to heaven; *a title to it,* and *a meetness for it.* Our only *title* to heaven is the blood and righteousness of the Son of God - that blood which "cleanseth us from all sin." (1 John 1. 7) and that righteousness which justifies us from all things from which we could not be justified by the law of Moses. (cf Acts 13. 39) Nothing unclean or defiled can enter heaven. This is God's own testimony: "There shall in no wise enter into it anything that defileth, neither whatsoever worketh abomination, or maketh a lie; but they which are written in the Lamb's book of life" (Rev. 21. 27). But besides the *title,* there must be also a *meetness* for this heavenly city, according to the words of the apostle: "Giving thanks unto the Father, which hath made us meet to be partakers of the inheritance of the saints in light" (Col.1. 12). Whilst here below, then, we must learn to sing some notes of that joyous anthem which will issue in full, uninterrupted harmony from the hearts and lips of the redeemed in the realms above, when that glorious company will ever cry, "Alleluia; Salvation, and glory, and honour, and power, unto the Lord our God" (Rev. 19. 1). If we are to sit down among those blessed ones who are called unto the marriage supper of the Lamb, not only must we be "arrayed in fine linen, clean and white, for the fine linen is the righteousness of saints" (Rev. 19. 8), but we must have had "the kingdom of God, which is righteousness, and peace and joy in the Holy Ghost" (cf Rom. 14. 17), set up in our hearts.

February 5

"Grace and truth came by Jesus Christ." – John 1. 17.

The way to learn truth is to be much in prayer to the Lord Jesus Christ; as you lie upon your bed, as engaged in your daily occupation, to be from time to time looking up to the Lord himself as he sits upon his throne of grace, and be begging of him to teach you himself, for he is the best teacher. The words which he speaks, "they are spirit and they are life" (John 6. 63). What he writes upon our hearts is written in characters which will

"stand every storm and live at last."

We forget what we learn from man, but we never forget what we learn from Jesus. Men may deceive; Christ cannot. You can trust no minister really and fully. Though you may receive truth from his lips, it is always mixed with human infirmity. But what you get from the lips of Jesus, you get in all its purity and power. It comes warm from Him; it comes cold from us. It drops like the rain and distils like the dew from his mouth; it comes only second-hand from ours. If I preach to you the truth, I preach indeed as the Lord enables me to speak. But it is he who must speak with power to your souls to do you any real good. Look then from me; look beyond me, to him who alone can teach us both. By looking to Jesus in the inmost feelings of your soul, you will draw living truth from out of his bosom into your own, from his heart into your heart, and thus will come feelingly and experimentally to know the blessedness of his own declaration: "I am the truth". (John 14. 6)

February 6

"Persecuted, but not forsaken; cast down, but not destroyed." – 2 Corinthians 4. 9.

You may be cast down by many doubts and fears, and lose the sense of the Lord's love to your soul, but you cannot lose the reality, nor is your faith destroyed by the hottest flame. It is like gold; the fire melts away and separates the dross and tin, but never touches the gold. In your hottest trials your faith will not have lost a particle. Neither will your hope be destroyed, however you may be cast down about your state or standing; for not a particle of hope, or of any one Christian grace can ever be lost. They may seem to suffer diminution as the apostle speaks, "If a man's work shall be burned, he shall suffer loss" (1 Cor. 3. 15); but it is no real loss, – it is merely the dross taken away, that he may come forth a vessel for the finer. The work of the Holy Spirit is as indestructible as the work of Christ; and thus every grace which he implants in the soul remains there untouched, unharmed in all its divine integrity. Love, patience, submission, and humility all remain unhurt in the flame, though the dross which is mixed with them is taken from them that they may shine all the brighter. Thus though you may be plunged into the hottest fires, you will not be destroyed, any more than the three children were destroyed in Nebuchadnezzar's furnace, or Jonah in the belly of the whale.

February 7

"In whom also after that ye believed, ye were sealed with that holy Spirit of promise, which is the earnest of our inheritance until the redemption of the purchased possession, unto the praise of his glory." – Ephesians 1. 13, 14.

Heaven is a prepared place for a prepared people. Holy are its inhabitants, holy its employments, holy its enjoyments. Therefore unless we know something of the teaching, the work, and witness of the Holy Spirit here, and are made partakers of a new, holy, spiritual, and heavenly nature we have no pledge or earnest of our interest in the inheritance of the saints in bliss. A carnal, unsanctified, unholy, unrenewed heart is utterly incapable of understanding, entering into, longing after, and loving an inheritance incorruptible, undefiled, and that fadeth not away. But every holy desire, heavenly affection, gracious longing, spiritual enjoyment, and believing hoping, loving, looking unto and cleaving to the Lord of life and glory by the power of the Holy Spirit, are all so many pledges and earnests of an interest in the glorious inheritance of the saints in light. The love, the joy, the peace, the calm tranquillity, and holy acquiescence in the will of God; the ravishing views of the glory of Christ which change the soul into the same image, from glory to glory; the delight felt in him, and the whole surrender of the heart and affections to the blessed Lord as the chiefest of ten thousand and the altogether lovely, are all so many earnests of the inheritance above, as being heaven begun below.

February 8

"These all died in faith." – Hebrews 11. 13.

When death came it did not rob them of their faith. They held with their believing hand in death every truth which they had held with their believing hand in life. It is in death that the gospel is such a blessing when held by a believing hand. What should we do upon a dying bed, with all our sins staring us in the face in all their awful magnitude, accused by Satan, condemned by conscience, terrified by a holy law, and frowned upon by an indignant God? What must be our end upon the bed of death if we had nothing to look to but a God who is a consuming fire, with nothing but the bitter recollection of past sins to agonise the mind and distress the conscience? O, if ever faith is needed, it will be needed then; if ever the gospel embraced, embraced then; if ever Christ looked to, looked to then; if ever laid hold of by the hand of faith, laid hold of then! Now if you know what faith is, and your faith has embraced the Son of God, and love has worked by that faith, and Christ in that faith has made himself precious, that faith will never give up the ghost in a dying hour. False faith will then expire; but the faith of God's elect will not leave you in the hour of death, but support you as you pass through the dark valley, and land you safe on that happy shore where faith is turned into sight, hope into enjoyment, and love abides in its fullest manifestation.

February 9

"Wherefore the rather, brethren, give diligence to make your calling and election sure; for if ye do these things, ye shall never fall." – 2 Peter 1. 10.

Have you any testimony to your effectual calling? Has grace indeed laid hold of your heart? O that you might know more fully – more powerfully – what a blessed hope of eternal life is laid up in the bosom of this heavenly calling, that it might cheer and encourage you to press on more and more to realise all that is given you in Christ, both for here and hereafter, in present grace and in future glory! In knowing what is the hope of their effectual calling, the saints of God learn that this hope embraces all things which are made theirs in Christ, whether life or death, or things present or things to come, that all are theirs; and for this blessed and all-sufficient reason, that they are Christ's and Christ is God's. It is by making sure our calling that we make sure our election, - for the one is the sure evidence of the other; and thus, if doubt and uncertainty hang over our calling, the same doubt and uncertainty must rest upon our election to eternal life. But as these doubts and fears are removed by the spirit of wisdom and revelation in the knowledge of Christ, and we can clearly see and fully believe that the grace of God effectually called us out of darkness into his marvellous light, then we see by faith what is laid up in the bosom of this calling, and what a glorious hope of eternal life is thereby afforded as an anchor of the soul, both sure and steadfast, and thus abound in hope through the power of the Holy Ghost.

February 10

"Lord, all my desire is before thee; and my groaning is not hid from thee." - Psalm 38. 9.

Many of the Lord's people cannot clearly read their names in the book of life; many are the doubts and fears that work in their bosom whether the Lord really has begun a work of grace upon their souls, and whether they truly are among the Lord's living family. But this thing they must know - whether at times and seasons they can lie in humility at the footstool of mercy, and appeal to a heart-searching God - "All my desire is before thee." They must know whether they ever fell down in humility and brokenness of heart before the divine Majesty, and felt these living desires going out of their bosom into the ears of the Lord of Sabaoth; and whether they can, with honesty, uprightness, and godly sincerity, say to the Lord in the language before us, "O

Lord, all my desire is before thee." "Thou seest my heart, and knowest everything that passes in my troubled breast." If you can say *that,* it is a mark of life. If that has been the feeling of your heart from time to time, you find it was the same feeling that worked in the bosom of David. And God saw fit that it should be written by the finger of the Spirit, and placed upon solemn record for the consolation and encouragement of souls in similar circumstances.

February 11

"My doctrine shall drop as the rain, my speech shall distil as the dew, as the small rain upon the tender herb, and as the showers upon the grass." – Deuteronomy 32. 2.

In the falling of the natural dew there is something soft, still, and gentle. We therefore read, "We will light upon him as the dew falleth on the ground" (2 Sam. 17. 12), that is, stealthily and unseen. It does not rush down like the pelting hail, but falls stilly and often imperceptibly; so that we scarcely know it has fallen, till we go out in the morning and see every blade of grass tipped with the sparkling dew-drops; by these bright gems we know that dew has fallen during the still hours of the night. So spiritually, the kingdom of God is not in noise, rant, or wild excitement. The Lord was not in the strong wind, nor in the earthquake, nor in the fire, but in the still small voice (1 Kings 19. 11, 12). And thus there may be a great deal of religious fire, but no presence of God felt; fleshly passions worked up into a storm, but no "still small voice" speaking to the conscience; a very earthquake of natural convictions, but no inward "demonstration of the spirit and of power." But when the spiritual dew falls, it drops gently, softly, and stilly into the heart, and it is only known by the sweet and blessed effects it produces.

Dew also has *a softening effect,* especially in warm climates, where it falls very copiously. We therefore read, "Thou makest it soft with showers" (Psalm 65. 10). It does not tear up the ground as with thunder-bolts, but by moistening and softening penetrates into the soil. And thus the dew of God's grace moistens and softens the heart, humbles, dissolves, and fertilises it; not by tearing it up with the thunderbolts of wrath and condemnation, but by dropping gently and stilly into it, so as to melt it into contrition, meekness, and godly sorrow before the throne of mercy and grace.

February 12

"In whom we have redemption through his blood, even the forgiveness of sins." – Colossians 1. 14.

Of all spiritual blessings made known to the soul by the power of God "a knowledge of salvation by the remission of sins" is the hardest to be obtained, and most prized when got. How many poor tried, exercised, distressed souls are at this very moment sighing and crying for the manifestation of this one blessing. These well know, and some of them by the painful experience of many years' hard bondage and travail, how hard it is to get forgiveness sealed on their heart. Not that it is really hard on the part of God now to forgive, that is, in experimental manifestation; for it is already done to and for all the elect of God: "And you, being dead in your sins and the uncircumcision of your flesh, hath he quickened together with him, *having forgiven* you all trespasses" (Colossians 2.13); and again, "In whom we *have"* (not "shall have," but "have," that is, now have) "redemption through his blood, the forgiveness of sins." Though he may not be able to lay hold of it for himself, appropriate it as a personal blessing, and feel sweetly and blessedly assured, in his own heart and conscience, of the forgiveness of all his sins; yet every quickened soul is really forgiven all his trespasses, past, present, and to come. It is one of the spiritual blessings with which he has been blessed, already blessed, in heavenly places in Christ Jesus.

February 13

"O send out thy light and thy truth: let them lead me; let them bring me unto thy holy hill, and to thy tabernacles." – Psalm 43. 3.

A living man cannot, in his right mind, bear the idea of standing still, that is to say, standing still so as to have no spiritual work going on within; and still less can he bear the idea of going backward. He wants to go forward. He is often dissatisfied with his state; he feels how little he knows; he is well certified of the shallowness of his attainments in the divine life, as well as of the ignorance and the blindness that are in him; and therefore, labouring under the feeling of his own shortcomings for the past, his helplessness for the present, and his ignorance for the future, he wants to go forward wholly and solely in the strength of the Lord, to be led, guided, directed, kept, not by the wisdom and power of the creature, but by the supernatural entrance of light and truth into his soul. The mercy-seat is continually covered with clouds; God hideth himself, and he cannot behold him; the truth seems obscured so that he cannot realise it. He often cannot find his way to Christ; he cannot perceive the path of life, nor whether his feet are in that path. He sees so few marks of grace in his soul, and feels so powerfully the workings of sin and corruption; he finds so few things for him and so many things against him, that he often staggers, and is perplexed in his mind, and seems almost to come to a feeling in his heart, that he is destitute of the grace of God altogether, that the secret of the Lord is not with him, but that he is a hypocrite in Zion, who has never had even the beginning of wisdom communicated to his soul.

February 14

"Which hope we have as an anchor of the soul, both sure and steadfast, and which entereth into that within the veil." – Hebrews 6. 19.

Anchors, you know, are made of different sizes. You may walk in the Queen's Dockyard, and there you may see anchors for a boat, and anchors for a three-decker. Yet all anchors are made in the same way, and are designed for the same purpose; and the little anchor that holds the boat is as useful and as much an anchor as that which holds the three-decker. So spiritually. There is hope in the heart of the babe. But the hope in the heart of a babe is but as the anchor of a boat; yet it holds that babe as firmly as the anchor holds the boat to which it is moored. But as the Lord increases hope, he increases the size of the anchor; and as the vessel and its anchor always bear a proportion to each other, so when he enlarges the size of the anchor he increases the size of the ship. Nay more, as he increases the size of the ship, he increases its burden, for these two are proportionate. Thus hope takes a more vigorous hold within the veil; it enters more deeply into the presence of God; it takes a firmer grasp of covenant engagements, electing love, the immutability of God's purposes, and the unchangeable nature of the great eternal I AM. Have you not felt at times your hope sweetly enlarged, so that it almost attained to the "full assurance of hope?" Scarcely a cloud remained between you and God; and you believed you should ride triumphantly into the haven of bliss and peace; and having these blessed sensations in your heart, you could part with life itself at that moment to fall into the embrace of your God.

February 15

"Then opened he their understanding, that they might understand the Scriptures." – Luke 24. 45.

Blessed opening, when He that hath the key of David puts in his hand by the hole of the door, and opens our heart to receive his own word. Then when we go to the Word of Truth, after it has come to us, our fingers drop with sweet-smelling myrrh upon the handles of the lock. It is said that "the dead shall hear the voice of the Son of God, and they that hear shall live." O, to hear the voice of the Son of God in our hearts! Surely it shall make our dead hearts, cold frames, withering hopes, drooping love, dying faith, languishing prayers, and fainting minds live; yea, revive as the corn and grow as the vine. What is all religion without a divine beginning, middle, and end, commencing, carried on, and accomplished with a heavenly power, supernatural life, and spiritual unction? Well may we be ashamed and sick of, and sorry for all our thoughts, words, and works, all our knowledge and profession that have not stood, or do not stand, in the power, teaching, and wisdom of God. All our talk has been but vain babbling, our prayers lip-service, our preaching wind and vanity, our profession hypocrisy, our knowledge the worst kind of ignorance, and all our religion carnality or delusion, if they have not been divinely communicated. Sir Isaac Newton, the wisest philosopher, is said to have remarked to one who congratulated him on his knowledge, "I have been like a little child on the sea-shore taking up a little water in a shell when the vast ocean of truth lay undiscovered before me." Much more may a spiritual man feel how little, how nothing he knows of the unsearchable riches of Christ, and the boundless stores of wisdom hid in them.

February 16

"I neither received it of man, neither was I taught it, but by the revelation of Jesus Christ." – Galatians 1. 12.

When I speak of a revelation of Christ, I am not contending for anything visionary. Dreams, voices, appearances in the air, sights and sounds, crosses in the sky, and apparitions at the bedside, I must leave to others. I believe that for the most part they are the portion of visionaries and enthusiasts, for we have all these in the visible Church of God, as well as Pharisees and hypocrites, Arminians and Antinomians. I will not indeed deny that the Lord may have wrought by them in some peculiar instances, as in the cases of Augustine and Colonel Gardiner. But taking the generality of God's people and the ordinary mode of divine operation, the revelation of Christ to the soul is a gracious internal discovery by the power of the Spirit, revealing him to the eyes of faith. Nothing is seen or heard by the bodily senses; and yet his glorious Person is as much seen, and his voice as much heard, as though eye and ear beheld his glory and listened to his words. It is altogether of grace, wholly heavenly and divine, and therefore nature, sense, and reason have no place here. It is a divine bringing into the heart of the power and presence, grace and glory, love and blood of Christ in a way that may be felt but never described. Under these spiritual operations and influences, – for it is the Spirit's work to take of the things of Christ and reveal them to the soul; it is his covenant office to testify of Jesus, – under these sacred influences, divine anointings, and gracious operations, Christ is made known unto the heart and looked unto, according to his own word: "Look unto me and be ye saved, all the ends of the earth."

February 17

"And we know that all things work together for good to them that love God, to them who are the called according to his purpose." – Romans 8. 28.

To look at all our varied circumstances; and then to believe that if we are the lovers of God, all things we experience are working together for our spiritual good, what a view does it give us of the wisdom, grace, and power of a wonder-working God! And we are to measure this good, not by what the creature thinks, but by what God himself has declared to be good in his word, and what we have felt to be good in our soul's experience. Have your trials humbled you, made you meek and lowly? They have done you good. Have they stirred up a spirit of prayer in your bosom, made you sigh, cry, and groan for the Lord to appear, visit, or bless your soul? They have done you good. Have they opened up those parts of God's word which are full of mercy and comfort to his afflicted people? Have they stripped off the covering that is too narrow? Have they made you more sincere, more earnest, more spiritual, more heavenly-minded, more convinced that the Lord Jesus can alone bless and comfort your soul? They have done you good. Have they been the means in God's hand of giving you a lift in hearing the preached word, of opening your ears to hear none but the true servants of God, those who enter into a tried path, and describe a gracious experience? Have they made the Bible more precious to you, the promises more sweet, the dealings of God with your soul more prized? They have done you good.

February 18

"Let Israel hope in the Lord: for with the Lord there is mercy, and with him is plenteous redemption." – Psalm 130. 7.

Let Israel hope in the Lord. Has she ceased to hope in the creature? Does she despair of salvation from any other source or quarter but the blood of the Lamb? Is she crying, sighing, longing, panting, and begging of the Lord to appear in her soul? "Let Israel," then, "hope in the Lord: for with the Lord there is mercy." He will not spurn his waiting Israel from his feet; he will not smite her with the lightnings of his wrath; he will show mercy to the poor, guilty sinner that comes with dust upon his head, clothed with sackcloth and ashes, mourning and lamenting his vileness before the Lord. There is no wrath in the bosom of the Lord against *him;* there is mercy, pardoning mercy in the bosom of Jehovah for Israel; therefore "let Israel hope in the Lord." If Israel look to herself, she cannot have one grain of hope; if she look to the law, she cannot have one ray of expectation; or if she look to an arm of flesh, none can do her good. But if Israel look "to the hills from whence cometh her help" – to God the Father, in his electing love – to God the Son, in his redeeming blood – to God the Spirit, in his sanctifying work; if Israel is thus enabled to anchor within the veil, thus to "hope in the Lord," her hope shall not be cut off, shall not be disappointed; it shall not be as "the hope of the hypocrite," a spider's web, that the first gust of eternal displeasure shall for ever sweep away.

February 19

"But of him are ye in Christ Jesus, who of God is made unto us wisdom, and righteousness, and sanctification and redemption." – 1 Corinthians 1. 30.

Consider what heavenly blessings there are for those who have a living union with the Son of God. Everything is provided for them that shall be for their salvation and their sanctification: not a single blessing has God withheld that shall be for their eternal good. View them as foolish, ignorant, unable to see the way, puzzled and perplexed by a thousand difficulties, harassed by sin, tempted by Satan, far off upon the sea. How shall they reach the heavenly shore? God, by an infinite act of sovereign love, has made his dear Son to be their *"wisdom"* so that none shall err so as to err fatally; none shall miss the road for want of heavenly direction to find it or walk in it. Their glorious Head, who is in heaven, is made of God unto them wisdom on earth to bring them to their heavenly inheritance. He opens up his word to their heart; he sends down a ray of light into their bosom, illuminating the sacred page and guiding their feet into the way of truth and peace. If they wander, he brings them back; if they stumble, he raises them up; and whatever be the difficulties that beset their path, sooner or later some kind direction or heavenly admonition comes from his gracious Majesty. Thus the wayfaring man, though a fool, does not err in the way of life, for his gracious Lord being his *"wisdom"* leads him safely along through every difficulty until he sets him before his face in glory.

February 20

"It is the spirit that quickeneth; the flesh profiteth nothing: the words that I speak unto you, they are spirit, and they are life." – John 6. 63.

It is through the word that the soul in the first instance is cleansed. It is by the word that the soul is begotten again unto eternal life. It is, too, by the word applied to the heart that the blessed Spirit from time to time keeps alive communion with the Lord Jesus Christ. Is it not so in vital experience? Some passage of Scripture drops into the soul, some promise comes warm into the heart, and as it comes it makes way for itself. It enters the heart, breaks down the feelings, melts the soul, and draws forth living faith to flow unto and centre alone in the "altogether lovely." There are many times and seasons when the word of God is to us a dead letter; we see and feel no sweetness in it. But there are other times, through mercy, when the word of God is made sweet and precious to us; when we can say, with the prophet of old, "Thy words were found, and I did eat them; and thy word was unto me the joy and rejoicing of mine heart" (Jer. 15. 16). It was so in the case of David. He says, they are "more to be desired than gold, yea, than much fine gold; sweeter also than honey and the honeycomb" (Psalm 19. 10). When this is felt, the sure effect is to bring the soul into communion with the Lord Jesus, who is the true word of God, and makes use of the written word to draw us near unto himself.

February 21

"Who loved me, and gave himself for me." – Galatians 2. 20.

Many of the saints of God may not be so highly favoured as to take up into their lips Paul's language of strong, personal assurance. They may hope, and at times may rise beyond a hope, into a sweet confidence, by the shining in of the Sun of righteousness, that the Son of God has loved them, and given himself for them. But the strength of Paul's persuasion and the full expression of his confidence so far outstrip both their assurance and their language, that many real saints of God confess they come short both in heart and tongue. Yet their coming short of this blessed certainty as an enjoyed reality in the heart, and as a declared confidence by the mouth – for conscience and tongue must move together where God works – does not affect the fact. Clouds and mists sometimes obscure the sun, but they do not blot him out of the sky. So the mists and fogs of unbelief may obscure the Sun of righteousness, yet they do not blot him out of the spiritual hemisphere. He still loved you and gave himself for you who believe in his name, though you may not be able to rise up to the faith of Paul, or speak with the same fulness of assurance. The bud has the same union with the vine as the branch, but not the same strength of union; the babe is as much a member of the family as the grown-up son, but has not the same knowledge of its relationship; the foot is as much a part of the body as the eye or the hand, though it has not the same nearness to the head, or the same honours and employments.

February 22

"I will bear the indignation of the Lord, because I have sinned against him." – Micah 7. 9.

It is a view of our sins against God that enables us to bear the indignation of the Lord against us and them. As long as we are left to a spirit of pride and self-righteousness, we murmur at the Lord's dealings when his hand lies heavy upon us. But let us only truly feel what we rightly deserve: that will silence at once all murmuring. You may murmur and rebel sometimes at your hard lot in providence; but if you feel what you deserve, it will make you water with tears of repentance the hardest cross. So in grace, if you feel the weight of your sins, and mourn and sigh because you have sinned against God, you can lift up your hands sometimes with holy wonder at God's long-suffering mercy that he has borne with you so long; that he has not smitten you to the earth, or sent your guilty soul to hell. You will see, too, that the heaviest strokes were but fatherly chastenings; that the rod was dipped in love; and that it was for your good and his glory that it was laid on. When this sense of merited indignation comes into the soul, then meekness and submission come with it, and it can say with the prophet, "I will bear the indignation of the Lord, because I have sinned against him." You would not escape the rod if you might. As Cowper says,

"Bastards may escape the rod,
  Sunk in earthly, vain delight;
But the true-born child of God
  Must not, would not if he might."

February 23

"He hath made with me an everlasting covenant, ordered in all things, and sure." – 2 Samuel 23. 5.

O the blessedness of having a manifest interest in the blood of the covenant, and thus to have a testimony that God has made a covenant with his dear Son upon our behalf; that our names are written in the book of life; and that Christ is our Mediator at the right hand of the Father! What are all earthly blessings compared with this? What are health and strength and riches and all the goods of this life; what is everything that the carnal heart can desire or the covetous mind grasp; what is all compared with an interest in the everlasting covenant, and in the love and blood and righteousness of the Lord the Lamb? What is earth, with all its attractions, compared with an interest in the precious, precious blood of a dying Jesus? You will find it so when you come to lie upon a bed of languishing and pain; when the cold drops of sweat stand upon your forehead, and the last enemy is about to grasp you by the throat. What will your anxious strivings to have something and be something more than you have or are, – aye, I may add, your successes, – what will they do for you then? Only be so many ghastly spectres of the past to terrify and alarm your conscience, to see what shadows you have been seeking to grasp to the neglect of solid substance. But in that solemn hour to have a testimony from God of pardon and peace, will make smooth a dying bed, will calm all anxious fears, and will take you safe through the dark valley of the shadow of death.

February 24

"As sorrowful, yet alway rejoicing." – 2 Corinthians 6. 10.

Though the Christian in himself is sorrowful, and has reason to be so all the day long, yet so far as he has any views by faith of the Lord Jesus Christ, any good hope through grace, or any manifestation of his Person, work, blood, and love, he may be always rejoicing. Nay, his very sorrow opens up a way for joy. There is no room in a worldly heart for spiritual joy, for the Lord gives joy in sorrow. When the heart is sunk in gloom and fear, and doubt and distress take possession of the mind, when family afflictions, or painful bereavements, or trying circumstances fill the heart with grief and dismay, that is the very time for the Lord to pour joy into the soul. As afflictions abound, so do consolations. Sorrow and joy are linked together as night and day, as sun and moon, as heaven and earth. Without sorrow there can be no joy, for joy is its counterpoise. If you had everything your heart could desire, what room would there be for spiritual joy? But when all sources of earthly joy dry up, and there is nothing but sorrow and trouble before you in this world, as long as life remains; when you are afflicted in body, poor in circumstances, tried in your family, distressed in your mind, and there is nothing but grief and misery, – then you have room made in your heart to receive the sweet consolations of God's grace.

February 25

"He will keep the feet of his saints." – 1 Samuel 2. 9.

The Lord sees his poor scattered pilgrims travelling through a vale of tears, journeying through a waste howling wilderness, a path beset with gins, traps, and snares in every direction. How can they escape? Why, the Lord keeps their feet, carries them through every rough place, as a tender parent carries a little child; when about to fall, graciously lays the everlasting arms underneath them, and when tottering and stumbling, and their feet ready to slip, mercifully upholds them from falling altogether. Thus the Lord keeps the feet of his saints. But do you think that he has not different ways for different feet? The God of creation has not made two flowers, nor two leaves upon a tree alike; and will he cause all his people to walk in precisely the same path? No; we have each our path, each our besetment, each our trials, each peculiar traps and snares laid for our feet. And the wisdom of the all-wise and only-wise God is shown by his eyes being in every place, marking the footsteps of every pilgrim, suiting his remedies to meet their individual case and necessity, appearing for them when nobody else could do them any good; watching so tenderly over them, as though the eyes of his affection were bent on one individual; and carefully noting the goings of each, as though all the powers of the Godhead were concentrated on that one person to keep him from harm.

February 26

"Tell me, O thou whom my soul loveth, where thou feedest, where thou makest thy flock to rest at noon: for why should I be as one that turneth aside by the flocks of thy companions? If thou know not, O thou fairest among women, go thy way forth by the footsteps of the flock, and feed thy kids beside the shepherds' tents." – Song of Solomon 1. 7, 8.

If you say that you want food and rest, to know Christ for yourself and to enjoy his presence and love, the Lord gives you two directions to attain to the enjoyment of these two blessings: 1. to tread in the footsteps of the flock, to walk in the way in which the saints of old have walked, in the path of tribulation and faith; 2. if you are favoured in any way to live within reach of the shepherds' tents, and have the privilege of hearing the gospel preached in its purity and power, to bring your kids in your arms beside the tent, and to put them down to feed on the juicy herbage. And be assured that if you come to the shepherds' tents with a prayerful spirit and a hungry soul, begging of God to open your heart to receive the word with power, and to crown it with his blessing, sooner or later you will find food and rest. But these things go together. If you want food you will go where it is to be got; if you want rest you will go where it is to be obtained. You will get neither in the world. But as you get food and rest beside the shepherds' tents you will find that it is really and truly Jesus himself who feeds, and Jesus himself who makes you lie down and rest. The shepherds are but servants. Christ is the Bridegroom, and he alone has the Bride. The shepherds' joy is to bring the sheep to Christ that they may find food and rest in him; and as your heart receives the joyful sound, and you feel the power of God's truth in your soul, there will be a doing what Christ bids as well as enjoying what Christ reveals.

February 27

"Remembering without ceasing your work of faith, and labour of love, and patience of hope in our Lord Jesus Christ, in the sight of God and our Father." – 1 Thessalonians 1. 3.

It is air and exercise that keep the body healthy. So it is spiritually. The graces of the Spirit need to be often exercised and well aired to keep them healthy – aired with the pure breath of heaven, and exercised with the operations of the Holy Ghost drawing them forth into activity and energy. And just as in nature a man gains health and strength by using his limbs and working his muscles, so in spiritual things these graces of the Spirit gain strength by use and exercise. Faith by working hard, hope by enduring much, and love by labouring long in the face of difficulties, become each more strengthened, more confirmed, more active, healthy, and energetic. It is a false faith to sleep all day in the sluggard's armchair; it is the hypocrite's hope who endures nothing for Christ's sake; it is love in lip and tongue and name that undergoes no labour to please the beloved Object. Look at these things in the light of your own experience. See whether you can find not only faith in your heart, but its work; not only hope, but its patience; not only love, but its labour. The Apostle remembered without ceasing their work of faith, and labour of love, and patience of hope. His eye was fixed not so much upon their Christian graces as their exercises of them, and as he saw their faith working diligently, their hope suffering patiently, and their love labouring unweariedly for the glory of God and the good of his people, he was satisfied they were the graces of the Spirit wrought in their heart by a divine power.

February 28

"God, who is rich in mercy." – Ephesians 2. 4.

Mercy well suits a sensible sinner; and the riches of God's mercy especially suit those who are brought down in real extremity of soul to see and feel how abundant he must be in mercy, how overflowing in the exceeding riches of his grace, that they may venture to entertain a hope of an interest in it, as freely coming down to them in their low and lost estate. We know mercy, feelingly and experimentally, before we know love. Love is first in God, but it is not first in our experience of it; nor do we go to God when made first to feel our need of mercy, as if we were objects of his love, or could venture to entertain the remotest idea that a God so holy could love a sinner so vile; but we go to him to obtain mercy, as the Apostle speaks: "Let us therefore come boldly unto the throne of grace, that we may obtain mercy, and find grace to help in time of need" (Hebrews 4. 16). Mercy is the first thing sought for at the throne of grace; and when this mercy is obtained, then grace is ever after continually sought for to help the helpless and dependent soul in every time of need, which need lasts all through life; and until grace is swallowed up in glory. Was not the simple plea for mercy the publican's prayer in the temple, "God be merciful to me a sinner"? And such has been the prayer of all and every one, whose heart has been touched by the finger of God.

February 29

"And hath put all things under his feet." – Ephesians 1. 22.

How vast, how numerous, how complicated are the various events and circumstances which attend the Church of God here below, as she travels onward to her heavenly home! But if all *things* as well as all persons are put under Jesus' feet, there cannot be a single circumstance over which he has not supreme control. Everything in providence and everything in grace are alike subject to his disposal. There is not a trial or temptation, an affliction of body or soul, a loss, a cross, a painful bereavement, a vexation, grief or disappointment, a case, state or condition, which is not put under Jesus' feet. He has sovereign, supreme disposal over all events and circumstances. As possessed of infinite knowledge he sees them, as possessed of infinite wisdom he can manage them, and as possessed of infinite power he can dispose and direct them for our good and his own glory. How much trouble and anxiety should we save ourselves, could we firmly believe, realise, and act on this! If we could see by the eye of faith that every foe and every fear, every difficulty and perplexity, every trying or painful circumstance, every looked-for or unlooked-for event, every source of care, whether at present or in prospect, are all, as put under his feet, at his sovereign disposal, what a load of anxiety and care would be often taken off our shoulders!

March 1

"Now our Lord Jesus Christ himself, and God, even our Father, which hath loved us, and hath given us everlasting consolation and good hope through grace, comfort your hearts, and stablish you in every good word and work." – 2 Thessalonians 2. 16, 17.

When the Lord is pleased to apply a promise, drop in a word of encouragement, speak home an invitation with power, he administers thereby consolation. It comforts the drooping heart; it speaks peace to a guilty conscience. And this consolation is "everlasting consolation;" for it flows from nothing less than such a source, viz. the eternal love of God; and flows onward to an everlasting ocean of infinite delight. Any intimation of an interest in the everlasting love of God is a blessing beyond all price; for the Lord never gives any such intimation but as a certain pledge, earnest, and foretaste of immortal bliss. He can neither disappoint nor deceive. Once blest, blest for ever. We may indeed for a long time together cease to enjoy the comfort, and even may fall into the greatest depths of darkness and confusion, so as to lose sight of almost all our evidences; but the foundation of God standeth sure: "The Lord knoweth them that are his." The river of eternal love may seem to flow by and not reach our breast, so high are the banks and hidden out of sight the stream. Still if ever it has watered our soul it will be one day "waters to swim in" of eternal delight.

March 2

"Blessed be the God and Father of our Lord Jesus Christ, who hath blessed us with all spiritual blessings in heavenly places in Christ." – Ephesians 1. 3.

O, could our faith but embrace a little, were it only a little, and O, could we daily come and drink but a few drops of this pure fountain of immortal joy, in the sweet realisation of being blessed, already blessed, fully blessed, unalterably, irreversibly blessed with all spiritual blessings in Christ, what strength and consolation would it impart to our often cast-down soul! Look at the words; examine them again and again; think over in your mind, one by one, the spiritual blessings that you most covet. Is it pardon? Is it peace? Is it the love of God shed abroad in your heart? Is it the spirit of adoption, enabling you to cry, "Abba, Father"? Is it communion with God? Is it the enjoyment of his presence and smiles? Is it deliverance from every doubt and fear? Is it a large measure of his fear in your heart, a subduing of all your lusts and corruptions, a godly, holy life, and a happy, blessed death? Are not these the spiritual blessings which you prize above house or land, wife or husband, child or relative, or any earthly good? With these, then, and with every other are you blessed, already blessed, if you are one of God's saints and a believer in Christ Jesus. God has not yet to bless you, beyond giving you a foretaste here and the full enjoyment hereafter. He has *already* blessed you with them all in Christ Jesus.

March 3

"Unto you that fear my name shall the Sun of righteousness arise with healing in his wings." – Malachi 4. 2.

Just as the sun rises in the east and gradually mounts up into the meridian sky, dispersing with every ray light, warmth, and gladness; so this blessed Lord Jesus, as the Sun of righteousness, is ever dispersing the beams of his grace and the rays of his favour; and whenever those beams come, and those rays fall, there is light and life, and everything to make the soul holy and happy. Now a man would act very foolishly if, wishing to have light in his room when the sun was shining at noonday, he should shut all the shutters, and strike a match to give him a little light for a few moments. Let us not then be so foolish as to look for happiness or comfort in our own performances when the glorious Sun of righteousness is at the right hand of God, and shining thence upon believing hearts. But when the veil is over the heart, it is like shutters in a room: there is no light to show who, what, or where Jesus is. And then need we wonder that men strike a light and make a fire, that they may "walk in the sparks of their own kindling"? But what is God's word against all such? "This shall ye have of mine hand, ye shall lie down in sorrow" (Isaiah 50. 11).

March 4

"In my Father's house are many mansions; if it were not so, I would have told you. I go to prepare a place for you." – John 14. 2.

O that we could lift our eyes to those blest abodes, those mansions of heavenly bliss, where no sorrow intrudes, where sin is unknown, where tears are wiped from off all faces, where there is no languishing body, no wasting sickness, no pining soul, no doubt, fear, darkness or distress; but one unmingled scene of happiness and pleasure, and the whole soul and body are engaged in singing the praises of God and the Lamb! And what crowns the whole, there is the eternal enjoyment of those pleasures which are at the right hand of God for evermore. But how lost are we in the contemplation of these things; and though our imagination may seem to stretch itself beyond the utmost conception of the mind, into the countless ages of a never-ending eternity, yet are we baffled with the thought, though faith embraces the blessed truth. But in that happy land, the immortal soul and the immortal body will combine their powers and faculties to enjoy to the uttermost all that God hath prepared for those that love him.

March 5

"He that hath an ear, let him hear what the Spirit saith unto the churches." – Revelation 2. 29.

These words extend the message beyond the church to which they were spoken, and address themselves to everyone to whom the word comes, and to whom an ear is given to hear and receive it. Thus each message sent to the churches becomes a message sent person-ally to us. If we have a spiritually circumcised ear, if we are willing to listen to the voice of the Lord, he speaks to us in every message as personally and as distinctly as he spoke to each individual church. It is indeed an unspeakable blessing to have this ear given to us that we may receive in humility, simplicity, and godly sincerity what the Lord speaks in the word of his grace. It is by his word that he knocks at the door of our hearts; and what a blessing he has pronounced on the man who hears his voice and opens the door when he hears the knock, like a fond and affectionate wife when she hears the knock of her husband at the door of his house: "Behold, I stand at the door, and knock: if any man hear my voice, and open the door, I will come in to him, and will sup with him, and he with me" (Rev. 3. 20).

March 6

"Thou hast delivered my soul from death." – Psalm 56. 13.

You may have been delivered from death, as much as David was, but not so fully in the assurance of the deliverance. God may have quickened your soul into life divine; he may have communicated his grace to your heart, and yet you have many doubts and fears whether it be a real work of grace upon your soul. It is not every child of God who has been delivered from death by regenerating grace who can use the words with the confidence expressed here: "Thou hast delivered my soul from death." But I will show you when he can. When God is pleased to bless him with a sense of his pardoning love; when Jesus is revealed to his heart, and manifested with power to his soul; when the blood of sprinkling is applied to purge his conscience from guilt, filth, and dead works, to serve the living God; when the Spirit of adoption is given, and he is enabled to cry, "Abba, Father;" when he can "read his title clear to mansions in the skies" by the witness of the Holy Ghost in his breast that he is a child of God; when he feels the presence of God, and a sweet flowing forth of love and affection to his heavenly Father, – at such favoured seasons as these, he can say in the sweet confidence of faith, "Thou hast delivered my soul from death."

March 7

"Love not the world, neither the things that are in the world." – 1 John 2. 15.

This is a very wide sentence. It stretches forth a hand of vast grasp. It places us, as it were, upon a high mountain, such as the Lord stood upon when tempted of Satan, and it says to us, "Look around you: now there is not one of these things which you must love." It takes us, again, to the streets of a crowded city; it shows us shop windows filled with objects of beauty and ornament; it points us to all the wealth and grandeur of the rich and noble, and everything that the human heart admires and loves. And having thus set before us, as Satan did before our Lord upon the high mountain, the kingdoms of the world, it says, not as he did, "All this will I give you," but, "All this I take from you. None of these things are for you. You must not love one of these glittering baubles; you must not touch one of them, or scarcely look at them, lest, as with Achan, the golden wedge and the Babylonish garment should tempt you to take them and hide them in your tent." The precept takes us through the world as a mother takes a child through a bazaar, with playthings and ornaments on every side, and says, "You must not touch one of these things." In some such similar way the precept would, as it were, take us through the world, and when we had looked at all its playthings and its ornaments, it would sound in our ears, "Don't touch any one of them; they are not yours; not for you to enjoy, not for you even to covet." Can anything less than this be intended by those words which should be ever sounding in the ears of the children of God, "Love not the world, neither the things that are in the world"?

March 8

"And you, being dead in your sins and the uncircumcision of your flesh, hath he quickened together with him, having forgiven you all trespasses." – Colossians 2. 13.

Christ's resurrection was the sure pledge and meritorious cause of the Church's regeneration. The whole body of the elect was "quickened together with Christ," as well as raised up together with him; that is, mystically quickened, as they were mystically raised, quickened in a mystical regeneration of soul, as well as raised up in a mystical regeneration of body. How wonderful is this, that every soul quickened into divine life in time is so because mystically quickened as a member of Christ when he was raised from the dead. View the whole body of the elect as dead in sin. Then view them quickened, one by one, in all their countless multitude, during the whole stretch of time. Consider the power put forth in the regeneration of each individual. Then take a view of the quickening of the dead body of Christ, as prior to the resurrection, and the whole body of the elect mystically quickened together with him. Do you see no act of infinite power, and power in harmony with love and grace here? Where are the eyes of your faith, if you see not this? Where your admiring love, if you do not adore this act of love to the Church, as in union with her covenant Head? Was not that a mighty act of power and love which, at one moment, and by one and the same act, mystically quickened millions of souls which shall live for ever in the presence of God?

March 9

"And thou shall remember all the way which the Lord thy God led thee these forty years in the wilderness, to humble thee, and to prove thee, to know what was in thine heart, whether thou wouldest keep his commandments, or no." – Deuteronomy 8. 2.

When you look back upon the way the Lord has led you these many years in the wilderness, can you not see how circumstance after circumstance, and event after event arose, to prove what was in you; whether godly fear, whether simplicity and sincerity, whether a desire to fear God, whether a dread to offend him, whether the life and power of vital godliness, or whether little else than an empty profession without the life-giving power of God in the soul? What a mercy for you to be able to look back and see how the Lord appeared for you, when without him you must have sunk; when you can feel, to your soul's comfort, that the Lord did uphold you in the trying hour, did appear for you in distressing circumstances, did make bare his right arm when you had no strength of your own, did guide you when you had lost all clue, did bring you safe through all when, without his help, you must have been utterly lost. What a mercy it is to be able, by the actings of living faith (and sure I am, there must be faith in exercise), to look back upon the way, and believe that indeed the grace of God was in your heart, that the Lord proved it, and showed it to be genuine by every circumstance that has taken place.

March 10

"He satisfieth the longing soul, and filleth the hungry soul with goodness." – Psalm 107. 9.

We find the living family of God sometimes set forth under the character of the hungry. Let us see what they are hungering after. Is it pleasure, honour, promotion, respectability? O no; these toys and baubles cannot satisfy the spiritual hunger of a living soul. They cannot hunger after that on which they cannot feed. They hunger then after righteousness, as the Lord said: "Blessed are ye that hunger and thirst after righteousness." They hunger after God himself in his blessed manifestations; they hunger after the bread of life which came down from heaven, that a man should eat thereof and not die. Christ in the letter of the word cannot satisfy their keen appetite. They must feed upon him internally, or their famine still continues. To these hungry, famishing souls, to have Christ in the letter is like a starving beggar standing outside a shop where there is plenty of provisions, and not having a farthing to buy them with. What is Christ in the letter? Will a sight of Christ in the word of God remove the burden of guilt, bring peace into the soul, purge the conscience or subdue the power of sin? Will the mere doctrine of Christ draw up the affections to him, cast out the world, dethrone self, or purify the heart? "Alas!" we say by painful experience, "not one jot, not one jot." But the presence of Christ in the soul can at once do all these things. Thus a hungry, famishing soul can only be pacified by Christ coming into his heart as the hope of glory.

March, 11

"This is the true God, and eternal life." – 1 John 5. 20.

O the blessedness, which eternity itself can never exhaust, of possessing eternal life! There is something to my mind so singularly blessed in the expression "eternal life," that I cannot help dwelling upon it. How the thought, the feeling of it expands the breast! Compared with it, how poor, mean, and low is our temporal life and all its concerns – the short span which God has allotted to us here below! And do observe how our eye is directed by holy John to the true God as being himself eternal life. He is not only the Giver, the Spring, the Subject, the Object of it; He himself is it all. O if he has but quickened our souls by his Spirit and grace, we carry now, even now, eternal life in our breast! for this eternal life is the precious fruit on earth of that eternal life in heaven which was with the Father and was manifested unto us (1 John 1. 2). But how shall we *know* that we have eternal life, you may ask? How do we know that we have natural life? By an inward consciousness that we are alive; by the pulse which beats, the lungs which breathe, the eye which sees, the ear which hears, the tongue which speaks, the hands which feel, by the warm play of blood through our veins, by the thoughts which pass to and fro through our mind. Similarly we know the possession of spiritual life by an inward consciousness of it and by its inward actings. And as where there is spiritual there is eternal life, as we feel the bubblings, springings, risings, and varied movements of this spiritual life in our bosom, we have a testimony that we have also eternal life; that this eternal life is in the Son of God, and from the Son of God has been breathed into and communicated unto our souls.

March 12

"Yet thou, O Lord, art in the midst of us, and we are called by thy name," – Jeremiah 14. 9.

If the Lord has ever been in our soul to manifest there a sense of his goodness and mercy, we can then make use of this as our plea, "Yet thou, O Lord, art in the midst of us." If he has ever heard your prayer he is with you; if he has ever given you a promise he is with you; if he has ever touched your heart with his finger he is with you; if he has ever favoured you with a smile he is with you. And though taking the general run of your experience he may be a stranger in the land, and as a wayfaring man that turneth aside to tarry for a night, or though even as it may seem, as if he were astonied at what you are – a mighty man that cannot save, still every token for good encourages you to cling, to cleave, to hang round him, to catch hold of his feet as the Shunamite caught Elisha by the feet, and would not be thrust away; for you cannot but feel that, with all that you are and have been, you dearly love him, and have a good hope, if not a clear testimony, that he loves you. Can you not sometimes look up to him, may I not say almost look at him in the face and say, "'Lord, thou knowest all things, thou knowest that I love thee'? And though my abominable sins have often made thee a stranger to me, yet in my heart of hearts, in the very depths of my soul thou knowest that I love thee." And if you can look at the Lord in the face, and appeal to his heart-searching eye that you do love him, depend upon it he loves you, for the word of truth declares, "We love him because he first loved us."

March 13

"Blessed is he, whosoever shall not be offended in me." – Matthew 11. 6.

What is the feeling of your heart toward Jesus? What is the solemn desire of your soul? that he would come and make your heart his abode? that he would visit your soul with the light of his countenance? that he would sprinkle his blood upon your conscience? that he would make himself very near, very dear, and very precious? Do you count one word from his lips worth a thousand worlds? a smile of his countenance worth thousands of gold and silver? Then you are blessed. You are not stumbling upon the dark mountains of error. You are not stumbling at the perfections of the Son of God. You are not offended at a free gospel, an unconditional salvation. No; the Lord in mercy has slaughtered your prejudices, subdued your enmity, and brought you to receive the gospel as a little child. "Well," but some may say, "I believe all this; but, then, I have doubts and fears whether the Lord has begun his work in me, whether I am one of his family. I cannot enjoy the power of truth as I could wish." But does not the Lord say, "Blessed is he, whosoever shall not be offended in me"? You are not offended and stumbled at Jesus. And he that is not offended in him, but is enabled to receive him as the Christ of God, to look to him, to believe in him, and at times to feel him precious – he comes under the blessing which maketh rich, and addeth no sorrow with it.

March 14

"An inheritance incorruptible, and undefiled, and that fadeth not away." – 1 Peter 1. 4.

Whatever you may have in this world, be it much or little, you must leave. And if you have no other inheritance than earth gives, where will be your portion in death and to all eternity? But if you are begotten again unto a lively hope, even if you do not enjoy the full assurance of faith, you have before you an inheritance which fadeth not away. We fancy some-times how happy we should be if we had this man's fine estate, or that man's large property; how much better we should spend it than he does, and what good we should do with it. And do you think that these men are happy with all their possessions, and that you would be happier or better if you had them? It is not in nature to be happy. These rich men have a canker which eats up all their happiness. And even if free from the heavier troubles of life, all satisfaction of the flesh fadeth away, for possession of itself rubs off all the bloom, and with possession come all the anxieties and cares connected with it. But this eternal inheritance "fadeth not away." The sweetest flowers fade and are thrown away as they become nauseous to sight and smell. But there is an abiding freshness, a constant verdure, a perpetual bloom, an unceasing fragrance, a permanent sweetness in this eternal inheritance, so that it is never flat or stale, but remains ever the same, or rather is ever increasing in beauty and blessedness, as more known, believed in, hoped unto, and loved.

March 15

"Being justified freely by his grace." – Romans 3. 24.

And it is because grace is free it can reach us. How free is the sun in sending forth its enlightening, warming beams; how free the clouds in discharging their watery treasures; how free the dew in falling from the face of heaven; how free the wind in blowing where it listeth. Now these are scriptural types and representatives of the free grace of God. It shines as freely as the sun; drops as freely as the rain; falls as freely as the dew; and blows as freely as the wind. But not in grace as in nature to all men. I mean not that; but all to whom it comes it comes freely. And whenever it so comes it communicates precious things with it. As the sun lights and warms, as the rain fertilises, as the dew softens, as the wind invigorates, so it is with the grace of God which comes out of the fulness of Christ. It enlightens the understanding, warms the heart, fertilises the soul, softens the spirit, and invigorates the whole new man of grace. And all this grace does freely, without charge or cost, without money or price, wanting nothing, asking nothing from us but a kindly return. The best debt to a benefactor is the debt of gratitude; the best return of kindness is the return of love; the best acknowledgment of a favour is good words and suitable deeds. The best thanks which the earth can give to the sun, rain, dew, and wind of heaven is to be fruitful – to manifest by the goodness of the crops, the goodness of what falls from heaven upon it. So it is in grace: "Whoso offereth praise glorifieth me" (Psalm 50. 23). A believing, loving heart, a prayerful, thankful lip, and a holy, godly life are the best returns for grace.

March 16

"Commit thy way unto the Lord; trust also in him; and he shall bring it to pass." – Psalm 37. 5.

What shall God bring to pass? The thing that lies deepest in the heart – *"thy way."* Does not thy way lie deepest in thy soul – the path that God has led, the path that God is now leading you by? You may be troubled in your soul, doubting and fearing in your mind, distressed in your feelings; you may sink down to the lowest point that a child of God can sink to; yet that way, in which you are so deeply sunk, if the Lord enable you from time to time to commit it to him, and trust in him, he will bring to pass above what your heart desires. Look at the movements of your heart God-ward; look at your embarrassments, temptations, and exercises; look at that which rolls backwards and forwards in your mind, that which is tossed to and fro on the waves of your anxious bosom, – what lies nearest, dearest, and deepest, – let honest conscience speak. *That,* whatever it be, the Lord tells you, and sometimes enables you to commit, to trust to him. Now whatever it be so committed and so trusted, the Lord has declared in his unerring word of truth, he "will bring it to pass;" he will fulfil it when his time has arrived. Does darkness envelope it? do mountains of difficulty stand up in the way of its fulfilment? Never mind; God will bring it to pass in the face of all, over mountains and through difficulties, in spite of, and in the midst of, all surrounding obstacles. He "will bring it to pass," – that which lies deepest in your heart, nearest your affections, and that which you are enabled in the actings of living faith sometimes to commit into the hands of the Lord God Almighty.

March 17

"God is faithful, by whom ye were called unto the fellowship of his Son Jesus Christ our Lord." – 1 Corinthians 1. 9.

When God calls his people by his grace, it is to make them partakers of the highest bliss and the greatest glory that he could confer upon the sons of men. And this not only in eternity, but in time; not only beyond, but this side of the grave. He appeals, therefore, to them by his prophet. "Have I been a wilderness unto Israel in a land of darkness?" (Jer. 2. 31.) When the Lord calls his people out of earthly pleasures, is it for no other purpose than to lead them into paths of affliction and sorrow? Does he make them leave the flesh-pots of Egypt to starve them in a waste howling wilderness? This was the complaint of the ancient murmurers, that Moses had brought them up out of Egypt to kill them with thirst (Exod. 17. 3). Does he take them from earthly delights to abandon them to misery and despair? O no! He calls them even in this time state to the greatest privilege and highest favour that his everlasting love could confer upon them, which is no less than "the fellowship of his Son, Jesus Christ our Lord," that they may have union and communion with the Son of God by grace here, and be partakers of his glory hereafter. God's dear Son is and always has been the object of his eternal delight. To glorify him has been from all eternity his fixed, his settled purpose; and in pursuance of this settled purpose, he gave him a people whom he formed for himself, that they might show forth his praise. Thus, therefore, the Redeemer addressed his heavenly Father – "And all mine are thine, and thine are mine; and I am glorified in them."

March 18

"To them that have no might he increaseth strength." – Isaiah 40. 29.

The Lord's people are often in this state, that they "have no might." All their power seems exhausted, and their strength completely drained away; sin appears to have got the mastery over them; and they feel as if they had neither will nor ability to run the race set before them, or persevere in the way of the Lord. Yet, even then, they have strength; for it says, *"he increaseth strength."* It does not say, 'he gives, bestows, communicates strength;' but " he *increaseth* strength." How can this be? We must have power to feel our weakness. God must put forth his power to enable us to fall down into nothingness and helplessness. It therefore says, "he *increaseth* strength." As though it would imply, 'Is not the very power to sink down into creature weakness, helplessness, and nothingness, *strength?'* It is so in God's mysterious dealings. And, therefore, "to them that have no might" (in other words, those who are sensible in their own consciences that they have no power at all, who are completely exhausted of nature's strength and wisdom), to these "he increaseth strength." Now the Lord "increaseth strength" in a very mysterious way. He often drops strength stilly and secretly into the soul. We are not always to expect very great manifestations. This is not the way in which the Lord usually increases strength. His visits to the soul are often better known by their fruits and effects, and by looking back upon them when they are past, than by any immediate impulse. The strength given is more easily felt than the hand seen which communicates it. In this respect it much resembles the new birth, of which the Lord says, "The wind bloweth where it listeth, and thou hearest the sound thereof, but canst not tell whence it cometh, and whither it goeth" (John 3. 8).

March 19

"Wherefore gird up the loins of your mind, be sober, and hope to the end for the grace that is to be brought unto you at the revelation of Jesus Christ." – 1 Peter 1. 13.

Hope chiefly regards *"the end;"* for that is "better than the beginning," the crowning consummation of all that faith believes, hope expects, and love enjoys. But through what dark and gloomy seasons has hope often to look before this end comes, being sometimes sunk so low as almost to despair even of life! How it has in these low spots to muster all its evidences, look back to this and that Ebenezer, this and that hill Mizar, this and that deliverance, manifestation, and blessing; how it has to hang upon the word of promise, cry out for help, and that mightily, as if at its last breath, and hope against hope in the very face of unbelief, infidelity, and despair. An end must come to all our struggles, trials, exercises, afflictions, and conflicts. We shall not be always struggling and fighting with a body of sin and death. We shall not be always exposed to snares and temptations spread in our path by sin and Satan, so as hardly to escape falling by them as if by the very skin of our teeth. Every day reminds us with warning voice that an end must come. But now comes the question, and often a very anxious question it is, What will that end be? Here hope comes in to sustain and support the soul, enabling it to look forward, that it may prove to be a hope that maketh not ashamed, a good hope through grace, and a hope of such a complete and enduring nature that the end may prove it was a grace of the Holy Spirit, and, as such, stamped with his own perfecting power.

March 20

"I will walk before the Lord in the land of the living." – Psalm 116. 9.

There is a distinction between walking *before* God and walking *with* God. To walk *before* God is to walk with an abiding sense of God's eye being upon us; to walk with a desire to do those things which are pleasing in his sight; to walk in his ordinances blameless; to walk before his people with our garments unspotted by the world; in a word, to walk before him in private as in public, alone and in company, before the Church and the world, by day and by night, as we should walk if we had a personal view of his glorious majesty in heaven before our eyes. Now if you carried about with you a deep and daily sense that God saw every thought, marked every movement, heard every word, and observed every action, this sense of his presence would put a restraint upon your light, trifling, and foolish spirit. You would watch your thoughts, your words, your actions, as living under a sense of God's heart-searching eye. This is to walk *before* God. But we read of Enoch that he "walked *with* God." This is a more advanced stage of the divine life. To walk *with* God is to walk with him in sweet familiarity, in holy confidence, in a blessed sense of interest in his love and grace, and thus to walk with him and talk with him as a man walketh and talketh with his friend. There are some who walk before God, but how few walk with God! Many live under a more or less deep and daily sense of God's heart-searching presence, who are not admitted into this sweet familiarity, nor enjoy the blessedness of this heavenly intercourse.

March 21

"I am the Lord that healeth thee." – Exodus 15. 26.

How does God heal the diseases of his people? He heals them chiefly by subduing them; for in this life they are never thoroughly healed. The promise runs: "He will subdue our iniquities" (Micah 7. 19). To subdue them is to restrain their power. Thus he sees one suffering under the power of unbelief. He gives him faith: this subdues his unbelief. Here is another poor languid patient, dying of exhaustion: he gives him strength. Here is a third mourning under his corruptions: he gives a drop of his blood to purge his conscience, and a taste of his love to warm his heart. He sees a fourth crying under the strong assaults of Satan: with one look Satan flies and the soul is set free. Thus with infinite wisdom blended with infinite love and power, he passes on from bed to bed of every sick patient, administering health wherever he goes. This blessed Physician has a remedy for every disease, and the remedy is always felt to be exactly suitable to the exigency of the case. It goes, so to speak, at once to the right spot; it heals the malady wherever it be, and whatever it be, just in the right way, and just at the right time. O then how good it is to bring all our diseases before the Lord! In a case of bodily sickness or painful complaint we uncover freely our malady to a physician whom we can trust; we tell him every circumstance and disclose every symptom. So should we go to the Lord with all our diseases, tell him all our complaints, unfold to him all our sorrows, and fully and freely lay before him everything that burdens the conscience, pains the mind, and distresses the soul, looking and waiting until he speaks the word, and every malady is healed.

March 22

"His bow abode in strength, and the arms of his hands were made strong by the hands of the mighty God of Jacob." – Genesis 49. 24.

Our ancestors, you know, were celebrated bowmen. Victories were won at Cressy and Agincourt by the English yeomanry, who were skilled in the use of the bow. Latimer says, in a sermon preached before the king, that no man could be a good archer who did not learn from his boyhood; and the custom he tells us was for the father to put his hands upon the son's hands, to teach him how to shoot, and throw the whole strength of his body into the bow. When the boy drew the bow, it was not the strength of his own arm that drew the string, nor was it the keenness of his eye that directed the arrow to the mark. The child appeared to draw the bow and to direct the arrow; but the hand of the father was upon the hand of the child, and the eye of the father was guiding the eye of the child; thus though the child seemed to draw the bow, it was the strength of the father that really pulled the string. So in the case of Joseph to whom our text refers, "the arms of his hands were made strong by the hands of the mighty God of Jacob." God put his hands upon the hands of Joseph, drew the bow for him, directed the arrow, and hit effectually the mark. Apply this to your experience. When you pray effectually, it is not you that pray; it is the Spirit of God that prays in you; for he helpeth our infirmities, and intercedeth for us with groanings which cannot be uttered. When you believe, it is the Spirit of God that works faith in you; when you hope, it is the Spirit of God that produces hope in you; when you love, it is the Spirit of God that sheds abroad love in you; it is the arms of his hands that are put upon your hands, and they are made strong by the hands of the mighty God of Jacob.

March 23

"Be not conformed to this world: but be ye transformed by the renewing of your mind, that ye may prove what is that good, and acceptable, and perfect will of God." – Romans 12. 2.

How shall we find the will of God acceptable? Only as we are renewed in the spirit of our mind, and are transformed and conformed to the suffering image of the sorrowing Son of God. How fearful, then, how dangerous, and yet how ensnaring is that worldly conformity which sets us in deadly opposition to that good and perfect will of God which was, and is "acceptable" to his dear Son, to all the holy angels round the throne, to the spirits of just men made perfect, to his spiritually-minded people on earth, and hateful to none but devils and carnal, ungodly men. And how truly blessed to be brought out of the power and prevailing influence of this worldly spirit, and to be cast into the gospel mould, where, being renewed in the spirit of our mind, we prove that the will of God is not only "good," pure goodness, and "perfect," worthy of all his glorious perfections, but "acceptable" to our heart and affections, which therefore tenderly embrace it, and thus, as it were, incorporate it into our will, making the two wills one. To bring us to this point is the grand object of all gospel discipline; and one may say that the ultimatum of gospel obedience is,

"To lie passive in his hand,
And know no will but his."

Here then only can we fully enter into the beauty and blessedness of gospel truth; here only can we submit to the weight of a daily cross, glory in tribulation, patiently endure afflictions, feel the sweetness of the promises, walk in obedience to the precepts, and tread the path that leads to endless glory.

March 24

"That at that time ye were without Christ, being aliens from the commonwealth of Israel, and strangers from the covenants of promise, having no hope, and without God in the world." – Ephesians 2. 12.

The Apostle here tells the Ephesians that in their natural state, before divinely quickened and made alive unto God, they were "without Christ," that is, without manifest union and communion with him. Though in the purposes of God, and by their eternal election in Christ, they were members of his mystical body, they had not been baptized into Christ by the Spirit so as to be made living members of his spiritual body, the Church (1 Cor. 12. 13), and therefore had not "put on Christ" (Gal. 3. 27). And as they were, such were we. We were "without Christ" in our Gentile days. He had no place in our thoughts. We knew nothing of his Person and work, blood and righteousness, beauty and blessedness, grace and glory. He was to us a root out of a dry ground, and in our eyes he had no form nor comeliness. His name might have been on our lips, but his Spirit and grace were not in our hearts. And if matters be in any way different now with us, if there be any faith on him, hope in him, or love to him, grace has wrought it all. Let us never forget what we were before we were called by grace. Let the remembrance of our sins and of the whole bent and current of our lives be bitter to us, that we may all the more prize and admire the riches of that sovereign grace which stooped to us in our low and lost estate. The paschal lamb was to be eaten with bitter herbs. The remembrance of Egyptian bondage should ever accompany the enjoyment of gospel liberty, and godly sorrow for sin the feeding on the flesh of Christ.

March 25

"All my children shall be taught of the Lord." – Isaiah 54. 13.

The teaching of God can only be known and realised by those who have seen an end of all creature perfection, and who are completely and experimentally destitute of all wisdom in the flesh. And God's teaching does not leave a man where it found him, dead, stupefied, worldly, unfeeling, and carnal. If he is in distress, it does not leave him in distress; if he feels guilty, it does not leave him guilty; if he is in darkness, it does not leave him in darkness; but it lifts him out of these evils. Thus God's people are continually led to come unto him for his instruction, because they feel that without his special teaching they can know nothing as they ought to know. Nay, the more they have, the more they want to have; for no sooner is the light withdrawn, than the darkness is more sensibly felt. If any text of Scripture has been opened up to them, it makes them want to have others made known in a similar way; if they have had any consolation, and it is taken away, it makes them want it again. So that the more wise and spiritual God's people become, the more foolish and carnal they appear in their own eyes; the stronger they are in the Lord and in the power of his might, the more sensibly do they feel the weakness of their flesh; and the more they are enabled to walk closely with the Lord, the more they discover the wretched wanderings of their base and sinful hearts.

March 26

"The Lord loveth the gates of Zion." – Psalm 87. 2.

What are gates for? Two purposes, entrance and exit. And Zion, too, has her gates of exit and entrance; she has her gates of access to God, entrance into the presence of the Most High; "the door of hope," opened in "the valley of Achor." And who has opened the door; or, rather, who has not only opened it and made it, but himself is the Door? "I am the Door," says Jesus. And was not "the door" opened through his rent flesh? As the Apostle speaks: "Having therefore, brethren, boldness to enter into the holiest by the blood of Jesus, by a new and living way, which he hath consecrated for us, through the veil, that is to say, his flesh." Through his bleeding wounds, through his pierced side, through his mangled feet and hands, there is now access to God:

> "A door of hope is opened wide
> In Jesus' pierced hands and side."

Is there any other access to God, but through the slaughtered Lamb? "Through him we have access by one Spirit unto the Father." There is no other; for he is "the way, the truth, and the life, and no man cometh to the Father but by him." Is not this an open way? Does not the soul through this door "walk in and out and find pasture," and enter into the immediate presence of God? Do you, my friends, ever find access to God, a heart to pray, a sense of acceptance in prayer, an open door, and power to enter therein? What opens it? *Merit?* Set up merit, and we are all damned to a man. It is not merit, great or little; it is the blood of the Lamb which alone has opened a way for poor lost sinners to draw near to God.

March 27

"Now we have received, not the spirit of the world, but the spirit which is of God; that we might know the things that are freely given to us of God." – 1 Corinthians 2. 12.

What thick clouds of darkness spread themselves at times over our souls; all things out of sight; our signs and tokens buried, as it were, in mist. It is like a sea fog, that comes out of the bosom of the vasty deep, and hides all objects from view. The ships are on the sea, notwithstanding, but this deep fog prevents their being seen. So with our souls at times, all is misty, cloudy, and no signs can be seen of the work of God upon our hearts. And yet we "know" them, by receiving the Spirit of God, for it is the only way whereby they can be known. We can only see light in God's light; only believe by God's faith; only love by God's love; therefore can only know the things freely given to us of God by the revelation of the Spirit. What we know savingly, experimentally, feelingly, we know only by divine teaching. How dark our mind often is; how low we sink at times; it is only the Son of God that can enable us to rise; only by the revelation of his Spirit can we believe that we are his. We know he is God when he shines forth, as we know the sun when it blazes forth in the summer sky. We know him by the teaching of the Spirit, but cannot see him till our eyes are divinely opened. The sun may shine in all its glory - does that communicate light to the eyes of the blind? or warm the corpse lying in the coffin? The blind see not; the dead hear not; the living, the living alone see and know the Son of God.

March 28

"Who are kept by the power of God through faith unto salvation." - 1 Peter 1. 5.

Those who are kept by the power of God through faith, are often in their minds troubled and anxious, fearing whether this salvation will ever reach their souls, - whether they may not prove castaways, - whether the work upon their heart is genuine, - whether they are under divine teachings. But the Lord says they are "kept by his power through faith *unto salvation:*" kept as in this garrisoned city, until salvation shall come in all its glory, sweetness, bliss and blessedness into their heart; preserved and encompassed by all the attributes of God from making shipwreck of faith, until they "receive the end of their faith, even the salvation of their souls." Then poor, doubting, distressed, fearing, guilty sinner, this promise is for thee. Thy soul is bound up in the bundle of life with the Lord thy God; thy character and thy name are contained here. And it is a promise suitable to you: yea, it is a promise suitable to us all. Suitable to us when we meet together, suitable when absent from each other, suitable for town, suitable for country; suitable for a child of God in a state of trial and temptation, and suitable when he enjoys a temporary respite from them; suitable for him in war, suitable for him in peace; suitable for him when the cannons roar and the earth trembles, suitable for him when he seems to have no enemy near, for the enemy then may be approaching by stratagem. Yea, could you point out a single moment when this promise is not suitable to you, that would be the very moment in which the promise would be wanted by you most. Could you ever arrive at such a spot as to say, "Now I want the promise no more," that very feeling would shew that you were on the brink of a fall, and therefore never needed the promise so much as then.

March 29

"Then the eyes of the blind shall be opened, and the ears of the deaf shall be unstopped." – Isaiah 35. 5.

That these miracles are effected by the power of the gospel is plain from the words that immediately precede, "Behold, your God will come with vengeance, even God with a recompence; he will come, and save you" (Isa. 35. 4). And how does God come and save but in the gospel, and by making it his own power unto salvation? If you look back at your experience you will see that one of the first effects of the power of the gospel upon your heart was, to open your ears to receive it as a message from God. When, for instance, you were first brought under its sound, and began to understand and feel what you heard, was there not given you, as it were, new ears to hear it, and a new heart to receive it? Were not those with you memorable days when you first heard the joyful sound of salvation by free grace; when it first dropped that blessed news into your soul which made your very heart thrill with unspeakable joy? God was then circumcising your ear, unstopping it, and conveying the gospel into your heart through it. "For faith cometh by hearing, and hearing by the word of God" (Rom. 10. 17). "As soon as they hear of me," says the Lord in prophecy, "they shall obey me: the strangers shall submit themselves unto me" (Psalm 18. 44). That gospel which was death to others was life to you; and that message at which others perhaps gnashed their teeth, came into your heart with an indescribable sweetness as the very voice of God to your soul.

March 30

"Herein is my Father glorified, that ye bear much fruit; so shall ye be my disciples." – John 15. 8.

The bearing of much fruit not only brings glory to God, but proves such rich fruit-bearers to be genuine disciples of the Lord Jesus. Now, though there is no merit in their bearing fruit, they sometimes get comfort from it, as proving an abiding union with Christ. "If ye keep my commandments, ye shall abide in my love; even as I have kept my Father's commandments and abide in his love." There is no maintaining of holy confidence in the soul but by walking in godly obedience; nor can there be any true spiritual communion with God whilst the guilt of disobedience lies hard and heavy on the conscience. To make straight paths for our feet; to walk in the fear of God; to live to his glory, are not only sweet tests of genuine discipleship, but faith, hope, and love cannot be maintained without them. And yet if we know anything of what gospel fruit is, and what we are as poor, vile sinners, must we not too often put our mouth in the dust? Instead of rejoicing in our fruitfulness, must we not often rather lament our barrenness, and cry out, "My leanness, my leanness, woe unto me!" Still, if we see and feel a deficiency in these points in ourselves and others, and, comparing our hearts, lips, and lives with the word of truth, must plead guilty, shall this utterly discourage us? No. This very discouragement may prove of service to us. It is good, at times, to be discouraged; because it makes us learn that "without Christ we can do nothing," and that it is only by his grace that we can produce fruit to his glory. It is, therefore, good to see and feel our barrenness and un-fruitfulness; for it is this very sight and sense of our own want of fruit that leads us in earnest desires to the Lord Jesus Christ to work in us to will and to do of his own good pleasure.

March 31

"For he hath made him to be sin for us, who knew no sin; that he might be made the righteousness of God in him." – 2 Corinthians 5. 21.

Our blessed Lord offered himself for sin; that is, that he might put away sin by the sacrifice of himself – "Who his own self bare our sins in his own body on the tree" (1 Pet. 2. 24). It was absolutely necessary either that the sinner should suffer in his own person, or in that of a substitute. Jesus became this substitute; he stood virtually in the sinner's place, and endured in his holy body and soul the punishment due to him; for he "was numbered with the transgressors." He thus, by the shedding of his most precious blood, opened in his sacred body a fountain for all sin and all uncleanness (Zech. 13. 1). The cross was the place on which this sacrifice was offered; for as the blood of the slain lamb was poured out at the foot of the altar, sprinkled upon its horns, and burned in its ever-enduring fire, so our blessed Lord shed his blood upon the cross. He there endured the wrath of God to the uttermost; he there put away sin by the sacrifice of himself; he there offered his holy soul and body, the whole of his pure and sacred humanity, in union with his eternal Deity, as an expiation for the sins of his people. Thus all their sin was atoned for, expiated, put away, blotted out, and will never more be imputed to them. This is the grand mystery of redeeming love and atoning blood. Here the cross shines forth in all its splendour; here God and man meet at the sacrifice of the God-man; and here, amidst the sufferings and sorrows, the groans and tears, the blood and obedience of God's dear Son in our nature, grace reigns through righteousness unto eternal life.

April 1

"That ye may approve things that are excellent; that ye may be sincere and without offence till the day of Christ." – Philippians 1. 10.

If divine light has enlightened your mind, divine life quickened your heart, and you love the Lord and his people, you must approve of the things that are excellent. For they are so commended to your con-science that you can no more do otherwise than you can tell a deliberate lie or call black white. And as you approve of them, you will disapprove of everything which is contrary to, or falls short of this excellency. Now this is what distinguishes us from the world and the spirit of it, and from all whose eyes are blinded by the god of this world – that whilst they approve of the things God abhors, we approve of the things that God loves. Here is the mind of Christ; here is the teaching of the Spirit giving us in some measure to see as Christ sees, to feel as Christ feels, to love as Christ loves, and to approve as Christ approves. We shall never go far wrong so long as we are approving the things that are excellent, and seeking, as the Lord may enable, to know the will of God and do it. But directly we lose sight of this spiritual standard and set up the opinion of men, then our eyes get blinded, our hearts hardened, our consciences benumbed, and instead of approving the things that are excellent, we may gradually and insensibly drift into the very spirit of ungodliness.

April 2

"I have chosen thee in the furnace of affliction." – Isaiah 48. 10.

According to God's own testimony, it is "through much tribulation" that we are to enter into the kingdom; and therefore there is no entering into the kingdom of grace here or the kingdom of glory hereafter without it. But let this be ever borne in mind, that whatever affliction befall the saints, it is laid upon them by the hand of God, and that for the express purpose of putting them into a situation and of making them capable of receiving those comforts which God only can bestow. None but Jesus himself and the Father can comfort a truly afflicted heart. And he can and does from time to time comfort his dear people by a sense of his presence; by a word of power from his gracious lips; by the light of his countenance; by the balm of his atoning blood and dying love; and by the work and witness of the Spirit within. And as they receive this consolation from the mouth of God, their hearts are comforted. How good the Lord is of his own free grace to bestow such blessings upon his redeemed family! May he give us much of them! And may he wherever he has bestowed upon any of us everlasting consolation, or even a good hope through grace, comfort our hearts as we journey through this vale of tears, and may our consolations be neither few nor small.

April 3

"Without holiness no man shall see the Lord." – Hebrews 12. 14.

To possess this holiness is a necessary and indispensable meetness for the inheritance of the saints in light; but this meetness must be wrought in us by the power of God's grace, for I am sure that in ourselves of it we have none. But see its necessity. What happiness could there be in the courts of bliss unless we had a nature to enjoy it? Unless we were made capable of seeing Christ as he is, and enjoying his presence for evermore, heaven would be no heaven to us. Nothing unclean or unholy can enter there. Sanctification therefore must be wrought in us by the power of God, to make us meet for the heavenly inheritance, and he therefore communicates of his Spirit and grace to give us heavenly affections, holy desires, gracious thoughts, tender feelings; and above all that love whereby he is loved as the altogether lovely. By the sanctifying operations of his Spirit, he separates us from everything evil, plants his fear deep in the heart, that it may be a fountain of life to depart from the snares of death; and works in us a conformity to his suffering image here that we may be conformed to his glorified image hereafter. Thus there is a perfect and an imperfect sanctification - perfect by imputation, imperfect in its present operations. But the one is the pledge of the other; so that as surely as Christ now represents his people in heaven as their holy Head, so will he eventually bring them to be for ever with him in those abodes of perfect holiness and perfect happiness which are prepared for them as mansions of eternal light and love.

April 4

"And when they were alone, he expounded all things to his disciples." – Mark 4. 34.

What is the exact meaning of the word disciple? It means properly a learner, one who is under a teacher, whose submissive and devoted pupil he has become, and from whom he receives continual instruction. And thus a disciple of Christ is one who is admitted by the Lord Jesus into his school, whom he himself condescends personally to instruct, and who therefore learns of him to be meek and lowly of heart. A disciple of Jesus is one who sits meekly at the Redeemer's feet, receiving into his heart the gracious words which fall from his lips. This was Mary's happy posture, whom the Lord commended for choosing the better part. Such is also the posture of all the saints of God, according to the ancient declaration, "Yea, he loved the people; all his saints are in thy hand: and they sat down at thy feet; every one shall receive of thy words" (Deut. 33. 3). But a true and sincere disciple not only listens to his Master's instructions, but acts as he bids. So a disciple of Jesus is one who copies his Master's example, and is conformed to his Master's image. A sincere disciple is also characterized by the *love* which he bears to his Master; so a disciple of Jesus is one who treasures up the words of Christ in his heart, ponders over his precious promises, and delights in his glorious Person, love, and blood. A disciple of Jesus is one who bears some reflection to the image of his heavenly Master; he carries it about with him wherever he goes, that men may take knowledge of him that he has been with Jesus; and as when Moses came down from the mount his face shone from the reflection of the heavenly glory which had streamed upon his countenance, so does the true disciple shine before men with some sparkles of the glory of the Son of God. To have some of these divine features stamped upon the heart, lip, and life, is to be a disciple of Jesus. To be much with Jesus is to be made like unto Jesus; to sit at Jesus' feet is to drink in Jesus' words; to lean upon Jesus' breast is to feel the warm heart of Jesus pulsating with love; and to feel this pulsation, causes the heart of the disciple to beat in tender and affectionate unison; to look up to Jesus, is to see a face more marred than the sons of men, yet a face beaming with heavenly beauty, dignity, and glory. To be a disciple, then, of Jesus, is to copy his example; to do the things pleasing in his sight; and to avoid the things which he abhors. To be a disciple of Jesus, is to be meek as he was; humble as he was; lowly as he was; self-denying as he was; separate from the world as he was; living a life of communion with God, as he lived when he walked here below. To take a worm of the earth and make him a disciple of Jesus is the greatest privilege God can bestow upon man. To select an obstinate, ungodly, perverse rebel, and place him in the school of Christ and at the feet of Jesus, is the highest favour God can bestow upon any child of the dust. How unsurpassingly great must be that kindness whereby the Lord condescends to bestow his grace on an alien and an enemy, and to soften and meeken him by his Spirit, and thus cause him to grow up into the image and likeness of his own dear Son. What are earthly honours and titles when compared with the favour thus conferred upon those whose foundation is in the dust? Compared with this high privilege, all earthly honours, stars and garters, titles and robes, sink into utter insignificance.

April 5

"To him that overcometh will I give to eat of the hidden manna." – Revelation 2. 17.

How often God's word is to you a sealed book; how often you hear from the pulpit the most encouraging preaching, yet get no encouragement from it; how often you hear Christ held forth in his Person, blood and righteousness, and go away as you came, without any sensible relief. What is the reason? Because you are overcome. Unbelief, bondage, darkness of mind, insensibility rest upon your spirit, and all these keep you from feeding upon the manna. But sometimes a gracious word comes over all these hills and mountains of unbelief, bondage, doubt and fear, and as this word drops into your heart, you begin to shout victory over all your foes and fears. Then the word of God begins to open itself up in its sweetness and blessed-ness. The Lord of the house brings out the hidden manna, and the word of God is made sweet and precious to the soul. Sometimes you read the word of God as a dry and barren task to satisfy conscience. When is that? When you are shut up in unbelief and bondage. But at other times the word of God is read with pleasure, and it is to you the joy and rejoicing of your heart. This is when you can believe it; and thus faith turns the word of God into manna. But if *you* are barren, then the word of God is barren; if dead, the word is dead; if cold and lifeless, the word is so too. But when the scene changes, when the clouds are dispersed, then you see light in God's light. Then it is a blessed Bible, a precious book, full of sweet promises and encouraging invitations. It is in this way the manna is given to the overcomer.

April 6

"And I will give him a white stone, and in the stone a new name written, which no man knoweth saving he that receiveth it." – Revelation 2. 17.

In ancient times they used to decide cases by white and black stones. The judges (for they were rather judges than jury) did not give their verdict upon the prisoner by oral testimony, "guilty," or "not guilty," as in our country, but by dropping into an urn a white stone to express their opinion that the prisoner was innocent, or a black stone to declare their judgment that the prisoner was guilty. The Lord has made use of this figure. He says, "To him that overcometh I will give a white stone;" that is, I will give into his con-science a sentence of acquittal. As the white stone was dropped into the urn, so peace and pardon are dropped into the sinner's bosom; and just as the judge, when he deposited the white stone in the urn, declared thereby the prisoner's innocence; so when the Lord is pleased to speak peace to the soul, he drops into the heart a white stone, to proclaim him discharged from the law's accusations, and interested in his love and blood.

"And in the stone a new name written." What is this new name? Is it not a new heart, a new nature – Christ in the soul the hope of glory? This is the "new name which no man knoweth saving he that receiveth it." New thoughts of Jesus, new openings up of Scripture, new meltings of heart, new softenings of spirit, every-thing made new by him who renews us "in the renewing of our mind" – no man knows these things saving he who receives them. It is all between the Lord and the soul, it is all between a pardoning God and a pardoned sinner; it is all mercy, all grace, all love, from first to last. Grace began, grace carries on, and grace finishes it; grace must have all the glory, and grace must crown the work with eternal victory.

April 7

"I will be as the dew unto Israel." – Hosea 14. 5.

Sometimes the Lord, without applying his word with any very great and distinguishing power to the heart, makes *his truth to drop* with a measure of sweetness into the soul. This is as rain or dew, according to his own gracious declaration, "My doctrine shall drop as the rain; my speech shall distil as the dew" (Deut. 32. 2). The dropping, then, of his doctrine, or, as the word means, his "teaching," as rain, and the distilling of his gracious speech as dew, kindle in the soul a love of the truth, and wherever this is felt there is salvation, for we read of those who perish that "they received not the love of the truth that they might be saved" (2 Thess.2. 10). There is a receiving of the truth, and a receiving of the love of the truth. These two things widely differ. To receive the truth will not necessarily save; for many receive the truth who never receive the love of the truth. Professors by thousands receive the truth into their judgment, and adopt the plan of salvation as their creed; but are neither saved nor sanctified thereby. But to receive the love of the truth by the truth as it is in Jesus being made sweet and precious to the soul, is to receive salvation itself. It is in this way that the gospel is made the power of God unto salvation; and therefore the Apostle, speaking of "the preaching of the cross," says that "it is to them that perish foolishness, but unto us which are saved it is the power of God" (1 Cor. 1.18). Now it is impossible that this power should be felt without its having an alluring effect upon the soul, whereby it comes out from every evil thing and cleaves to the Lord with purpose of heart.

April 8

"If ye were of the world, the world would love his own: but because ye are not of the world, but I have chosen you out of the world, therefore the world hateth you." – John 15. 19.

If you walk in the fear of God, and follow in the footsteps of a persecuted and despised Jesus, the world will hate and despise you as it hated and despised him, as he himself declares, "If the world hate you, ye know that it hated me before it hated you" (v. 18). God himself has put enmity between the seed of the woman and the seed of the serpent (Gen. 3. 15); and nothing will secure you from the manifestation of this enmity if you are on Christ's side. Neither rank, nor property, nor learning, nor education, nor amiability, nor the profusest deeds of liberality, nor the greatest uprightness of conduct, will stave off the scorn of men, if you are a sincere follower of the Lord Jesus Christ, and carry out in practice what you hold in principle. If you are not conformed to Jesus here in his suffering image, you will most certainly not be conformed to Jesus hereafter in his glorified likeness. But if by living for and unto Jesus and his cross, your name be cast out as evil, wear it as your distinguishing badge, as adorning the breast of a Christian warrior. If men misrepresent your motives or actions, and seek to hunt you down with every calumny that the basest malignity can invent, do not heed it as long as you are innocent. They cannot find you a better or more honourable crown, if indeed your godly life provoke the cruel lie. It is a crown that your Master bore before you when they crowned his head with thorns. If you feel as I have felt, you will at times count yourself even unworthy to suffer persecution for his name's sake.

April 9

"Heal me, O Lord, and I shall be healed; save me, and I shall be saved: for thou art my praise." – Jeremiah 17. 14.

If we feel that we have ruined our own souls, that no human arm can save us, that we cannot bring salvation into our own consciences, nor of ourselves see any beauty, glory, sweetness, or suitability in the Lord Jesus Christ, and yet are striving with prayer and supplication to touch the hem of his garment, to taste the sweetness of his dying love, to feel the efficacy of his atoning blood, to be wrapped up in his glorious robe of righteousness, and to know him in the sweet manifestations of his grace, we too can say, "Save me, and I shall be saved." Here is this sin! save me from it; here is this snare! break it to pieces; here is this lust! Lord, subdue it; here is this temptation! deliver me out of it; here is my proud heart! Lord, humble it; my unbelieving heart! take it away, and give me faith; give me submission to thy mind and will; take me as I am with all my sin and shame and work in me everything well-pleasing in thy sight, for "Thou art my praise." If ever I have blessed thee, it has been for thy goodness to my soul; if ever my heart has been tuned to thy praise, if ever my lips have thanked thee, it has been for the riches of thy grace, and the manifestations of thy mercy. I am nothing, and never shall be anything but a poor guilty sinner in thy eyes; but I have to praise thee for all that is past, and to hope in thee for all that is to come; "for thou," and thou alone, O Lord, "art my praise."

April 10

"I will rejoice in the Lord, I will joy in the God of my salvation." – Habakkuk 3. 18.

If ever, as we pass through this wilderness, we feel one drop of solid joy, of true happiness, it must flow, it *can* flow only from one source – the manifestation of Christ to our souls. This joy may be very transient: we may have to look upon it through a vista of many years; and doubts and fears may becloud the mind whether we ever rejoiced truly in Christ, or whether our joy might not have been "the joy of the hypocrite" that perisheth. And yet we are brought to this point – we can find joy and peace in Him alone. Sin, the world, the things of time and sense, business, amusement, pleasure so called, afford now no joy; there is an aching void, a feeling of dreariness and misery connected with everything short of communications of mercy, favour, and love. So that though we may not be enabled to say, 'we greatly rejoice at all times, in all places, at all seasons, in the Lord;' yet we can come to this point - we can rejoice in no other; we can take real pleasure in nothing else. One smile from the Lord, one word from his lips, one gracious breaking in of the light of his countenance does, while it lasts, communicate joy; and from no other quarter, from no other source can a moment's joy be drawn.

April 11

"Hold fast that which is good." - 1 Thessalonians 5. 21.

There are two things especially which every saint of God is called upon to hold fast: these are, first, *the beginning of God's work* upon his soul; and, secondly, his *deliverance.* Any manifestation too that you have had of the Lord Jesus Christ; any application of his atoning blood; any discovery of his glorious Person or shedding abroad of his love; hold that fast, for it is good. And so I may say, hold fast any promise you have ever had applied; any answer to prayer you have ever received; any felt blessing that may have been wrought in your heart by a divine power. All this is good. It comes from a good God; it works in a good way; it leads to a good end; it will make a good deathbed, and will land you in a most blessed eternity. Therefore "hold fast that which is good." Everything which is commended to your conscience as really good; every good man; every good minister; every child of God with whom you feel union or communion; every good precept, word, and work; in short, whatever is fully commended to your conscience as spiritual and divine, hold that fast, and you will find the benefit of it. Discard and reject everything bad, unbecoming, inconsistent, ungodly, erroneous, or heretical; discard them all - show them no mercy. In heart but not in hand, hew them down, as Samuel hewed down Agag in Gilgal.

April 12

"He that dwelleth in the secret place of the most High shall abide under the shadow of the Almighty." – Psalm 91. 1.

What is "the secret place of the most High"? It is the same spot, of which Asaph speaks in the seventy-third Psalm (v. 17) – "Until I went into the sanctuary of God; then understood I their end." It is the spot, of which the Lord speaks in Ezekiel – "I will be to them as a little sanctuary in the countries where they shall come." Then this "secret place" is the secret bosom of God. It is an entrance by faith into Jehovah, by a spiritual manifestation of him, leading us into a spiritual acquaintance with him. "The secret place of the most High" is that solemn spot, where Jehovah meets with the sinner in Christ, and where he opens up to him the riches of his mercy, and leads him into his bosom, so as to read the secrets of his loving heart. It is called a "secret" place, as only known to the persons to whom it is especially communicated. It is called a "secret" place, because none can get into it, – no, nor desire to get into it, – except the Lord himself, with his own mysterious hand, opens up to them a part in it, sets them down in it, and sweetly blesses them in it. Then to be in "the secret place of the most High" is to be brought into something like fellowship and acquaintance with God – something like communion, spiritual worship, divine intercourse; so as to know some-thing of him experimentally, and "run into" him, as "a strong tower," and there feel solemn safety.

April 13

"But now is Christ risen from the dead, and become the first-fruits of them that slept. For since by man came death, by man came also the resurrection of the dead. For as in Adam all die, even so in Christ shall all be made alive." – 1 Corinthians 15. 20, 21, 22.

Christ risen is the firstfruits of that mighty crop of buried dead whose remains still sleep in the silent dust, and who will be joined by successive ranks of those who die in him, till all are together wakened up in the resurrection morn. The figure is that of the sheaf of the firstfruits which was waved before the Lord before the harvest was allowed to be reaped (Lev. 23. 10, 11). This offering of the wave sheaf was the consecration and dedication of the whole crop in the field to the Lord, as well as the manifest pledge that the harvest was fully ripe for the reaper's sickle. The firstfruits represented the whole of the crop, as Christ is the representative of his saints; the offering of them sanctified what was still unreaped in the field, as Christ sanctified or consecrated unto God the yet unreaped harvest of the buried dead; and the carrying them into the tabernacle was the first introduction therein of the crop, as Christ entering heaven as the firstfruits secures thereby the entrance of the bodies of the saints into the mansions prepared for them before the foundation of the world. Thus Christ rising from the dead presented himself before the Lord as the firstfruits of the grand harvest of the resurrection yet unreaped, and by doing so consecrated and dedicated the whole crop unto God. As, then, he rose from the dead, so shall all the sleeping saints rise from the dead at the last day, for his resurrection is the firstfruits, the pledge, and the earnest of theirs.

April 14

"As having nothing, and yet possessing all things." – 2 Corinthians 6. 10.

How do we possess all things? In possessing Christ who is heir of all things. If we possess Christ, what have we not in him? We have wisdom to teach us, righteousness to justify us, sanctification to make us holy, and redemption to deliver us from sin, death, and hell. If we have him, we have the favour and love of God; we have the pardon of our sins, the reconciliation of our persons, the casting behind God's back of all our backslidings, and a title to a heavenly crown. If we have him, we have everything in him, for Christ is ours, and Christ is God's. Therefore in him we possess all things. We shall have in providence things sufficient to carry us to the grave. He will give us everything that is for our good, and keep back nothing that is for our benefit. If we possess him, what have we not in him? Now the world, when death comes, what has it? Nothing to look to but the anger of God, and a fearful judgment. But the saint of God, when death comes to him, what has he to look to? A crown of life, a mansion in the skies, a smiling God, and a blessed assurance that he shall sit down at the marriage supper of the Lamb. Thus though the saints of God have nothing, yet they possess all things; and possessing a heavenly crown, what can God give them more?

April 15

"And so will I go in unto the king, which is not according to the law: and if I perish, I perish." – Esther 4. 16.

When we are in darkness, under distress of conscience, or when guilt lies hard and heavy upon the soul, these things do, and must until removed, keep us back from the Lord. But are we ever to give heed to these enemies of our soul's peace? Are we never to press through the crowd? How was it with the man who was paralysed for so many years? He might for ever have lain helpless upon his bed, had he not been brought into the presence of Jesus. How with the woman with the issue of blood? She might for ever have tarried on the skirts of the crowd, a poor, polluted, self-condemned wretch. But she pressed through the crowd, and got to touch the hem of Jesus' garment. So with us. Shall we ever dwell in the outskirts – in the outer court of the temple? Shall we merely walk round Zion's bulwarks and tarry at her doors, or shall we venture into the holiest itself? Shall we, driven out by fear, act like Cain, and go out from the presence of the Lord? Or shall we, with all our sins and discouragements, still draw near? The Apostle encourages us to come with holy boldness to the throne of grace, and to venture into the presence of the King of kings. Esther would have ruined herself and all her nation had she given way to the weakness of the flesh; but she said, "I will go in unto the king; and if I perish, I perish." She went in with that resolution. The king held forth the sceptre; Esther touched it, and she and the people were saved. So in grace. Shall we ever keep away through guilt, and sin, and shame? Now the Holy Ghost not only in the word of truth encourages, but he himself from time to time enables us to draw near. And when we draw near under his divine operations, we feel the blessedness of so doing. Liberty is given, access, holy freedom, a spirit of prayer, power to take hold of God, to wrestle for the blessing, and sometimes to agonize with earnest sighs and groans and the energy of one of old: "I will not let thee go except thou bless me."

April 16

"Jesus Christ the same yesterday, and today, and for ever." – Hebrews 13. 8.

The eye of our faith must be ever fixed on Jesus, for the Person of Christ is the grand object of faith, and to lose sight of him is to lose sight of the Way, the Truth, and the Life. Is he not the same Jesus now that he was on earth? He is exalted, it is true, to an inconceivable height of glory, so that when John saw him, even as if in some measure veiled, he fell at his feet as dead. But he is the same Jesus now as when he was the man of sorrows and acquainted with grief; and as he wears the same human body, so he has the same tender, compassionate heart. All that he was upon earth as Jesus, he is in heaven still. All that tenderness and gentleness, all that pity to poor sensible sinners, all that compassion on the ignorant and on them that are out of the way, all that grace and truth which came by him and were manifest in him, all that bleeding, dying love, all that sympathy with the afflicted and tempted, all that power to heal by a word all manner of sickness and disease, all that surpassing beauty and blessedness whereby he is to those who have seen him the chiefest among ten thousand and the altogether lovely, he not only retains in the highest heavens, but is, so to speak, endowed with greater capacity to use them, for all power is given to him in heaven and earth, and all things are put under his feet, and that not only for his own sake, but that he might be the Head over all things to the Church.

April 17

"Thou therefore endure hardness, as a good soldier of Jesus Christ." – 2 Timothy 2. 3.

We often get into states and frames of mind, where we need something else besides consolation. A child would not grow, if it were always fed upon sweet-meats. It must have exercise, and be exposed to the weather, and have the cold winds blow upon its face, and be hardened, so as to enable it to bear the chill winter and the nipping frosts. So the child of God is not always petted, and fed upon love-tokens. He is not always carried in the warm bosom, or sucking the breasts of consolation, but he has to learn lessons to fit him to be a soldier. The soldier, we know, has to endure hardships. He has to lie all night upon the wet grass; to be pinched with hunger, parched with thirst, and nipped with cold; to make harassing marches; to hear the roar of the cannon and the whistling of the bullets, "the thunder of the captains and the shouting;" to see the flash of the sabre uplifted to cut him down, and the glitter of the bayonet at his breast, aye, and to feel painful and dangerous wounds. So with the spiritual soldier in God's camp. He has to hunger and thirst, to suffer cold, nakedness, and hard privations, to be shot at by the arrows of calumny and the fiery darts of Satan, to make harassing marches through an enemy's country, to suffer painful wounds, and by these very exercises learn to be a soldier. Only so far as he is thus exercised spiritually can he learn the art of war, can he know how to fight and make effectual battle under the banners of the Lord against the enemies of his salvation.

April 18

"But the salvation of the righteous is of the Lord: he is their strength in the time of trouble." – Psalm 37. 39.

Times of trouble try the saint of God, and they are meant to do so; that is the very purpose why they are sent, for "the Lord trieth the righteous." Still the promise holds good: "he is *their strength* in the time of trouble." When he breaks up the fountains of the great deep of sin and iniquity, he strengthens his people that they may not be carried away by the flood. When he hides his face, he strengthens them to say, "Though he slay me, yet will I trust in him." When temptation besets them sore, when they are put into the furnace, the Lord is with them there, as he was with the three men whom Nebuchadnezzar cast in. The Son of God is there with them, so that not a hair of their head is singed, nor does the smell of fire pass upon them (Dan. 3. 27). In all their afflictions he is afflicted, and by sharing it with them supports them under it. He is thus their strength; for he strengthens them with strength in their soul. He enables them to bear the weighty cross – to sustain the heavy load of trial and affliction – to put their mouth in the dust as needing and deserving his chastising strokes, and submit to his righteous dispensations and dealings as plainly sent by a gracious and loving hand. And ever and anon he drops in a sustaining word, gives an encouraging look, bestows a soft and healing touch, and thus helps them to wait in faith and hope until in due time he sends full deliverance. Thus he helps and delivers, and will do so in every time of trouble down to their dying bed, when he will give them their full and final deliverance from the body of sin and death and a world full of iniquity and sorrow.

April 19

"The election hath obtained it, and the rest were blinded." – Romans 11. 7.

Those that are blinded by the god of this world, have no knowledge of what power and feeling and savour and dew are; they see not these things, they are blind to their reality, they are dead to their importance; but the living family of God, who are brought by his blessed Spirit into some apprehension of eternal realities, have eyes to see what power is, and hearts too, to desire to feel its manifestation. Nay, it is the very seeing what reality and power are which makes them desire to experience the savour of eternal things in their conscience; and because they do not feel them as they wish, it makes them often fear that they are blind altogether (Isaiah 59. 10). But the very inquiry, the very anxious cry, the very groaning desire, the very fervent supplication to the Lord that he would not let them live and die without a testimony from himself, that he would lift up the light of his countenance and grant them the life of his favour – these very cries are a proof of life. Were you blind, you would not see these things; were you deaf, you would not spiritually hear these things; were you dead, you would not feel these things. And, therefore, that which you seem to take as an evidence against you, is, in reality, an evidence for you; and the very sensations of trepidation, anxious inquiry, godly fear, and the crying out before the Lord that he would search and try you and really make your heart right in his sight – these very things are the symptoms of life, the evidences of a work of grace upon the heart, and are the spiritual breathings of the quickened soul, the Lord himself having communicated these feelings unto it.

April 20

"And hath put all things under his feet, and gave him to be the head over all things to the church, which is his body, the fulness of him that filleth all in all." – Ephesians 1. 22, 23.

In the mind of God, and as chosen in Christ, the Church is a perfect body. It is, therefore, the fulness of Christ. Just as our head and members, in their union with each other, form one perfect harmonious body, so it is with Christ and the Church. As the natural head would be incomplete without the body, as the body would be incomplete without the head, so it is with Christ mystical, and his body the Church. Each lacks the other, and the union of both makes the whole complete. The Son of God, by becoming incarnate, needed a body of which he should be the Head. Without it, he would be as a bridegroom without the bride, a shepherd without the sheep, a foundation without the building, a vine without the branches. He did not need the Church as the Son of God, but he needed her as the Son of man. In her all his love is complete, his work complete, his grace complete, his glory complete; and when she is brought home to be for ever with him in glory, then all the purposes of God, all his eternal counsels of wisdom and grace, will be complete. In this sense we may understand the expression, "the fulness of him that filleth all in all." What a wonderful thought it is that he who, as the Son of God, filleth all in all - filleth all places with his omnipresence - should yet deign to have a relative fulness in his body the Church!

April 21

"And seekest thou great things for thyself? seek them not."
- Jeremiah 45. 5.

Whatever schemes and projects the Lord's people may devise that they may prosper and get on in the world, he rarely suffers their plans to thrive. He knows well to what consequences it would lead; - that this ivy creeping round the stem would, as it were, suffocate and strangle the tree. The more that worldly goods increase, the more the heart is fixed upon them; and the more the affections are set upon idols, the more is the heart drawn away from the Lord. He will not suffer his people to have their portion here below. He, therefore, says to them in his providence, as well as in his word, "Seek them not." But you will perhaps say, "What are we then to seek?" I will tell you in one word, - *Realities.* What are these great things that you are seeking after? say in religion. Could you see them in their right light, you would see that they are but shadows. You feel, for instance, your deficiency in gift in public when you are called upon to pray, or in private when you converse with those who possess readier speech, and you want what are commonly called *gifts,* such as a greater fluency of utterance, more ability to quote Scripture, and a more abundant variety of expressions, so as to make a deeper impression on the hearers - the real want being that you might stand higher in their estimation. But what would these gifts, if you had them to the fullest extent, so that men might almost worship you for them, do for you when you shall be called upon to lie upon a death-bed - when eternity is in view, and your soul has to deal with God only? You will want no gifts then. Grace will be the only thing which can do you any good.

April 22

"The entrance of thy words giveth light; it giveth understanding unto the simple." - Psalm 119. 130.

The word "simple" means literally something which is not folded or twisted together. But owing to the treacherous and desperately deceitful heart of man, all, without exception, in a state of nature are the reverse of this. All their plots and contrivances for worldly profit or fleshly pleasure are tangled and complicated; and they are continually twisting together some thread or other of carnal policy. But when God the Holy Ghost begins the work of grace upon the souls of the elect, he proceeds (if I may use the expression) to untwist them. He takes hold of that rope which Satan and their own hearts have been twisting together for years, and he untwists it throughout its whole length, so as to leave the strands not intertwined as before, but riven, separated, and torn from each other. The light that shines into the soul out of the fulness of Jesus discovers to a man the tortuousness, the crookedness, the complicated deceit and hypocrisy of which he is guilty. A man then is made "simple," when the folds and rumples of his heart are shaken out, and he is brought to see and feel that God looks into him; that his eye penetrates into every recess of his bosom; and that there is not a thought in his heart, nor a word in his tongue, but the Lord knoweth it altogether (Psalm 139. 4). This character is aptly represented by Nathaniel. He had gone through this untwisting work in his soul. He had been under the fig-tree, and whilst kneeling and praying there, the eye of God looked into him, and just as a flash of lightning runs, in a moment, through a coil of wire, so, when the eye of God looked into Nathaniel's soul, that instantaneous flash unravelled and untwisted the devices of his heart, and made him a simple man before him – "an Israelite indeed, in whom is no guile" (John 1. 47).

April 23

"Pass the time of your sojourning here in fear." – 1 Peter 1. 17.

Our life here is but a vapour. We are but pilgrims and strangers on this earthly ball, mere sojourners, without fixed or settled habitation, and passing through this world as not our home or resting-place. The Apostle, therefore, bids us pass this time, whether long or short, of our earthly sojourn, under the influence and in the exercise of godly fear. We are surrounded with enemies, all seeking, as it were, our life, and therefore we are called upon to move with great caution, knowing how soon we may slip and fall, and thus wound our own consciences, grieve our friends, gratify our enemies, and bring upon ourselves a cloud of darkness which may long hover over our souls. Our life here below is not one of ease and quiet, but a warfare, a conflict, a race, a wrestling not with flesh and blood alone, but with principalities and powers and spiritual wickedness in high places. We have to dread ourselves more than anything or anybody else, and to view our flesh as our greatest enemy. This fear is not a slavish, legal fear, such as that which John speaks of, and of which he says that "it hath torment," but that holy, godly, and filial fear which is the firstfruit and mark of covenant grace, and is "a fountain of life, to depart from the snares of death." How needful, then, it is to pass the time of our sojourning here in the exercise of this godly, reverential fear! And let no one think that this filial fear is inconsistent with faith even in its highest risings, or with love in its sweetest enjoyments.

April 24

"By the fear of the Lord men depart from evil." – Proverbs 16. 6.

There is a very close and intimate connection between godly fear and being "holy in all manner of conversation." When do we drop into levity in conversation? When do light and frothy words fall from our lips? When do any of those hasty bursts of temper, or those fretful expressions, or that mere carnal, worldly talk to which we are naturally prone, hover upon our lips and break forth, more or less unguardedly, from our tongue? Is it not when this godly fear is not playing its streams as a fountain of life to well water the soul and soften it into humility and love, and is not springing up in wholesome checks and godly admonitions to keep the tongue as with a bridle and to rule that little member which, though so little, if untamed, defileth the whole body? But if this fear be in exercise, it will restrain that levity of speech which not only grieves and wounds our own conscience, but is often a stumbling-block to the world, a bad example to the family of God, and a weapon in the hands of Satan to bring death into the soul. We should do well to ponder over those words of the Apostle, and to carry them with us when we are brought into conversation with others in the daily walks of life: "Let no corrupt communication proceed out of your mouth, but that which is good to the use of edifying, that it may minister grace unto the hearers. And grieve not the Holy Spirit of God, whereby ye are sealed unto the day of redemption" (Eph. 4. 29, 30).

April 25

"Elect according to the foreknowledge of God the Father, through sanctification of the Spirit, unto obedience and sprinkling of the blood of Jesus Christ: Grace unto you, and peace, be multiplied." – 1 Peter 1. 2.

Peter declares that we are "elect unto obedience." Election unto eternal life, unto salvation, unto the blood of sprinkling many gladly hear of, receive, and profess. This, they say, is sweet and precious doctrine. And so indeed it is. But do they find or feel any similar sweetness and preciousness in being chosen and ordained to know and do the will of God? Do they see and feel the blessedness of the precept being secured by divine decree, as well as the promise; and that there is a constraining power in the love of Christ under which they experience a holy and sacred pleasure in no longer living unto themselves, but unto him who died for them and rose again, similar in kind, if not in degree, to the pleasure which they experience in knowing they were ordained unto eternal life? But until this obedience be rendered, until these good works be brought forth, half of the sweetness and blessedness of real religion and of salvation by grace is not felt or known, nor the liberty of the gospel thoroughly realised or enjoyed, for the gospel must be obeyed and lived, as well as received and believed, that its full, liberating, sanctifying influences may be experienced, as sweetening the narrow and rugged path of doing and suffering the whole will of God.

April 26

"Thou hast set our iniquities before thee, our secret sins in the light of thy countenance." – Psalm 90. 8.

Thus Moses the man of God testified, and so Job found it: "For thou writest bitter things against me, and makest me to possess the iniquities of my youth" (Job 13. 26). But though the Lord sets his people's sins in the light of his countenance, and brings them to bear with weight and power upon their conscience, and thus for a time at least lets them sink and fall into distress and grief, he will support them under the heavy load, that they may not altogether be crushed by it. I do think, that if there is one single grace more overlooked than another in the Church of God at the present day, it is the grace of repentance. Though it lies at the very threshold of vital godliness, though it was one main element in the gospel that Paul preached, for he "testified both to the Jews, and also to the Greeks, repentance toward God, and faith toward our Lord Jesus Christ" (Acts 20. 21), yet how it is passed by. Men speak of faith, hope, and love; but repentance, contrition, godly sorrow for sin, how much this part of God's work upon the soul is passed by. But the Lord will not pass it by. Books may pass it by; men may pass it by; ministers may pass it by; but the Lord will not pass it by. He will bring out these secret sins and set them in the light of his countenance; and when he lays them upon the sinner's conscience, he will make him feel what an evil and bitter thing it is to have sinned against the Lord.

April 27

"That the righteousness of the law might be fulfilled in us, who walk not after the flesh, but after the Spirit." – Romans 8. 4.

A person may be "in the flesh," as indeed we all are, and yet not "walk after it." To walk after it implies, a setting it up as a pattern, and walking in accordance with it. But a person may be dragged after another, as we see sometimes a child is dragged unwillingly along by its mother, who does not willingly walk with her. The child is not walking after its mother, nor hand in hand with her, nor side by side; but is compelled against its will to go a road which it hates, as to go to school when it fain would go to play. So in a sense it often is with the child of grace; he is often dragged on by the flesh. He does not go after it willingly; he does not sin wilfully, but is entangled by the strength of the flesh, dragged on contrary to his best wishes, and sometimes in spite of his earnest cries, tears, groans, and desires. He does not walk after it as in Alpine countries tourists walk through the snow after a guide, setting his feet deliberately in every step which the flesh has made before him. The saint of God, therefore, though he is in the flesh, does not walk after the flesh; for if he so walked he could not fulfil the law of love, and therefore the righteousness of the law could not be fulfilled in him. But, as enabled by grace, he does from time to time walk after the Spirit, for as the Spirit leads, he follows; as the Spirit prompts, he obeys; and as the Spirit works, he performs. When the Spirit reveals Jesus, he loves him with a pure heart fervently; when the Spirit applies a promise, he believes it; and when he makes known the truth of God to his soul, he feeds upon and delights in it.

April 28

"My soul followeth hard after thee." – Psalm 63. 8.

The Lord (we would speak with reverence) does not suffer himself at first to be overtaken. The more the soul follows after him, the more he seems to withdraw himself, and thus he draws it more earnestly in the pursuit. He means to be overtaken in the end: it is his own blessed work in the conscience to kindle earnest desires and longings after himself; and therefore he puts strength into the soul, and "makes the feet like hinds' feet" to run and continue the chase. But in order to whet the ardent desire, to kindle to greater intensity the rising eagerness, the Lord will not suffer himself to be overtaken till after a long and arduous pursuit. This is sweetly set forth in the Song of Solomon, 5. 2-8. We find there the Lord coming to his bride; but she is unwilling to open to him till "he puts his hand in by the hole of the door." She would not rise at his first knocking, and therefore he is obliged to touch her heart. But "when she opened to her Beloved, he was gone"; and no sooner does he withdraw himself, than she pursues after him; but she cannot find him; he hides himself from her view, draws her round and round the walls of the city, until at length she overtakes, and finds Him whom her soul loveth. This sweetly sets forth how the Lord draws on the longing soul after himself. Could we immediately obtain the object of our pursuit, we should not half so much enjoy it when attained. Could we with a wish bring the Lord down into the soul, it would be but the lazy wish of the sluggard, who "desireth, and hath not." But when the Lord can only be obtained by an arduous pursuit, every faculty of the soul is engaged in panting after his manifested presence; and this was the experience of the Psalmist, when he cried, "My soul followeth hard after thee."

April 29

"Wherefore doth a living man complain, a man for the punishment of his sins? Let us search and try our ways, and turn again to the Lord." – Lamentations 3. 39, 40.

I believe in my conscience there are thousands of professors who have never known in the whole course of their religious profession what it is to have "searched and tried their ways"; to have been put into the balances and weighed in the scales of divine justice; or to have stood cast and condemned in their own feelings before God as the heart-searching Jehovah. From such a trying test, from such an unerring touchstone they have ever shrunk. And why? Because they have an inward consciousness that their religion will not bear a strict and scrutinizing examination. Like the deceitful tradesman, who allures his customers into a dark corner of his shop, in order to elude detection when he spreads his flimsy, made-up goods before them, so those who have an inward consciousness that their religion is not of heavenly origin, shun the light. As the Lord says, "Every one that doeth evil hateth the light, neither cometh to the light, lest his deeds should be reproved. But he that doeth truth cometh to the light, that his deeds may be made manifest, that they are wrought in God" (John 3. 20, 21). Now if you know nothing of having from time to time your ways searched and tried by God's word, or if you rise up with bitterness against an experimental, heart-searching ministry that would try them for you, it shews that there is some rotten spot in you – something that you dare not bring to the light. The candle of the Lord has not searched the hidden secrets of your heart; nor have you cried with David, "Search me, O God, and know my heart: try me, and know my thoughts. And see if there be any wicked way in me, and lead me in the way everlasting" (Ps. 139. 23, 24).

April 30

"Lead me in thy truth, and teach me." – Psalm 25. 5.

What wonderful things does God sometimes show us in his word! How our eyes sometimes seem to be anointed with eyesalve "to behold wondrous things out of God's law!" (Psalm 119. 18.) Sometimes in reading a chapter we see such beauty, such fulness, such sweetness, such glory in it, that it seems, as it were, to fill our very hearts. And what our souls want (I am sure my soul wants it, and it is my frequent cry to the Lord in secret that I may feel it) is to have this blessed truth taken out of the word of God, and applied to and sealed upon our hearts by the Spirit of God. I want no new revelation. Day by day I seem more satisfied of this, and more established in it – that all saving truth is in the word of God. I seek no visions, I desire no dreams, I want no airy speculations; but when my heart is brought to lie at the footstool of mercy, this seems to be the panting and breathing of my soul – to know experimentally and spiritually the blessed truths that my eyes see in the word of God, to have them opened up to my understanding, brought into my heart, grafted into my soul, applied to my conscience, and revealed with such supernatural and heavenly power that the truth as it is in Jesus may be in me a solemn and saving reality, that it may bring with it such a divine blessing as to fill me with grace, enlarge my heart into the enjoyment of the gospel, gird up my loins with spiritual strength, give and increase faith, communicate and encourage hope, shed abroad and draw forth love, and fill me with joy and peace in believing.

May 1

"I say unto you, Ask, and it shall be given you; seek, and ye shall find; knock, and it shall be opened unto you." – Luke 11. 9.

Wherever there is true prayer, there is importunity. Wherever the Lord brings trials upon the soul, he pours out upon it the spirit of grace and supplications. He thus encourages and enables the soul to be importunate with him. The blessings and benefits of perseverance and importunity in prayer the Lord has brought prominently before us in two parables – one, of the man in bed with his children, who would not get up and relieve his friend, but yet was overcome by his importunity; and the other, of the woman, who had a cause at issue, and went before the judge, who feared not God, neither regarded man; yet by her continual going to him, overcame him at last by her importunity (Luke 11. 5-8; 18. 1-7). Thus importunity and perseverance form the very feature of true prayer. If the child of God has a burden – if he is labouring under a strong temptation – if his soul is passing through some pressing trial – he is not satisfied with merely going to a throne of grace and coming away. There is at such times and seasons, as the Lord enables, real importunity; there is a holy wrestling; there are fervent desires; there are unceasing groans; there is a labouring to enter into rest; there is a struggling after deliverance; there is a crying unto the Lord, until he appears and manifests himself in the soul.

May 2

"Who shall separate us from the love of Christ?" – Romans 8. 35.

Be this never forgotten, that if we have ever been brought near to the Lord Jesus Christ by the actings of living faith, there never can be any final, actual separation from him. In the darkest moments, in the dreariest hours, under the most painful exercises, the most fiery temptations, there is, as with Jonah in the belly of hell, a looking again toward the holy temple. There is sometimes a sigh, a cry, a groan, a breathing forth of the heart's desire to "know Him, and the power of his resurrection"; that he would draw us near unto himself, and make himself precious to our souls. And these very cries and sighs, groanings and breathings, all prove that whatever darkness of mind, guilt of conscience, or unbelief we may feel, there is no real separation. It is in grace as it is in nature; the clouds do not blot out the sun; it is still in the sky, though they often intercept his bright rays. And so with the blessed Sun of righteousness; our unbelief, our ignorance, our darkness of mind, our guilt of conscience, our many temptations - these do not blot out the Sun of righteousness from the sky of grace. Though thick clouds come between him and us and make us feel as though he was blotted out, or at least as if we were blotted from his remembrance, yet, through mercy, where grace has begun the work, grace carries it on: "Being confident of this very thing, that he which hath begun a good work in you will perform it until the day of Jesus Christ" (Phil. 1. 6).

May 3

"In the world ye shall have tribulation: but be of good cheer; I have overcome the world." - John 16. 33.

Has not our path been one of tribulation, more or less, since the Lord was first pleased to turn our feet into the narrow way? But have we found, do we ever find, peace in Jesus? Do we desire to find peace there? Do we look for peace, do we expect to enjoy peace, from any other quarter? Dare we think, for a single moment, of peace in self, peace in the world, or peace in sin? Is our heart so fixed upon Jesus, our eyes so up unto him, the desires of our soul so after the manifestations of his mercy and love, that we are sure there is no peace worth the name except what is found in him? Our seasons of peace may not have been long – they may have been transient, very transient; yet sweet while they lasted, and sufficient to shew what true peace is, sufficient to give us longings after a clearer manifestation of it, and make us desire a fuller enjoyment of it. And yet the Lord winds it all up with the solemn and blessed declaration that though our appointed path is one of tribulation in the world, yet he has overcome it; sin shall not be our master, the world shall not be our conqueror, the things of time and sense shall not gain a victory over us. May He give us a sweet assurance that he will fight our battles, and bring us off more than conquerors.

May 4

"He staggered not at the promise of God through unbelief; but was strong in faith, giving glory to God; and being fully persuaded that, what he had promised, he was able also to perform." – Romans 4. 20, 21.

This, then, was Abraham's faith. It was a firm credence in the promise of God made to him, and yet a faith that lived under opposition, hoping against hope, and being fully persuaded that what God had promised he would perform. Our faith, then, if it be genuine, must resemble that of Abraham. It must anchor in the truth of God as made life and spirit to our soul. It must meet with every opposition from without and within; from sin, Satan, and the world; from nature and flesh and reason all combined against it. But in spite of all, it must hope against hope, and be fully persuaded that what God has promised he is able to perform; and thus by perseverance and patient waiting obtain the victory. Take another example, that of Moses: his faith was of this nature. "By faith Moses, when he was come to years, refused to be called the son of Pharaoh's daughter; choosing rather to suffer affliction with the people of God, than to enjoy the pleasures of sin for a season" (Heb. 11. 24, 25). The peculiar character of the faith of Moses was this, that though he was highly exalted and might have enjoyed all the treasures and pleasures of Egypt, yet he deliberately preferred to suffer affliction with the people of God, than to enjoy all that wealth could offer or carnal pleasure present; "having respect to the recompence of the reward."

May 5

"Know ye not, that to whom ye yield yourselves servants to obey, his servants ye are to whom ye obey; whether of sin unto death, or of obedience unto righteousness?" – Romans 6. 16.

There is a blessedness in obedience. It does not give us, but it manifests our interest in the finished work of the Son of God. There is nothing in the highest acts of faith or obedience that we can take any joy in as accomplished by us, nothing that we can boast of as our own; and yet there is a sacred blessedness in obeying the gospel by believing in the Son of God, by walking in the fear of God, and doing the things, as well as professing them, which are pleasing in God's sight. Walk in carnality, pride, and self-righteousness; live after worldly customs and conform yourself to worldly opinions, and if there be a grain of godly fear, or one spark of the life of God in your heart, you will do the best thing you can to bring your soul into misery and bondage. Therefore, though we can take no merit from and make no boasting of any obedience we may render, yet is the path of godly obedience so safe, so blessed, so honouring to God, and so comforting to the soul thus favoured, that it should be and will be the desire of all who truly fear God to be ever found walking in it. And O the blessedness, if we are enabled in any measure to obey the will of God by believing in his dear Son and by walking in his fear, to find under every temptation and trial in life, death, health, and sickness, that we have a gracious and sympathising High Priest, "the author of eternal salvation to all them that obey him"! (Heb. 5. 9)

May 6

"The Lord hear thee in the day of trouble; the name of the God of Jacob defend thee; send thee help from the sanctuary, and strengthen thee out of Zion." – Psalm 20. 1, 2.

When the soul has to pass through the trying hour of temptation, it wants help from the sanctuary. And nothing but help from the sanctuary can ever stand it in any stead. All other help leaves the soul just where it found it. Now why does the Lord send help from the sanctuary, but because the soul to whom help is sent stands interested in the Father's love, the Saviour's blood, and the Spirit's teachings – interested in the eternal covenant transactions of the Three-One Jehovah. Help is sent him from the sanctuary, because his name has been from all eternity registered in the Lamb's book of life, graven upon the palms of his hands, borne on his shoulder, and worn on his heart. He was in the sanctuary when his covenant Head stood up on his behalf, and in the Lord's book all his members were written when as yet there was none of them. He was then *virtually* in the sanctuary before all time, and he will be personally in the sanctuary after all time. But he must be "made meet to be a partaker of the inheritance of the saints in light" (Col. 1. 12). As he is predestinated to inhabit that sanctuary, he must have a nature suited for its holy delights. Now it is receiving help from the sanctuary that fits him to inhabit it. Communications of life and grace out of it make him a new creature, and produce spirituality and heavenly-mindedness. The breath of heaven in his soul draws his affections upward, weans him from earth, and makes him a pilgrim and a sojourner here below, " looking for a city which hath foundations, whose builder and maker is God" (Heb. 11. 10).

May 7

"The Lord hath appeared of old unto me, saying, Yea, I have loved thee with an everlasting love: therefore with lovingkindness have I drawn thee." – Jeremiah 31. 3.

There can be no new thought in the mind of God. New thoughts, new feelings, new plans, new resolutions continually occur to our mind; for ours is but a poor, fallen, fickle, changeable nature. But God has no new thoughts, feelings, plans or resolutions; for if he had he would be a changeable Being, not one great, eternal, unchangeable I AM. All his thoughts, therefore, all his plans, all his ways are like himself, eternal, infinite, unchanging and unchangeable. So it is with the love of Christ to the Church. It is eternal, unchanging, unchangeable. And why? Because he loved as God. Never let us lose sight of the glorious Deity of Jesus. He loved her in eternity as the Son of God, prior to his incarnation. That was but the fruit of his love. We can, therefore, assign no beginning to the love of Christ, for it existed when he existed, which was from eternity. Neither can we put any end to that love, for it can only end with himself; and as he had no beginning, so he has no ending. His love then is as himself, which as it knew no beginning shall know no end. O what a mercy it is for those who have any gracious, experimental knowledge of the love of Christ, to believe it is from everlasting to everlasting; that no incidents of time, no storms of sin or Satan, can ever change or alter that eternal love, but that it remains now and will remain the same to all eternity!

May 8

"The substance of a diligent man is precious." – Proverbs 12. 27.

If the Lord has done anything for our souls by his Spirit and grace, and given us anything to taste, handle, realise, and enjoy for ourselves, we know there is a substance and reality in the things that we believe. Religion is our chief employment; our daily meditation or exercise – the main concern of our thoughts and what lies with the greatest weight upon our minds. And justly so; for it is our all. If we have religion, the religion of God's giving, it will be uppermost in our heart. It is true we are surrounded with and often hampered by a body of sin and death; we have many worldly cares and anxieties which will intrude upon our minds; and those engaged in business have many things especially to drag them down from heaven to earth. Still, religion will be for the most part uppermost in a man's soul, where God has begun and is carrying on a gracious work. Not but what he is often very cold and dead, lifeless in his prayers, and unfeeling in his affections; not but what he may be carried away by the things of time and sense and dragged down into darkness, carnality, and death; but with it all, there is something in his bosom that struggles upward – there is that in his heart which goes after the precious things of Christ, and the solemn realities of eternity.

May 9

"Thou gavest also thy good spirit to instruct them, and withheldest not thy manna from their mouth, and gavest them water for their thirst." – Nehemiah 9. 20.

When we are thoroughly emptied of ourselves – when our knowledge is shown to be ignorance, our wisdom folly, our righteousness filthy rags, and our strength weakness – then we begin to long after the teachings of the blessed Spirit. We must be purged and tried before we can value and receive the treasures of grace. When we are well exercised and tried in our souls, then we begin to long after the teachings of the Holy Spirit, that he would shed abroad the love of God in our soul, visit and guide us, overshadow us with his holy presence, and drop into our hearts his secret unction. Before we are brought here, we know not the personality of the Holy Ghost. We have no evidence in our conscience that he is God; we cannot worship and adore him as the Third Person in the blessed Godhead. But when we are brought to this spot, that we know nothing without his teaching, feel nothing without his giving, and are nothing without his making – this makes us pant and sigh after his teachings and leadings; and we are brought to wait in the posture of holy adoration and still quietness for the dew and unction of the Spirit to fall upon our conscience.

May 10

"Every one that loveth him that begat loveth him also that is begotten of him." – 1 John 5. 1.

Where there is love to Jesus, there will be love to those who are his by redemption, his by regeneration, and his by personal possession. The more, too, that we see and the more that we know of the beauty and blessedness of the Lord of life and glory, the more we shall love his image as we behold it visibly marked in his dear people, and the more we shall cleave to them as being Christ's with tender affection. It is our dim, scanty and imperfect knowledge of God the Father in his eternal love, and of the Lord Jesus Christ in his grace and glory, which leaves us so often cold, lifeless, and dead in our affections towards him; and with the declension of love towards the Head comes on decay of love towards his members. If there were more blessed revelations to our soul of the Person and work, grace and glory, beauty and blessedness of the Lord Jesus Christ, it is impossible but that we should more and more warmly and tenderly fall in love with him; for he is the most glorious object that the eye of faith can see. He fills heaven with the resplendent beams of his glorious majesty; and has ravished the hearts of thousands of his dear family upon earth by the manifestations of his bleeding, dying love. So that if we love him not, it is because we know him not. If, then, to those who know him he makes himself precious, it is evident that just in proportion to our personal, spiritual, experimental knowledge of him will be our love to him.

May 11

"I will not let thee go, except thou bless me." – Genesis 32. 26.

It is encouraging to the Lord's people as they are from time to time placed in similar circumstances of trial, exercise, perplexity, sorrow or distress with Jacob, to see the blessed result of his wrestling with the angel. He crosses the ford of Jabbok all weakness; he recrosses it all strength. He leaves his family, and wrestles alone, a fainting Jacob; he returns to them a prevailing Israel. He goes to the Lord in an agony of doubt and alarm, fearing every moment lest he and all that was dear to him should be swept off from the face of the earth; he returns with the Lord's blessing in his soul, with the light of the Lord's countenance lifted up upon him. And is not this instance recorded for the instruction and consolation of the Lord's living family? Are they not from time to time in circumstances experimentally which resemble Jacob's circumstances literally? Have they not similar difficulties and similar necessities? And does not the Lord from time to time raise up in their heart the same faith to lay hold? the same importunity to keep hold? And shall He who gave Jacob such a merciful deliverance – shall He who has recorded in his holy word this remarkable event in Jacob's life for the edification and instruction of his people in all times – hear Jacob, and not hear them? It is derogatory to the sympathising "Man of Sorrows"; it is treason against the Majesty of heaven to believe, that a child of God in similar circumstances can go to the Lord in a similar way and not get a similar blessing.

May 12

"But I am poor and needy; yet the Lord thinketh upon me." – Psalm 40. 17.

Are there not solemn seasons in your soul, when you think upon the Lord? When you lie awake, perhaps at midnight, thinking upon God, upon his truth, his love, his word, his dealings with your soul, and your desires, prayers, and breathings all flow forth to his sacred Majesty – is not this some evidence that you are thinking upon his name? And be assured that if you think upon him, he has thought upon you. Look at the giddy multitude. Do they think upon God? Is Jesus ever felt to be precious to their souls? Do they pant after him as the hart after the water brooks? No; their language is, "There is no God." It is not their spoken language, but it is their inward language. But through mercy you can say, that you think upon God; and thus there is some evidence, though you cannot rise up to the assurance of it, that he thinketh upon you. And if he thinks upon you, his thoughts are thoughts of good, thoughts of peace, and not of evil. Does he not read your heart? Does not his holy eye look into the very secret recesses of your soul? And if he thinks upon you, will he leave you, give you up, abandon you in the hour when you need him most? No; he who thought upon you in eternity, will think on you in time, in every trial, every temptation, every sickness, and in the solemn hour when soul and body part. Through life and death he will still think on you; and will bring you at last to that heavenly abode where these two things will be blessedly combined – the Lord's ever thinking upon his Zion, and his Zion ever thinking upon him.

May 13

"Say unto my soul, I am thy salvation." – Psalm 35. 3.

To keep water sweet, it must be perpetually running; and to keep the life of God up in the soul, there must be continual exercises. This is the reason why the Lord's people have so many conflicts, trials, painful exercises, sharp sorrows, and deep temptations – to keep them alive unto God; to bring them out of, and to keep them out of that slothful, sluggish, wretched state of carnal security and dead assurance in which so many seem to have fallen asleep – fallen asleep like the sailor upon the top of the mast, not knowing what a fearful gulf is boiling up below. The Lord, therefore, "trieth the righteous." He will not suffer his people to be at ease in Zion; to be settled on their lees, and get into a wretched Moabitish state. He therefore sends afflictions upon them, tribulations, and trials, and allows Satan to tempt and harass them. And under these feelings the blessed Spirit, from time to time, raises up in them this sigh and cry, "Say unto my soul, I am thy salvation." None but thyself, Lord, can save me; nothing short of thy voice can whisper peace to my conscience; nothing short of thy blood can speak away guilt from lying as a heavy burden upon my heart; nothing short of thy love shed abroad by the Holy Ghost can make my soul happy in thyself.

May 14

"Ye are not your own." – 1 Corinthians 6. 19.

There is a blessed sense in these words, "Ye are not your own." Remember you must be some one's. If God be not your master, the devil will be; if grace do not rule, sin will reign; if Christ is not your all in all, the world will be. It is not as though we could roam abroad in perfect liberty. Someone will have us. We must have a master of one kind or another; and which is best, a bounteous benevolent Benefactor such as God has ever shewn himself to be; a merciful, loving, and tender Parent; a kind, forgiving Father and Friend; and a tender-hearted, compassionate Redeemer, able to save us to the uttermost; or a cruel devil, a miserable world, and a wicked, vile, abominable heart? Which is better, to live under the sweet constraints of the dying love of a dear Redeemer; under gospel influences, gospel principles, gospel promises, and gospel encouragements; or to walk in fancied liberty, with sin in our heart, exercising dominion and mastery there; and binding us in iron chains to the judgment of the great day? Even taking the present life, there is more real pleasure, satisfaction, and happiness in half an hour with God, in sweet union and communion with the Lord of life and glory, in reading his word with a believing heart, in finding access to his sacred presence, in knowing something of the droppings in of his favour and mercy, – there is more solid happiness in half an hour thus spent in the real service of God, than in all the delights of sin, all the lusts of the flesh, all the pride of life, and all the amusements that the world has ever devised to kill time and cheat self, thinking, by a death-bed repentance, at last to cheat the devil.

May 15

"Ye are bought with a price." – 1 Corinthians 6. 20.

How deep, how dreadful, of what awful magnitude, of how black a dye, of how ingrained a stamp must sin be, to need such an atonement - no less than the blood of him who was the Son of God - to put it away. What a slave to sin and Satan, what a captive to the power of lust, how deeply sunk, how awfully degraded, how utterly lost and undone must guilty man be to need a sacrifice like this. "Ye are bought with a price." Have you ever felt your bondage to sin, Satan, and the world? Have you ever groaned, cried, grieved, sorrowed, and lamented under your miserable captivity to the power of sin? Has the iron ever entered into your soul? Have you ever clanked your fetters, and as you did so, and tried to burst them, they seemed to bind round about you with a weight scarcely endurable? But have you ever found any liberty from them, any enlargement of heart, any sweet going forth from the prison-house, any dropping of the manacles from your hands, and the fetters from your feet, so as to walk in some measure of gospel liberty? "Ye are bought with a price." Ye were slaves of sin and Satan; ye were shut up in the dark cell, where all was gloom and despondency; there was little hope in your soul of ever being saved. But there was an entrance of gospel light into your dungeon; there was a coming out of the house of bondage; there was a being brought into the light of God's countenance, shining forth in his dear Son. Now, this is not only being bought with a price, but experiencing the blessed effects of it.

May 16

"And a man shall be as an hiding place from the wind, and a covert from the tempest." – Isaiah 32. 2.

Who is this man? Need I ask the question? Is there not a response in every God-fearing breast? It is the man Christ Jesus - the man who is God's fellow. How blessed it is to have a scriptural and spiritual view of the humanity of the Lord Jesus Christ, to see him not merely as God, truly essential God, one in essence, glory, and power with the Father and the blessed Spirit, but also man, made in all things like unto us, sin only excepted. And what a suitability there is in the humanity of the Lord Jesus, when we view it in union with this glorious Deity! As man he suffered, as man he bled, as man he died, as man he stands a Mediator for his fellow men between God and man; as man, he has for human distress an affectionate, compassionate, sympathising heart; as man, he obeyed the law in every particular; as man, he bore all the sufferings of humanity, and thus became the Brother born for adversity, flesh of our flesh, and bone of our bone; yet perfectly pure, harmless, undefiled, separate from sinners, and now exalted higher than the heavens. But what beauty, grace, glory, and suitability do we see in the man Christ Jesus, till he is revealed to the soul by the blessed Spirit? None. It is he who takes the humanity of Christ Jesus and shows it to the eye of faith. And this humanity he shows not as mere humanity, but as in union with, though distinct from, his eternal Deity. O this blessed man! - this man of sorrows; this suffering, agonizing, crucified man. View him on the cross, bleeding for thy sins; and then lift up thine eyes and see him as the same man at the right hand of God. This was Stephen's dying sight just before he passed into his presence: "Behold, I see the heavens opened, and the Son of man standing on the right hand of God" (Acts 7. 56).

May 17

"We are saved by hope." – Romans 8. 24.

What is the meaning of being saved by hope? It does not mean saved actually, but instrumentally; not saved as regards our eternal security, but as regards our experience of salvation. By hope we are instrumentally saved from despair, saved from turning our backs upon Christ and the gospel, saved from looking to any other Saviour, or any other salvation; and especially saved from making this world and this life our happiness and home, as "waiting patiently for what we see not", even "the redemption of our body". Now it is by hope that we hang upon and cleave to the Lord Jesus, and thus by this grace we abide in him. It is therefore spoken of as an "anchor of the soul, both sure and steadfast, and which entereth into that within the veil" (Heb. 6. 19). What holds the ship firm in the storm, and prevents it falling upon the rocks? The anchor. The ship abides firm as long as the anchor holds. So by hope the soul abides in Christ. He is within the veil; we are without, and, it may be, tossed up and down on a sea of doubt and fear, distress and anxiety, and yet there is a bond of union between him and us firmer than the Atlantic Cable.

May 18

"I will put my fear in their hearts, that they shall not depart from me." – Jeremiah 32. 40.

As the fear of God springs up in a believing soul, and is maintained and kept alive by the influences which come out of Christ as a covenant Head, it produces, as its effects, an abiding in him. We cannot depart from him through the fear of God. It is therefore called "a fountain of life to depart from the snares of death." If a fountain of life, it must be fed out of him who is the life; and as it departs from the snares of death, it cleaves more fully and closely to him as these snares are broken to pieces and left behind. If we examine the movements of godly fear in our hearts, we shall see that all its tendencies are toward life and the Source of life; toward hatred of sin and love of holiness; toward a desire after the enjoyment of heavenly realities, and a deadness to the things of time and sense; toward a knowledge of Christ in the manifestation of himself, and a longing to live more to his praise, to walk more in his footsteps, and to be more conformed to his suffering image. Now, as none of these things can be produced but by union with Christ and abiding in him, we see how the fear of God helps forward and is needful to this abiding. For directly that the fear of God burns low in the soul, there is a gradual withdrawing from, and a sensible declining of this abiding in Christ.

May 19

"Let the word of Christ dwell in you richly in all wisdom." – Colossians 3. 16.

This surely means something more than merely reading the word in a careless, formal manner. It is "to dwell in us," that is, take up its firm and lasting abode in our heart, and that "richly"; not poorly and niggardly, but copiously and abundantly, unfolding to us and putting us into possession of the wealth of its treasures; and that in "all wisdom," making us wise to salvation, opening up to us the manifold wisdom of God, and how it displays itself in the great mystery of godliness. Now we shall not attain to this rich and heavenly wisdom unless we search and study the Scriptures with prayer and supplication to understand what the Holy Ghost has revealed therein, and what he is pleased to unfold therefrom of the will and way of God for our own personal instruction and consolation. We very easily fall off from abiding in Christ; nor can we expect to keep up sensible union and communion with the Lord Jesus if we neglect those means of grace which the Holy Ghost has provided for the sustentation of the life of God in the soul. When we get cold, sluggish, and dead, to read the word of God is a task and a burden; but not so, when the life of God is warm and gushing in the soul. Then, to read his holy word with prayer and supplication, entering by faith into its hidden treasures, and drinking into the mind of Christ as revealed therein, is a blessed means of maintaining the life of God in the heart, and keeping up union and communion with Christ.

May 20

"Thou wilt cast all their sins into the depths of the sea." – Micah 7. 19.

When God takes all our iniquities with his own hand, and casts them with his own arm into the depths of the sea, they will never come out of those depths to witness against the family of God in the great and terrible day. Your sins now may seem to be all alive in your breast, and every one of them to bring accusation upon accusation against you. This sin is crying out for vengeance, and that for punishment. This slip, this fall, this backsliding, this foolish word, this wrong action, are all testifying against you in the court of conscience. Do what you may, be where you may, live how you may, watch and pray how you may, keep silent and separate from the world or even from your own family how you may, sin still moves, lives, acts, works, and often brings you into guilt and bondage. But if God has had mercy upon us he has cast all our sins with his own hands into the depths of the sea, and those sins have no more eyes to look at us with angry indignation, have no more tongues to speak against us in voices of accusation, have no more life in them to rise up and testify that they have been committed by us, that God's law has been broken by them, and that therefore we are under its condemnation and curse. And there is no truth in God's word more certain than the complete forgiveness of sins, and the presentation of the Church of Christ at the great day faultless before the presence of his glory with exceeding joy.

May 21

"O satisfy us early with thy mercy; that we may rejoice and be glad all our days." – Psalm 90. 14.

Many of the dear children of God are tossed up and down on a sea of great uncertainty, doubt and fear, because they have not had sensible manifestations of Christ to their soul. He has not come into them in the power of his love; still they often say, "When wilt thou come unto me? O visit me with thy salvation; speak a word to my soul; it is thyself, and thyself alone, I want to hear, to see, and to know!" Now these are drawings of the gracious Lord, the secret beginnings of his coming, the heralds of his approach, the dawning of the day before the morning star arises and the sun follows upon his track. But when the Lord does come in any sweet manifestation of his presence or of his power, then he will abide where he has come, for he never leaves or forsakes a soul which he has once visited. He may seem to do so; he may withdraw himself; and then who can behold him? But he never really leaves the temple which he has once adorned and sanctified with his presence. Christ is formed in the hearts of his people the hope of glory; their body is the temple of the Holy Ghost, and Christ dwells in them by faith. Though we often mourn over his absence and do not feel his gracious presence as we would, still he is there, if he has once come.

May 22

"For whatsoever is born of God overcometh the world: and this is the victory that overcometh the world, even our faith." – 1 John 5. 4.

If we are to be saved our faith must gain the day; we must have a faith that shall triumph over death and hell and gain a glorious conquest over every internal and external and infernal foe. This is just the state, then, in which the matter stands: we must either conquer or be conquered; we must either gain the day and be crowned with an immortal crown of glory, or else sink in the strife, defeated by sin and Satan. But none of God's people will be defeated in the fight; and yet they often seem, as it were, to escape defeat by the very skin of their teeth; yet faith will sooner or later gain the day, for Jesus is its finisher as well as its author. He will crown the faith of his own gift with eternal glory. He will never suffer his dear family to be overcome in the good fight of faith, for he will give strength to every weak arm and power to every feeble knee, and has engaged to bring them off more than conquerors. Thus as the Lord the Spirit is pleased to work in the soul by his living energy, he strengthens faith more and more to believe in the name of the only begotten Son of God, to receive more continual supplies out of his fulness, to wrestle more earnestly with God for a spiritual blessing, to stand more firmly in the evil day against every assaulting foe, to fight more strenuously the good fight of faith, and never cry quarter until faith gains its glorious end, which is to see Jesus as he is in the realms of eternal day.

May 23

"Trust in him at all times; ye people, pour out your heart before him." – Psalm 62. 8.

Have we not sometimes been enabled to pour out our hearts at the throne of grace, and tell the Lord what we really wanted, what we really asked for, and tell him that nothing but that which he alone could give would satisfy our souls? There have been such times of access to the God of grace. And afterwards perhaps we have forgotten the things we told him of; we have been heedless of the prayers we laid at his feet; and though very earnest at the time in seeking after certain blessings, we left them at the Lord's feet and forgot them all. But the Lord does not forget them; they are treasured up in his heart and memory; and in his own time he brings them to light, and gives the fulfilment of them. But before he does it, he will bring us into the spot where we want them again; and then we have to tell him, and supplicate and ask him again, ashamed of ourselves perhaps that we should have asked the Lord for these blessings and been as heedless of them as though we did not care to receive them at his hand; but still, under trouble, under soul necessity, under grief, we go and tell him again. And then the Lord, in his own time and way, brings about the very things we desired of him; opens up ways, lifts out of trials, removes burdens, makes a way in the deep, which no eye but his could see, and no hand but his could open, – leads the soul into it, brings the soul through it, – and then hides all glory from the creature, by making us fall down before his feet, and ascribe glory and honour and power and thanksgiving and salvation unto God and the Lamb.

May 24

"Set your affection on things above, not on things on the earth." – Colossians 3. 2.

Everything upon earth, as viewed by the eyes of the Majesty of heaven, is low and paltry. Earth is after all but a huge clod of dust, and as such, apart from its having been once the place of the Redeemer's sufferings and sacrifice, being now the habitation of his suffering people, and to be hereafter the scene of his glory, as insignificant in the eyes of its Maker as the small dust of the balance or the drop of the bucket. What, then, are its highest objects, its loftiest aims, its grandest pursuits, its noblest employments, short of the grace of the gospel, in the sight of him who inhabits eternity, but mean and worthless? Nay, even in our eyes is there not one consideration that when felt stamps vanity upon them all? – that all earth's pursuits, whatever high attainments men may reach in this life, be it of wealth, rank, learning, power, or pleasure, end in death? The breath of God's displeasure soon lays low in the grave all that is rich and mighty, high and proud; "for the day of the Lord of hosts shall be upon every one that is proud and lofty, and upon every one that is lifted up; and he shall be brought low" (Isaiah 2. 12). Thus that effectual work of grace on the heart, whereby the chosen vessels of mercy are delivered from the power of darkness and translated into the kingdom of God's dear Son, may well be termed a "high calling," for it calls them out of those low, grovelling pursuits, those earthly toys, those base and sensual lusts in which the children of men seek at once their happiness and their ruin, unto the knowledge and enjoyment of those things which are above, where Christ sitteth on the right hand of God.

May 25

"As dying, and, behold, we live." – 2 Corinthians 6. 9.

Though we die, and die daily, yet, behold, we live; and in a sense, the more we die, the more we live. The more we die to self, the more we die to sin; the more we die to pride and self-righteousness, the more we die to creature strength; and the more we die to nature, the more we live to grace. And this runs all the way through the life and experience of a Christian. Nature must die, that grace may live. The weeds must be plucked up, that the crop may grow; the flesh be starved, that the spirit may be fed; the old man put off, that the new man may be put on; the deeds of the body be mortified, that the soul may live unto God. As then we die, we live. The more we die to our own strength, the more we live to Christ's strength; the more we die to creature hope, the more we live to a good hope through grace; the more we die to our own righteousness, the more we live to Christ's righteousness; and the more we die to the world, the more we live to and for heaven. This is the grand mystery, that the Christian is always dying, yet always living; and the more he dies, the more he lives. The death of the flesh is the life of the spirit; the death of sin is the life of righteousness; and the death of the creature is the very life of God in the soul.

May 26

"I will overturn, overturn, overturn it: and it shall be no more, until he come whose right it is; and I will give it him." – Ezekiel 21. 27.

Are there not seasons in our experience when we can lay down our souls before God, and say, "Let Christ be precious to my soul, let him come with power to my heart, let him set up his throne as Lord and King, and let self be nothing before him"? Well, we utter these prayers in sincerity and simplicity, we desire their fulfilment; but oh, the struggle! the conflict! when God answers these petitions. When our plans are frustrated, what a rebellion works up in the carnal mind! When self is cast down, what a rising up of the fretful, peevish impatience of the creature! When the Lord does answer our prayers, and strips off all false confidence; when he does remove our rotten props, and dash to pieces our broken cisterns, what a storm - what a conflict takes place in the soul! Angry with the Lord for doing the very work we have asked him to do, rebelling against him for being so kind as to answer those petitions that we have offered up, and ready to fume and fret against the very teaching for which we have supplicated him. But he is not to be moved; he will take his own way. " 'I will overturn,' let the creature say, let it think what it will. Down it shall go to ruin, it shall become a wreck, it shall be overthrown. My purpose shall be accomplished, and I will fulfil all my pleasure. But I will overturn, not to destroy, not to cast into eternal perdition, but I will overturn the whole building to erect a far more goodly edifice. Self is a rebel, who has set up an idolatrous temple, and I will overturn and bring the temple to ruin, for the purpose of manifesting my glory and my salvation, that I may be your Lord and your God."

May 27

"If any man come to me, and hate not his father, and mother, and wife, and children, and brethren, and sisters, yea, and his own life also, he cannot be my disciple. And whosoever doth not bear his cross, and come after me, cannot be my disciple." - Luke 14. 26, 27.

There is no middle path to heaven - there is no intermediate state between hell and heaven; no purgatory for that numerous class who think themselves hardly good enough for heaven, yet hardly bad enough for hell. No; there is no intermediate road nor state. We must win Christ as our own most blessed Jesus, and with him enjoy the happiness and glory of heaven, or sink down to hell with all our sins upon our head beneath his most terrible frown. The soul then that has been charmed with the beauty and blessedness of Jesus longs to win him, and that not for a day, month, or year, but for eternity; for in obtaining him, it obtains all that God can give the soul of man to enjoy as created immortal and for immortality. Under the influence of his grace, it feels at times, even here below, all its immortal powers springing forth into active, heavenly life, and looks forward in faith and hope to a glorious eternity, where it will be put into possession of the highest enjoyment which God can give to man, even union with himself by virtue of union with his dear Son, according to those wonderful words of the Redeemer himself – "That they all may be one; as thou, Father, art in me, and I in thee, that they also may be one in us" (John 17. 21).

May 28

"Remember me, O Lord, with the favour that thou bearest unto thy people: O visit me with thy salvation." – Psalm 106. 4.

How is a man brought and taught to want to be "visited with" God's salvation? He must know some-thing first of condemnation. Salvation only suits the condemned. The Son of man came to seek and to save that which was lost; and therefore salvation only suits the lost. A man must be lost – utterly lost – before he can prize God's salvation. And how is he lost? By losing all his religion, losing all his righteousness, losing all his strength, losing all his confidence, losing all his hopes, losing all that is of the flesh; losing it by its being taken from him, and stripped away by the hand of God. A man who is brought into this state of utter beggary and complete bankruptcy – to be nothing, to have nothing, to know nothing – he is the man, who in the midnight watches, in his lonely hours, by his fireside, and at times, well-nigh night and day, is crying, groaning, begging, suing, seeking, and praying after the manifestation of God's salvation to his soul. "O visit me with thy salvation." He wants a visit from God; he wants God to come and dwell with him, take up his abode in his heart, discover himself to him, manifest and reveal himself, sit down with him, eat with him, walk with him, and dwell in him as his God. And a living soul can be satisfied with nothing short of this. He must have a visit. It profits him little to read in the word of God what God did for his saints of old; he wants something *for himself,* something that shall do *his* soul good; he wants something that shall cheer, refresh, comfort, bless, and profit him, remove his burdens, and settle his soul into peace. And therefore he wants a visitation – that the presence and power, the mercy and the love of God should visit his soul.

May 29

"That I may see the good of thy chosen." – Psalm 106. 5.

Did you ever see any good in God's chosen? Oh! "how goodly are thy tents, O Jacob, and thy tabernacles, O Israel!" Did you ever see what good God has blessed his people with, and how good it is to be one of them? All God's people see that there is a "good" in God's chosen family, peculiar to them, and *that* they sigh and long for. But some will say, Had David never seen it when he penned this psalm? Aye, surely; he had seen it. But did he not want to see it again? Yes; he had lost the sight of it, the sweet vision of it had retired, the old veil had come back, his eyes were dim, he wanted fresh "eye-salve". So with us; we have seen, we trust, at times "the good of God's chosen", have felt our affections drawn towards them, and drawn up towards God, and have said, "Whom have I in heaven but thee? and there is none upon earth that I desire beside thee." That was to enjoy the sweet foretastes of heaven. But all these sweet foretastes became clouded; fogs and mists rested upon them, and hid them from our eye. Fresh sin brought fresh guilt, and darkness and deadness and doubts and temptations and fears and besetments came on of various kinds; and all these beclouded our sight. But we cannot forget the past; we cannot forget the solemn moments when we walked with God and talked with God, nor the sweet feelings that his presence enkindled. However dark, however dead, however disconsolate, however tried, harassed, and tempted, we cannot forget that. And having "seen the good of God's chosen" we want to see again the good sight, to taste again that heavenly banquet. "That I may see the good of thy chosen."

May 30

"That I may rejoice in the gladness of thy nation." – Psalm 106. 5.

What is *"the gladness of God's nation?"* To be saved "without money and without price"; to be saved by grace - free, rich, sovereign, distinguishing grace, with-out one atom of works, without one grain of creature merit, without anything of the flesh. This is "the gladness of God's nation"; to rejoice in free grace, grace superabounding over the aboundings of sin, grace reigning triumphant over the dreadful evils of our heart. It is grace that "gladdens" a man's heart. Oh! sweet grace! blessed grace I when it meets our case and reaches our souls. Oh! what a help, what a strength, what a rest for a poor toiling, striving, labouring soul, to find that grace has done all the work, to feel that grace has triumphed in the cross of Christ, to find that nothing is required, nothing is wanted, nothing is to be done. It is a full and perfect, complete and finished work. Oh! sweet sound, when it reaches the heart and touches the conscience, and is shed blessedly abroad in the soul.

This is "the gladness of God's nation;" this makes their heart glad, that the work is finished, that the warfare is accomplished, that the Church of God "hath received of the Lord's hand double for all her sins"; this is the comforting sound wherewith God comforts his people; this makes the nation glad, and their heart to leap and dance for joy. Has *your* heart never leaped at the sound? – only for a moment? Has grace never sounded sweetly in your soul, and made your very heart dance within you? If it has, you know what is "the gladness of God's nation."

May 31

"That I may glory with thine inheritance." – Psalm 106. 5.

The Church is Christ's *inheritance.* He purchased it with his own blood. He went into captivity for it, and he redeemed it by pouring out his precious blood. Now this inheritance *glories:* "That I may glory with thine inheritance." And in whom does it glory? It glories in its covenant Head. It does not glory in itself – in its pious self, righteous self, strong self, religious self; "let not the wise man glory in his wisdom, neither let the mighty man glory in his might, let not the rich man glory in his riches: but let him that glorieth glory in this, that he understandeth and knoweth me." "He that glorieth, let him glory in the Lord." The glory of the Church is to glory in her covenant Head – to glory in Christ and in Christ alone; to glory in his strength, love, blood, grace, and righteousness; and to glory in him, herself being covered with shame. None can glory in Christ, until he is stripped of his own glory. There is no putting the crown of glory on the head of self and on the head of the Mediator. There is no saying, "I have procured this by my own strength", and putting the crown upon that head. There is no saying, "I obtained this by my own exertions", and putting the crown upon those exertions. No; a man to glory in Christ must be covered with shame and confusion. He must be abased in his feelings; he must have his mouth in the dust; he must loathe himself in dust and ashes before God; he must see and feel himself to be the chief of sinners, and "less than the least of all saints"; he must know and feel himself to be a wretch indeed. And then when he lies in the dust of abasement, if a sight of the dear Redeemer's glory catches his eye and inflames his heart, he glories in him, and in him alone. And all the "inheritance" of God glory in him; they can glory in nothing else, and their highest attainment is to place all the glory of salvation from first to last simply upon his head, to whom that glory belongs.

June 1

"Open thy mouth wide, and I will fill it." – Psalm 81. 10.

When the Lord favours your soul with sweet access at the throne of grace, make the most of it. What should we think of the master of a vessel coming up the river, if, when the wind was favourable and the tide served, he would not heave her anchor, or hoisted but her fore-sail to the breeze, and would not take full advantage of wind and tide? Now it is so sometimes with our souls; a gale blows, a gale of grace on the soul, and the tide of faith rises. Is it not our wisdom, and is it not our mercy, at such a rare season, to make the most of it? If the Lord deign to give us an ear, is it not our mercy to tell him all that our souls desire? Do you recollect what the prophet said to the king who only struck his arrows three times on the ground, and then stayed? "The man of God was wroth with him, and said, Thou shouldest have smitten five or six times; then hadst thou smitten Syria till thou hadst consumed it; whereas now thou shalt smite Syria but thrice" (2 Kings 13. 19). Sometimes it is so with us. When the Lord gives us some little access unto himself, we do not make the most of it. Satan casts in some fiery dart, some worldly circumstance distracts our mind, some filthy imagination rises up in our bosom; and instead of resisting the devil that he may flee from us, we give way to him; the opportunity is gone, the sweet moment is lost, and it may be months before we get the ear of the King again. It will, therefore, be your wisdom and your mercy, when the gale blows, and the tide rises, to spread every sail, and to get as far as you can on your course to the haven of eternal rest and joy.

June 2

"Who verily was foreordained before the foundation of the world, but was manifest in these last times for you." – 1 Peter 1. 20.

By "these last times" is meant this present dispensation, the dispensation of grace under which we live, and they are called the last times chiefly for two reasons: 1. Because Christ was manifested in the last days of the legal dispensation of the old covenant, which now, as decaying and waxing old, was ready to vanish away (Heb. 8. 13), which it did when at the destruction of Jerusalem the whole of the temple service, including the sacrifices offered there, was brought to an end. But 2. Another reason why the dispensation under which we live is called "the last days" is because it is the final revelation of God. It is "the time accepted", "the day of salvation", of which all the prophets have spoken (2 Cor. 6. 2; Acts 3. 24). Christ is now upon his throne of grace; the great, the glorious, the only Mediator between God and men is now at the right hand of the Father; the Intercessor who is able to save to the uttermost all that come unto God by him, seeing he ever liveth to make intercession for them, still lives to plead, as an Advocate with the Father, Jesus Christ the righteous, as the great High Priest over the house of God. But he will leave the throne of grace to take his seat on the throne of judgment; and then "these last days" will close in all the glories of salvation to his friends, in all the horrors of destruction to his foes.

June 3

"Then I said, I am cast out of thy sight; yet I will look again toward thy holy temple." – Jonah 2. 4.

When poor Jonah spake these words he uttered them in the very bitterness of his heart; he felt that he was cast out of God's gracious presence. But he must have known something experimentally of the sweet-ness of God's manifested presence; he must have tasted that heaven was in it, and that all his happiness centred there. He must have enjoyed this in order to know if God's presence were not felt in the soul, there was but one barren scene of gloom and death; and that to be " cast out of his sight" was the commencement of hell upon earth. Now here a living soul differs from all others, whether dead in sin, or dead in a profession. The persuasion that in God alone is true happiness; the feeling of misery and dissatisfaction with everything else but the Lord, and everything short of his manifested presence, is that which stamps the reality of the life of God in a man's soul. Mere professors of religion feel no misery, dissatisfaction, or wretched-ness, if God shine not upon them. So long as the world smiles, and they have all that heart can wish, so long as they are buoyed up by the hypocrite's hope, and lulled asleep by the soft breezes of flattery, they are well satisfied to sail down the stream of a dead profession. But it is not so with a living soul; he is at times panting after the smiles of God; he is thirsting after his manifested presence; he feels dissatisfied with the world, and all that it presents, if he cannot find the Lord, and does not enjoy the light of his countenance. Where this is experienced, it stamps a man as having the grace of God in his heart.

June 4

"I lead in the way of righteousness." – Proverbs 8. 20.

How does the Lord Jesus – who speaks here under the name of Wisdom – lead his saints "in the way of righteousness"? By casting a mysterious light into their souls, whereby they see what the word of God has revealed, and shedding abroad a mysterious power in their hearts, whereby faith is created, to receive, lay hold of, and credit that which God has made known. We may read the word of God for ever in vain, unless that word is made life and light to our souls; but when the Lord the Spirit, whose covenant office and work it is to take of the things of Jesus and reveal them to the heart, sheds a mysterious and blessed light upon those Scriptures which speak of Jesus as the law-fulfiller, as having brought in a glorious righteousness, and at the same moment is pleased to raise up faith and power in the heart to receive, credit, embrace, and handle what he has thus revealed, then by his own persuasive power he leads the soul "in the way of righteousness." And O what a wonderful way it is! that God should ever find out such a way, as to make all his people righteous, by imputing to them another's righteousness! It will be the wonder, the song of saints through all eternity; it will exhaust all the depths of their finite wisdom to look into these secrets of wisdom, love, and power. Yea, the angels themselves, who so far exceed men in wisdom, are represented as "desiring to look into" these things, and therefore when the ark was made, and the mercy seat put over the tables which were enclosed therein, the seraphim were framed as looking down upon this golden mercy seat, representing how the height, breadth, length, and depth of these mysteries overpass even the faculties of the angels themselves.

June 5

"Alas! for that day is great, so that none is like it: it is even the time of Jacob's trouble; but he shall be saved out of it." – Jeremiah 30. 7.

This "day of trouble" is when sin is laid as a heavy burden upon a man's conscience; when guilt presses him down into the dust of death, when his iniquities stare him in the face, and seem more in number than the hairs of his head; when he fears he shall be cast for ever into the bottomless pit of hell, and have his portion with the hypocrites. This "day of trouble" is not literally a day, a portion of time meted out by the rising or setting sun, a space of twenty-four hours. The hands of a clock, or the shadow of a dial, cannot regulate spiritual troubles. A day here means a season, be it long or short; be it a day, week, month, or year. And as the season cannot be measured in length, so the trouble cannot be measured in depth. The only wise God deals out various measures of affliction to his people. All do not sink to the same depth, as all do not rise to the same height. All do not drink equally deep of the cup; yet all, each in their measure, pass through this day of trouble, wherein their fleshly religion is pulled to pieces, their self-righteousness marred, their presumptuous hopes crushed, and they brought into the state of the leper, to cry, "Unclean, unclean." Until a man has passed through this day of trouble, until he has experienced more or less of these exercises of soul, and known guilt and condemnation in his conscience; until he has struggled in this narrow pass, and had his rags of creature righteousness torn away from him, he can know nothing experimentally of the efficacy of Jesus' atoning blood, nor feel the power of Christ's resurrection.

June 6

"Though I be nothing." – 2 Corinthians 12. 11

Paul did not mean to say that he had no religion, but none in himself. 'What! could not Paul stand against temptation?' Not more than you or I, unassisted by the grace of God. 'Could not Paul pray more than I can?' No, not at all, except so far as the spirit of grace and supplications was given to him. 'Could not Paul love more than I do?' Not a bit more, nor think a spiritual thought more, as far as self was concerned. I do not mean to say that Paul did not pray, believe, and love more than any of us do; but he did not perform these actions in himself one whit more than we can. He says, expressly, "In me, that is, in my flesh, dwelleth no good thing;" and therefore not the good thing of faith, or love, or divine communion.

Now when the Lord has brought a soul down to be nothing, he then makes his strength perfect in that nothingness; he communicates strength to pray, strength to believe, strength to hope, to love, to receive the gospel. Just like the poor man with the withered hand, to whom Jesus said, "Stretch forth thine hand." It was withered, he could not do it of himself. But Christ's strength was made perfect in weakness: when he spake the word, the withered hand was stretched forth, and became whole as the other. So with the dead Lazarus – he was asleep in death; but when the voice of love and power penetrated into the tomb, "Lazarus, come forth," life was made perfect in the dead corpse. So with the Old Testament worthies, who "out of weakness were made strong" (Heb. 11. 34). And so, each in our measure, it is with us; our weakness, helplessness, and inability are the very things which draw forth the power, the strength, and the grace of Jesus.

June 7

"Ye believe in God, believe also in me." – John 14. 1.

To believe in God is to believe in him as he has manifested himself in his dear Son in all the fulness of his love, in all the riches of his grace, and in all the depth of his mercy. God must be seen, not in the terrors of a holy law, but in the mercy and truth of the glorious gospel of the Son of God, and thus be approached and believed in as the God and Father of our Lord Jesus Christ, and our Father in him. How few see and realise this, and yet how sorely exercised are many of the living family upon this point! To believe in God in such a way as to bring pardon and peace into their conscience; to believe in God so as to find manifest acceptance with him; to believe in God so as to call him Abba, Father, and feel that the Spirit itself beareth witness with our spirit that we are his children; to believe in God so as to find him a very present help in trouble; to receive answers to prayer, to walk in the light of his countenance, to have his love shed abroad in the heart, to be manifestly reconciled to him, and feel a sense of his manifested goodness and mercy – this is to believe in God through Jesus Christ. And O how different is this from merely believing about God from what we see in nature that he is the Creator of all things, or from what we may have realised of his footsteps in providence that he watches over us as regards the things that perish, or from seeing in the letter of the word that he is the God of all grace to those who fear his name!

June 8

"For our light affliction, which is but for a moment, worketh for us a far more exceeding and eternal weight of glory." – 2 Corinthians 4. 17.

O ye suffering saints of God! ye tried and afflicted children of the most High! raise up your thoughts as God may enable you – lift up your eyes, and see what awaits you. Are you tried, tempted, exercised, afflicted? It is your mercy. God does not deal so with everyone. It is because you are his children, that he lays on you his chastening hand. He means to conform you to the image of his Son in glory, and therefore he now conforms you to the image of his Son in suffering. 'O but,' you say, 'I cannot believe it is so!' No; if you could, it would not be much of a trial. This is the trial of faith – to go groaning on, struggling on, sorrowing on, sighing on; believing against unbelief, hoping against hope; and still looking to the Lord, though there is everything in nature to damp the hopes and expectations of your waiting souls. Yet all will end well with the people of God. Their life here is a life of temptation, of suffering and trial; but heaven will make amends for all. And if our faith is now tried as "with fire," it will one day "be found unto praise and honour and glory at the appearing of Jesus Christ." In that day when the secrets of all hearts will be brought to light, the faith of thousands will be found to be little else than presumption; but the faith of God's dear family will then be crowned with "praise and honour and glory"; and they shall see the Lamb as he is face to face, when all tears are wiped away from all faces.

June 9

"If we confess our sins, he is faithful and just to forgive us our sins, and to cleanse us from all unrighteousness." – 1 John 1. 9.

Has the Lord made sin your burden? Has he ever made you feel guilty before him? Has he ever pressed down your conscience with a sight and sense of your iniquities, your sins, your backslidings? And does the Lord draw, from time to time, honest, sincere, unreserved confession of those sins out of your lips? What does the Holy Ghost say to *you?* What has the blessed Spirit recorded for your instruction, and for your consolation? "If we confess our sins, he is faithful and just to forgive us our sins." Not merely on a footing of mercy; still less because you confess them. It is not your confessing them, but it is thus – your confessing them is a mark of divine light; your confessing them springs from the work of grace upon your heart. If, then, you possess divine life, if you have grace in your soul, you are a child of God, Jesus obeyed for you – Jesus suffered for you – Jesus died for you – Jesus has put away your sin. And, therefore, you being a child of God, and Jesus having done all these things for you, God is now "faithful" to his promise that he will receive a confessing sinner; and "just" to his own immutable and veracious character. And thus, from justice as well as mercy, from faithfulness as well as compassion, he can, he will, and he does pardon, forgive, and sweetly blot out every iniquity and every transgression of a confessing penitent.

June 10

"My soul, wait thou only upon God; for my expectation is from him." – Psalm 62. 5.

I believe that the Lord, before ever he communicates a real blessing to the souls of his poor and needy children, not merely convinces them by the Spirit of the depth of their poverty, of their truly ruined and lost state by nature, of the destitution of everything good in them; but he opens their eyes in a mysterious manner to see certain blessings which are stored up in Christ; for instance, righteousness to cover their nakedness, blood to atone for their transgressions, grace to superabound over all the aboundings of sin, faith to be the evidence of things not seen, hope to anchor within the veil, and love to be a foretaste of eternal bliss. These and similar blessings the Lord presents before their eyes, and gives them a spiritual understanding that these mercies are stored up in Christ; and as he gives them this perception of what the blessing is, and shows them that these blessings are not in the creature, but in Christ, he draws forth the desires and sighs and ardent affections of their souls after these blessings, so that nothing but these special mercies can really satisfy them, ease their minds, assuage their troubles, bind up their wounds, and pour oil and wine into their conscience. And thus he brings them to be suppliants, he lays them at his feet as beggars. Yet, base though they feel themselves to be, black though they know they are, there is that mysterious attraction of the Spirit, as well as that mysterious fitting together of their poverty and Christ's righteousness, their nakedness and Christ's justifying robe, their helplessness and his almighty strength, that they never can be satisfied, unless an experienced and enjoyed union of the two takes place in their conscience.

June 11

"In whom ye also are builded together for an habitation of God through the Spirit." – Ephesians 2. 22.

These words will apply both to the whole body of Christ viewed collectively, and to each separate member of that body viewed individually; and what the

Church of God is in its completeness in Christ, as it will be in heaven above, and what it is in its visible and militant state on earth now, so is every individual member of that Church in this time state; and it is this solemn truth which makes the words before us to have such a forcible application to every individual believer. As we shall all have to answer for ourselves, "to die", as one said, "alone," and as religion is a personal matter, how careful should it make each individual believer so to walk before God and man that he may have both an inward and outward evidence that his body is the temple of the Holy Ghost (1 Cor. 6. 19), and that he is a habitation of God by the Spirit. If he realise this, and live under its solemn weight and influence, how careful he will be not to defile that body which is the temple of the Holy Ghost; how desirous and anxious not to defile his eyes by wandering lusts, nor his ears by listening to worldly and carnal conversation, nor his lips by speaking guile, or indulging in light and frothy talk, nor his hands by putting them to anything that is evil, nor his feet by running on errands of vanity and folly; but to view his body as a member of Christ (1 Cor. 6. 15), and therefore sanctified to his service and to his glory.

June 12

"Follow after righteousness." – 1 Timothy 6. 11.

We may understand two things by this expression. First, the discovery to the conscience of Christ's imputed righteousness, in the way of justification; and secondly, the communication to the soul of a divine or righteous nature, whereby it brings forth the fruits of sincerity and uprightness before God. Both are to be followed after. But it may be asked, Why the first, if a man has a knowledge of his justification, and a sense of his acceptance with God? But may not a sense of interest in Jesus' glorious righteousness, and the inward testimony of the Spirit be lost in the enjoyment of them, or at least considerably diminished, for a time? We read (Luke 15. 8) of the woman who lost a piece of silver. Was there not a lighting of the candle, a sweeping of the house, and a diligent search into every corner till it was found again? The woman's piece of money was not really lost; it was still in the house; but as to her feelings, it was as much lost as though she were never to receive it again into her possession. So a sense of acceptance and justification by Christ's righteousness, this precious coin from heaven's mint may be lost for a time in feeling, though not really lost out of the heart. And what will the soul do that has lost it but diligently search the house in every corner, by the candle of the Spirit, till it find the piece of money again?

June 13

"I have surely heard Ephraim bemoaning himself." – Jeremiah 31. 18.

The spiritual feeling of sin is indispensable to the feeling of salvation. A sense of the malady must ever precede, and prepare the soul for, a believing reception and due apprehension of the remedy. Wherever God intends to reveal his Son with power, wherever he intends to make the gospel "a joyful sound" indeed, he makes the conscience feel and groan under the burden of sin. And sure am I that when a man is labouring under the burden of sin, he will be full of complaint. The Bible records hundreds of the complaints of God's people under the burden of sin. "My wounds stink and are corrupt", cries one, "because of my foolishness. I am troubled; I am bowed down greatly; I go mourning all the day long" (Psalm 38. 5, 6). "My soul", cries another, "is full of troubles: and my life draweth nigh unto the grave" (Psalm 88. 3). " He hath led me," groans out a third, "and brought me into darkness, but not into light" (Lam. 3. 2). A living man needs must cry under such circumstances. He cannot carry the burden without complaining of its weight. He cannot feel the arrow sticking in his conscience without groaning under the pain. He cannot have the worm gnawing his vitals without complaining of its venomous tooth. He cannot feel that God is incensed against him without bitterly complaining that the Lord is his enemy. Spiritual complaint then is a mark of spiritual life, and is one which God recognises as such. "I have surely heard Ephraim bemoaning himself." It shows that he has something to mourn over, something to make him groan being burdened; that sin has been opened up to him in its hateful malignancy; that it is a trouble and distress to his soul; that he cannot roll it like a sweet morsel under his tongue, but that it is found out by the penetrating eye, and punished by the chastening hand of God.

June 14

"Work out your own salvation with fear and trembling." – Philippians 2. 12.

None but God's people under the teachings of the Spirit know what it is to "work out their own salvation." And all who work out their own salvation will work it out "with fear and trembling." For when a man is taught by God to know what he is; when he feels what a deceitful heart he carries in his bosom; when the various snares, temptations, and corruptions by which he is daily encompassed are opened up to him; when he knows and feels what a ruined wretch he is in self, then he begins to fear and tremble lest he should be damned at the last. He cannot go recklessly and carelessly on without "making straight paths for his feet," without "examining himself whether he be in the faith." And whenever a man's dreadfully deceitful heart is opened up to him; whenever the hollowness of an empty profession is unmasked; whenever he feels how strait is the path, how narrow the way, and how few there are that find it; whenever he is brought to see how easily a man is deceived, and how certainly he must be deceived unless God teach him in a special manner; - whenever a man is brought to this point, to see what a rare thing, what a sacred thing, and what a spiritual thing religion is, that God himself is the author and finisher of it in the conscience, and that a man has no more religion than God is pleased to give him, and cannot work a single grain of it in his own soul; when he stands on this solemn ground, and begins to work out that which God works in, it will always be "with fear and trembling;" with some "fear" lest he be deceived, until God assures him by his own blessed lips that he is not deluded; and "with trembling," as knowing that he stands in the immediate presence of God, and under his heart-searching eye.

June 15

"For it is God which worketh in you both to will and to do of his good pleasure." – Philippians 2. 13.

When God has worked in a man "to will", and not only worked in him "to will", but also worked in him "to do"; when he has made him willing to flee from the wrath to come; willing to be saved by the atoning blood and justifying righteousness of Jesus; willing to be saved by sovereign grace as a sinner undone without hope, and glad to be saved in whatever way God is pleased to save him; willing to pass through the fire, to undergo affliction, and to walk in the strait and narrow path, willing to take up the cross and follow Jesus, willing to bear all the troubles which may come upon him, and all the slanders which may be heaped upon his name; when God has made him willing to be nothing, and to have nothing but as God makes him the one, and gives him the other: and besides working in him "to will", has worked in him "to do", worked in him faith to believe, hope whereby he anchors in the finished work of Christ, and love whereby he cleaves to him with purpose of heart; when all this has been "with fear and trembling", not rushing heedlessly on in daring presumption, not buoyed up by the good opinion of others, not taking up his religion from ministers and books; but by a real genuine work of the Holy Ghost in the conscience; when he has thus worked out with fear and trembling what God has worked in, he has got at salvation; at salvation from wrath to come, from the power of sin, from an empty profession; at salvation from the flesh, from the delusions of Satan, from the blindness and ignorance of his own heart; he has got at a salvation which is God's salvation, because God has worked in him to will and to do of his good pleasure.

June 16

"Wherein ye greatly rejoice, though now for a season, if need be, ye are in heaviness through manifold temptations." – 1 Peter 1. 6.

As everything by nature in us is contrary to the life of God, there is a needs-be for manifold trials and temptations to bring us out of those things which are opposed to the grace of God, and to conform us to the image of his dear Son. Thus we need trial after trial, and temptation upon temptation, to cure us of that worldly spirit, that carnality and carelessness, that light, trifling, and empty profession, that outside form of godliness, that spirit of pride and self-righteousness, that resting short of divine teachings, heavenly blessings, and spiritual manifestations, that settling on our lees and being at ease in Zion, that being mixed up with all sorts of professors, that ignorance of the secret of the Lord which is with them that fear him – all which marks of death we see so visibly stamped upon the profession of the day. There is a needs-be to be brought out of all this false, deceptive, hypocritical, and presumptuous profession, whether high or low, sound in doctrine or unsound, so as to be made simple and sincere, honest and upright, tender and teachable, and to know something experimentally of that broken and contrite spirit in which the Lord himself condescends to dwell. And as the Lord works this spirit of humility and love for the most part through trials and temptations, there is a needs-be for every one, of whatever nature it may be, or from whatever quarter it may come.

June 17

"For we which have believed do enter into rest." – Hebrews 4. 3.

We enter into rest by ceasing from our own works, and resting on Christ's; according to the words, "For he that is entered into his rest, he also hath ceased from his own works, as God did from his." Now when you can fully rest upon the finished work of the Son of God, and believe by a living faith that your sins were laid upon his head; that he bore them in his body on the tree; that he has washed you in his precious blood, clothed you with his righteousness, and is sanctifying you by his Spirit and grace, then you can rest. There is something here firm and solid for the conscience to rest on. Whilst the law thunders, whilst Satan accuses, whilst conscience condemns there is no rest. But you can rest where God rests. God rests in his love; in the finished work of his dear Son; in the perfection of Christ's humanity; in his fulfilment of all his covenant engagements; in the glorification of his holy law; in the satisfaction rendered to his justice; in the harmonising of all his attributes; in the revelation of his grace and his glory to the children of men; for he is his beloved Son, in whom he is well pleased. The tabernacle in the wilderness, and afterwards the temple on Mount Zion, was a type of the pure and sacred humanity of the Lord Jesus. There God rested in a visible manner by a cloud upon the mercy seat, called by the Jewish writers the Shekinah. This, therefore, was the place of his rest, as he speaks, "For the Lord hath chosen Zion; he hath desired it for his habitation. This is my rest for ever: here will I dwell; for I have desired it" (Psalm 132. 13, 14).

June 18

"Therefore they shall come and sing in the height of Zion." – Jeremiah 31. 12.

Until the redeemed know something of the efficacy of atoning blood and have their consciences purged from guilt and filth by its application, they cannot come and sing in the height of Zion. But when they are redeemed from the hand of him who is stronger than they; when atoning blood is applied to their consciences to purge away guilt and filth; when Christ is revealed and made experimentally known; when his gospel in the hands of the Spirit becomes a word of power, and a view of the King in his beauty is granted to the believing heart, then, drawn by the cords of love and the bands of a man, they come to Zion, where the King sits enthroned in glory. It is called "the height of Zion," not only because Zion was high literally, but because the Lord of life and glory is exalted to the highest place of dignity and power. God's ancient promise was, "Behold, my servant shall be exalted and extolled, and be very high" (Isaiah 52. 13); and the Apostle says, "Wherefore God also hath highly exalted him, and given him a name which is above every name" (Phil. 2. 9); and again, "Far above all principality, and power, and might, and dominion, and every name that is named, not only in this world, but also in that which is to come" (Eph. 1. 21). But why do they come? It is to commune with him, to worship him in the beauty of holiness, to get words from his lips, smiles from his face, touches from his hand, and whispers from his lips. And when he is graciously pleased to speak a word to them as Prince of peace, to reveal himself to their souls in the glory of his divine Person as God-man, and to shed abroad his love in their hearts, then they can sing, and in them is the promise fulfilled, "They shall come and sing in the height of Zion."

June 19

"For he shall stand at the right hand of the poor, to save him from those that condemn his soul." – Psalm: 109. 31.

How cheering, how comforting it is, to have a friend to stand by us when we are in trouble. Such a friend is Jesus. In the hour of necessity, he comes as a friend to stand by the right hand of the poor creature, whose soul is condemned by guilt and accusations. But he stands in a far higher relation than that of a friend; he stands too as a *Surety and a Deliverer.* He goes, as it were, into the court; and when the prisoner stands at the bar, he comes forward and stands at his right hand as his surety and bondsman; he brings out of his own bosom the acquittal of the debt signed and sealed with his own blood, he produces it before the eyes of the court, and claims and demands the acquittal and absolution of the prisoner at whose right hand he stands. He stands there, then, that the prisoner may be freely pardoned, and completely justified from those accusations that "condemn his soul." O sweet standing! – O blessed appearance! Unbelief, the workings of a desperately wicked heart, and the fearful suggestions of the enemy, come forward to condemn us; but Christ Jesus, this Mediator betwixt God and man, "stands at the right hand of the poor," and produces his own glorious righteousness. Are we pressed down with unbelief? He communicates faith. Is our mind sinking into despair? He breathes into it hope. Is the soul bowed down with guilt, at a distance from God, unable to approach him on account of its heavy temptations? He puts his own arm under this poor dejected soul and lifts up his bowed-down head, and then the soul looks upwards, and instead of wrath sees the countenance of the Father beaming mercy and love, because the Surety is "standing at the right hand of the poor."

June 20

"Who crowneth thee with lovingkindness and tender mercies." – Psalm 103. 4.

The coronation of a king puts the last and highest seal upon his reigning authority. This made the spouse say, "Go forth, O ye daughters of Zion, and behold king Solomon with the crown wherewith his mother crowned him in the day of his espousals, and in the day of the gladness of his heart" (S. of S. 3. 11). And what a day will that be when the anti-typical Solomon is crowned Lord of all. Thus there is a crown put upon the soul which is healed of all its diseases, and whose life is redeemed from destruction. It is as if God could not be satisfied till he had put the crown of his lovingkindness upon the soul, until he had himself crowned the heart with his own love. And what is the effect? The soul puts a crown of glory upon his head. So the soul has the crown of grace, and God has the crown of glory. This is being crowned with lovingkindness and lender mercies. And O what a crown it is! How it crowns all our iniquities, hides them from God's sight as a crown covers a monarch's brow. How it crowns all our trials that we have had to pass through, severe and cutting as they were at the time to the flesh. How it crowns all our bereavements by putting upon the bereaved heart the crown of God's lovingkindness. How it crowns all our prayers by enabling us to see their gracious answers. How it crowns all God's dealings with us in providence and in grace, and stamps lovingkindness upon them all; for the crown includes everything in it. As the Queen's crown includes her royalty, her dignity, her power - for all are symbolised thereby - so God's lovingkindness, put upon the heart as a crown, includes and secures every blessing for time and eternity.

June 21

"Blessed be the God and Father of our Lord Jesus Christ, which according to his abundant mercy hath begotten us again unto a lively hope by the resurrection of Jesus Christ from the dead." - 1 Peter 1. 3.

The resurrection of Jesus Christ was God's grand attestation to the truth of his divine mission and Sonship, for by it he was " declared to be the Son of God with power." It therefore set a divine stamp upon his sacrifice, blood-shedding, and death, showed God's acceptance of his offering, and that sin was thus for ever put away. Now, just think what would have been the dreadful consequences if Christ had not been raised from the dead, or if we had no infallible proofs (Acts 1. 3) of his resurrection. There would have been, there could have been no forgiveness of sin (1 Cor. 15. 17); and therefore, when the conscience became awakened to a sense of guilt and condemnation, there could have been nothing before it but black and gloomy despair. But Christ being raised from the dead and having gone up on high to be the High Priest over the house of God, and the Holy Spirit bearing witness of this both in the word and through the word to the soul, a door of hope is opened even in the very valley of Achor. The Holy Ghost, who would not have been given had not Christ risen from the dead and gone to the Father, now comes and testifies of him to the soul, takes of the things which are his, reveals them to the heart, and raises up faith to look unto and believe in him as the Son of God, and thus, according to the measure of the revelation, it abounds in hope through the power of the Holy Ghost (Rom. 15. 13).

June 22

"Jesus saith, Go to my brethren, and say unto them, I ascend unto my Father, and your Father; and to my God, and your God." – John 20. 17.

Why your Father? Because my Father. Why your God? Because my God. As his only-begotten Son from all eternity, God was the God of our Lord Jesus Christ; as the Father's messenger and servant, doing his will upon earth, even in his lowest humiliation, God was his God; and now that he is risen from the dead and gone up on high to be the great High Priest over the house of God, now that he is entered into his glory and ever lives to make intercession for us, God is still his God. This view of Jesus is most strengthening and encouraging to faith. The great and glorious God, the great self-existent I AM, the God in whom we live and move and have our being, the God before whom we stand with all we are and have, the God against and before whom we have so deeply and dreadfully sinned – this great and glorious God is "the God of our Lord Jesus Christ." We may, therefore, draw near unto him with all holy boldness, present our supplications before him, call upon his holy name, and worship him with all reverence and godly fear as the God of our Lord Jesus Christ, and our God in him. A believing view of God, as revealing himself in the person of his dear Son, as reconciling us to himself by his precious blood, as accepting us in the Beloved, and not imputing our trespasses unto us, disarms God of all his terrors, removes the bondage of the law out of our hearts and the guilt of sin from our consciences, enlarges, comforts, and solaces the soul, soothes the troubled spirit, and casts out that fear which hath torment.

June 23

"The just shall live by faith." – Romans 1. 17.

A life of faith in Christ is as necessary to our present and experimental salvation as his death upon the cross was to our past and actual salvation. If you are alive to what you are as a poor fallen sinner, you see yourself surrounded by enemies, temptations, sins, and snares; and you feel yourself utterly defenceless, as weak as water, without any strength to stand against them. Pressed down by the weight of unbelief, you see a mountain of difficulty before your eyes, sometimes in providence and sometimes in grace. You find, too, that your heart is a cage of unclean birds, and that in you, that is, in your flesh, there dwelleth no good thing; neither will nor power have you in yourself to fight or flee. How then shall this mountain become a plain? How shall you escape the snares and temptations spread in your path? How shall you get the better of all your enemies, external, internal, infernal, and reach heaven's gate safe at last? If you say, "By the salvation already accomplished," are you sure that salvation belongs to you? Where is the evidence of it if you have no present faith in Christ? How can that past salvation profit you for present troubles unless there be an application of it? It is this application and manifestation of salvation which is being saved by his life (Rom. 5. 10). See how it works; and what a suitability is in it. You are all weakness, and he is and has all strength, which he makes perfect in your weakness. You are all helplessness against sin, temptation, and a thousand foes. But help is laid upon Christ as one that is mighty; he therefore sends you help from the sanctuary and strengthens you out of Zion (Psalm 20. 2), that these sins and enemies may not get the better of you.

June 24

"Forasmuch as ye know that ye were not redeemed with corruptible things, as silver and gold, from your vain conversation received by tradition from your fathers; but with the precious blood of Christ, as of a lamb without blemish and without spot." – 1 Peter 1. 18, 19.

O the unspeakable depths of the goodness and mercy of God! O the riches of his super-abounding grace! When there was no other way of redemption, God sent his only-begotten Son, that by his precious blood, as of a lamb without blemish and without spot, we might be redeemed from all the consequences of our vain conversation received by tradition from our fathers; and not only from all its consequences, but from its power and practice. It is a knowledge, a personal, experimental knowledge of this redemption, which lays us under a spiritual obligation to walk worthy of our high calling. And it acts in this way. A view by faith of the bleeding, dying Lamb of God, a seeing and feeling what he suffered in the garden and on the cross to redeem us from hell, will ever make sin hateful in our eyes, and holiness longed after as the soul's happiest element. If ever sin is mourned over, hated, confessed, and forsaken; if ever there be ardent desires after a conformity to Christ's image; if there ever be a longing after union and communion with him, it is at the foot of his cross. By it and it alone is the world crucified unto us, and we unto the world; and well may we say that our highest attainment in grace is to have the experience of the Apostle: "I am crucified with Christ: nevertheless I live; yet not I, but Christ liveth in me: and the life which I now live in the flesh I live by the faith of the Son of God, who loved me, and gave himself for me" (Gal. 2. 20).

June 25

"At that day shall a man look to his Maker, and his eyes shall have respect to the Holy One of Israel." – Isaiah 17. 7.

In the very name "the Holy One of Israel," there is something the sweetness of which melts the heart of a poor sensible sinner. For what is he in himself as a fallen child of Adam? A filthy, defiled, polluted wretch, unfit for the presence of God. And what can fit such an unclean, unworthy, deformed sinner for the eternal presence and enjoyment of the Triune Jehovah, but such a Saviour as the Holy One of Israel, whose blood, as a holy fountain, cleanseth from all sin? The soul that stands in him, stands complete, without spot or blemish. And must not his heart leap and dance when with a measure of faith he is able to lay hold of this Holy One of Israel? But this living faith in and spiritual reception of the only Mediator between God and man cannot exist until a man is brought into circumstances in which he needs the Holy One of Israel. Until he is emptied and stripped of all creature strength he cannot truly understand how, nor really desire that the strength of Christ may be made perfect in his weakness. So with Christ's wisdom; his righteousness; his blood; so with his love; his gracious presence; – all are mere words, loose and floating ideas, dim, dreamy conceptions, until poverty and need lie hard upon the soul, and the blessed Spirit makes known "the unsearchable riches of Christ," as so many experimental realities. It is this gracious discovery which endears to him the Holy One of Israel. There is no divine faith, no going out of hope, no flowing of affection toward the Holy One of Israel, till "that day," when he has no one else to look to, no hope in the creature; till all his righteousness fails him, and he feels that he must be saved by free grace, or eternally perish.

June 26

"The Spirit searcheth all things, yea, the deep things of God." – 1 Corinthians 2. 10.

The Spirit of God which dwelleth in a man, making his body his temple, searcheth the deep things of God; for there is in these deep things a most heavenly treasure, which is to be searched into that it may be found. What depths do we sometimes see in a single text of Scripture as opened to the understanding, or applied to the heart; what a depth in the blood of Christ: how it "cleanseth from all sin", and if from all sin it must cleanse away millions of millions of the foulest sins of the foulest sinners. What a depth in his bleeding, dying love that could stoop so low to lift us so high! What a depth in his pity and compassion to extend to such guilty, vile transgressors as we are! What depth in the eternal counsels and unspeakable wisdom of God to contrive such a plan as was accomplished and brought to light in the incarnation and death of his dear Son, that thus mercy and justice might meet together without jar or discord, every attribute of God be fully honoured, and yet that those who deserved hell should be lifted up into the enjoyment of heaven. What depths, too, there are in our own heart, not merely of sin but of grace, for true religion has its depths which the Spirit searches and brings to view. Thus if we have any faith, it lies very deep, for it is hidden in the heart, and sometimes so hidden as to be almost, if not altogether, out of sight. The Spirit then searches for it, and brings it out and up. So if we have any love, it strikes its root into the inmost recesses of our affections, and therefore needs to be searched into; or any hope, it lies like the anchor at the bottom of the sea. It therefore has to be searched into that it may be made manifest that it is sure and steadfast and enters within the veil.

June 27

"And they that use this world, as not abusing it: for the fashion of this world passeth away." – 1 Corinthians 7. 31.

Nothing is real but that which has an abiding substance. Health decays, strength diminishes, beauty flees the cheek, sight and hearing grow dim, the mind itself gets feeble, riches make to themselves wings and flee away, children die, friends depart, old age creeps on, and life itself comes to a close. These fugitive, transitory things are then mere shadows; there is no substance, enduring substance in them. Like our daily food and raiment, house and home, they support and solace us in our journey through life. But there they stop; when life ends, they end with it. But real religion – and by this I understand the work of God upon the soul – abides in death and after death, goes with us through the dark valley, and lands us safe in a blessed eternity. It is, therefore, the only thing in this world of which we can say that it is real. Is not this John's testimony? "All that is in the world, the lust of the flesh, and the lust of the eyes, and the pride of life, is not of the Father, but is of the world. And the world passeth away, and the lust thereof: but he that doeth the will of God abideth for ever" (1 John 2. 16, 17). And who is that man, that blessed man, who lives when all dies, who abideth for ever when all others pass away into the outer darkness? It is he who doeth the will of God. But how and when do we the will of God? "And this is the will of him that sent me, that every one which seeth the Son, and believeth on him, may have everlasting life: and I will raise him up at the last day" (John 6. 40). If, then, you have seen the Son, and believed in him, you have now everlasting life, and Jesus will raise you up at the last day.

June 28

"God is the Lord, which hath shewed us light." – Psalm 118. 27.

If God the Lord hath showed us light, he hath showed us light both with respect to himself and with respect to ourselves. He hath showed us with respect to himself who he is; he hath stamped something of himself upon our consciences; he hath discovered something of his glorious character to our souls; and brought us, under the operation of the Holy Spirit, into his presence, there to receive communications of life out of Christ's inexhaustible fulness. Thus in this light we see and feel that we have to do with a heart-searching God; in this light we see and feel that we have to do with a sin-hating God; with a God who will not be mocked nor trifled with; in this light we see and feel that every secret of our heart, every working of our mind is open before him; and in this light, so far as he is pleased to manifest it, we see what we are in his holy and pure eyes – a mass of sin, filth, and corruption, without help, without strength, wisdom, or righteousness, without creature comeliness, without anything of which we can say that it is spiritually good. Again, God the Lord, showing us light, hath showed us more or less of the way of salvation through Jesus Christ. He has not only showed us what we are by nature, but he has in a measure condescended to show us what we are by grace; not merely brought into our hearts some acquaintance with himself as a God of perfect justice, but he has also brought, more or less, into our souls some acquaintance with him as a God of mercy; and has thus brought us, in some solemn measure, to know him the only true God, and Jesus Christ, whom he hath sent; and, thus, to have the springing up of spiritual life more or less, each according to his measure, in our souls.

June 29

"O Lord, correct me, but with judgment; not in thine anger, lest thou bring me to nothing." – Jeremiah 10. 24.

Fury is not in me, saith the Lord. No; there is no wrath in the bosom of God against the persons of his people. They are for ever "accepted in the Beloved," and stand in him before the throne of God without spot or wrinkle; but there is displeasure against their sins; and this displeasure their kind and gracious Father makes them feel when he withdraws from them the light of his countenance, and sends his keen reproofs and sharp rebukes into their conscience. But these very "judgments" help them (Ps. 119. 175), for they lead to deep searchings of heart; and as the same blessed Spirit who sets home the reproof communicates therewith repentance, they sorrow after a godly manner, and this godly sorrow worketh repentance to salvation not to be repented of (2 Cor. 7. 10). If, then, our afflictions, crosses, losses, bereavements, family troubles, church trials, and more especially if the rebukes and reproofs of God in our own conscience have been a means of humbling our proud hearts, bringing us to honest confession of, and godly sorrow for our sins and backslidings, if they have instrumentally separated us more effectually from the world, its company, its ways, its maxims, and its spirit; if they have, in the good hand of God, stirred up prayer and supplication in our hearts, led us into portions of the word of truth before hidden from view, laid us more feelingly and continually at the footstool of mercy, given us a deeper insight into the way of salvation, made mercy more dear and grace more sweet, have these trials and afflictions been either unprofitable or unseasonable?

June 30

"The Spirit of the Lord spake by me, and his word was in my tongue." – 2 Samuel 23. 2.

We read that "no prophecy of the scripture is of any private interpretation"; that is to say, it is the public property of the whole family of Jehovah; and "holy men of God spake as they were moved by the Holy Ghost"; the Holy Ghost so influencing and working upon their minds as to make them bring forth out of their hearts that which should be suitable to the whole family of God. For instance, we read in Psalm 51, David's confession of sin; but David's confession of sin applies to every soul that is condemned on account of sin. When Job, too, poured out his piteous complaints, he was speaking, though he might know it not, for the children of God to the remotest time. So when the Lord said to Joshua, "I will never leave thee, nor forsake thee," it was a promise specially given to Joshua; it seemed to be confined to that individual; it appeared to be of private interpretation, as though Joshua, and Joshua alone, was entitled to that promise. But we find the apostle Paul bringing forward this promise as the general property of the whole Church of God: "Let your conversation be without covetousness; and be content with such things as ye have: for he hath said, I will never leave thee, nor forsake thee" (Heb. 13. 5). "He hath said"? to whom? To Joshua; but in saying it to Joshua, he said it to the Church of God; in giving Joshua the promise, he gave that promise to every soul that needed with Joshua his help, that feared with Joshua to be forsaken, that wanted with Joshua his sustaining hand; and therefore this private promise to Joshua was not of private interpretation, but, when applied by the blessed Spirit, suits every living soul that is placed in similar circumstances with the individual to whom that promise was addressed.

July 1

"My grace is sufficient for thee: for my strength is made perfect in weakness." – 2 Corinthians 12. 9.

How mysterious are God's dealings! That such a highly favoured man as Paul should come down from the "third heaven" to the very gates of hell (that is not too strong an expression, for "the messenger of Satan" came from hell), that he should sink in soul-feeling to the very gates of hell, there to be buffeted by "the messenger of Satan"; and all to teach him a lesson that heaven did not teach him, *the strength of God is made perfect in weakness!* Do you not think, that if we are to learn our weakness, we must learn it in the same way? How did Paul get his religion? And must we not get ours, in our feebler measure, through the same channels, by the same means, and by the same inward teachings? If we are to learn the secret of Christ's strength, it is not by making daily advances in fleshly holiness, and getting stronger in self day by day. It is not by old nature being so mended and improved, as bye and bye to be shaded off into grace, just as the colours in the rainbow are so harmoniously blended that you can scarcely tell where the one ends and the other begins. For this is what is really meant by "progressive sanctification", that the old nature is so gradually softened and blended into grace, that we can scarcely tell where the old man ceases and the new nature commences. Did the Apostle learn Christ's strength in that way? No; but by being buffeted by Satan's messenger, and thus being beaten out of his own strength, he found Christ's strength made perfect in his weakness.

July 2

"Draw me, we will run after thee." Song of Solomon 1. 4.

How many of us can take the words of the bride into our lips, or have ever been able at any one time of our life to use such an expression? We must have had some sight and sense of the preciousness and loveliness of Jesus before ever we can cry, "Draw me," from the depth of a sincere heart. For the sincere soul is afraid to approach the holy Jehovah, whose eyes are as a flame of fire, and insult him with mock petitions and words that it does not feel. But if ever that desire has been kindled, and that prayer raised up in your soul, "Draw me, we will run after thee," it must have been the work of the Holy Ghost in your hearts, to raise up those feelings and to give you a living faith in the Son of God. And "he that believeth shall be saved." Whatever doubts, whatever fears, whatever temptations, whatever exercises beset the path, "he that believeth shall be saved." He that has had given him one grain of spiritual faith in Christ's glorious person, who has had one sight of his atoning blood, one sip of divine love shed abroad in his heart, is sure to go to glory; he is saved with an everlasting salvation, in his covenant Head. The Lord that has kindled these strong desires after himself in his soul, will surely fulfil them. As we find he did in the case of the bride; he said to her, after a little time, "Rise up, my love, my fair one, and come away. For, lo, the winter is past, the rain is over and gone; the flowers appear on the earth; the time of the singing of birds is come, and the voice of the turtle is heard in our land. Arise, my love, my fair one, and come away."

July 3

"Which holdeth our soul in life." – Psalm 66. 9.

It is indeed an unspeakable mercy for the heirs of promise that the life given them in Christ and communicated by the Holy Spirit to their souls cannot be extinguished. It may sink very low – one can hardly say how low, but so low as to sink out of sight and almost out of feeling; and yet if it has once been breathed into the soul from the mouth of God, it can never die. Still it is most desirable that this divine life should be maintained in strength and vigour, and not sink so low as to be scarcely perceptible either to ourselves or others, for if so, we have little comfort of it in our own breast, and are of little use or service to the people of God. It is a sad thing to be satisfied with a low, lean, and lifeless state of soul, or be placing our religion in external activity and zealous attention to forms and mere externals, just to preserve a clean outside, when within there is little else but darkness, bondage, and death. How the Lord seems, as it were, obliged to plunge us into trials and afflictions to bring us out of carnality and death, and to keep us from settling on our lees like Moab! (Jer. 48. 11)

July 4

"Yea, I will rejoice over them to do them good." – Jeremiah 32. 41.

God rejoices as much in saving your soul as you can rejoice in your soul being saved. Say I "as much"? His joy is infinite, and yours is finite; his the joy of God, and yours but the joy of man. Do you believe that God rejoices to save, delights in saving? Why else should he have given his dear Son? Do the angels rejoice over repenting sinners? Is there no joy then in the bosom of

God to save a sinner too? How this takes us up, as it were, into the very realms of bliss, and reveals to us the wondrous character of God in his Trinity of persons and Unity of essence, that there is a rejoicing in the salvation of the Church, so that God himself, so to speak, is filled with eternal joy in the salvation of his people. When his dear Son offered himself as a sacrifice for sin, and thus put away the transgressions and iniquities of the Church by his own blood-shedding and death, overcame death and hell, and washed us in his blood from all our filth and guilt and shame, God, so to speak, rejoiced with infinite joy in the completion of the work of his dear Son. It was the fulfilment of his eternal purposes of wisdom and grace. It was the manifestation of his glory to men and angels. It was the triumph of good over evil, of holiness over sin, of mercy over judgment, of love over enmity, of wisdom over craft, of the counsels of God over the devices of man, and, above all, of the Son of God in his weakness over Satan in his might. It was peopling heaven with an innumerable multitude of saints by whom eternal anthems of praise should be sung to God and the Lamb. Thus we may see how the God of heaven even now rejoices with holy joy over every one whom he brings to the enjoyment of a salvation so free, so great, so glorious.

July 5

"We must through much tribulation enter into the kingdom of God." – Acts 14. 22.

What are the promises? Are not all the promises suited to the Lord's poor and needy family? What are the promises of pardon, except to the guilty? What are promises of salvation, except to the lost? What are promises of consolation, except to the afflicted? What are promises of grace, except to those who feel themselves altogether undone? Thus it is "through much tribulation" we enter into the sweetness of the promises. Then they come with power into the heart; they are manifested with life and feeling to the soul; and we begin, like Jeremiah of old, to find God's word and eat it; and feel it to be the very joy and rejoicing of our heart. This is the effect of passing through tribulation in providence and in grace, – of cutting trials; of severe, harassing temptations; of frowns from the world; of blows from sinners and saints; of learning the workings of a heart deceitful above all things and desperately wicked; to lead us "into the kingdom of God"; and into those sweet manifestations of loving-kindness and tender mercy which alone can satisfy us whose consciences God's finger has touched. And I believe you that are honest, you that are sincere, you that fear to be deceived, you that know there is a secret in vital godliness, and long to know it more deeply, and feel it more powerfully; I am sure there is an inward witness in your soul that you never entered into any one mystery of the kingdom of God set up in your heart except through tribulation. Was it not through tribulation you understood the word, and felt it applied to your conscience by the power of God? And was it not by and through tribulation, through the medium of suffering, that you were made to value more and more the manifestation of God to your soul? and feel that nothing could satisfy you, nothing content you, but a blessed discovery of dying love?

July 6

"Who by him do believe in God, that raised him up from the dead, and gave him glory; that your faith and hope might be in God." – 1 Peter 1. 21.

Observe the special mark which is here given of those for whom Christ was manifested. It is said of them that "by him they believe in God." If this be their distinctive mark, we may well inquire what is intended by it. It must surely be a very great thing to believe in God with a faith that brings salvation with it. It is easy to believe that there is a God in nature, or a God in providence, or a God in grace, according to the mere letter of the word, and this is what thousands do who have no manifested interest in redeeming love and atoning blood. In fact, it is the great delusion of the day, the religion of that religious multitude who know neither God nor themselves, neither law nor gospel, neither sin nor salvation. All this is a believing *about* God, or a believing *of* God, such as that he exists, or that he is such a God as the Scriptures represent him to be; but this is a very different thing from believing *in* God. This is a special and peculiar faith, and implies a spiritual and saving knowledge of God, such as our Lord speaks of (John 17. 3); and as none can thus know him unto eternal life but from some discovery of himself, some personal manifestation of his presence, some coming nigh of himself in the power of his word and the operations of his grace, so none can believe in him without a faith of divine operation. To believe, therefore, in God is not an act of the natural mind, but it is the gift and work of God, bestowed upon us through the mediation of Christ, and therefore, as the Apostle says, "given in the behalf of Christ" (Phil. 1. 29).

July 7

"For what is the hope of the hypocrite, though he hath gained, when God taketh away his soul? Will God hear his cry when trouble cometh upon him? Will he delight himself in the Almighty? Will he always call upon God?" – Job 27. 8-10.

Many of God's people are at times exercised as to their hypocrisy, and sometimes they may think themselves the most consummate hypocrites that ever stood in a profession. But if you are exercised with these painful surmises, these doubts and fears, just see (and the Lord enable you to bring it to the light of his countenance) these two features of a spiritual character. Do not talk about your hope; it may be "a spider's web". Do not boast of your gifts; they may be altogether in the flesh. Do not bring forward the good opinion of men; they may be deceived in you. But just see if, with the Lord's blessing, you can feel these two tests in your soul, as written there by his own hand. If so, you are not a hypocrite; God himself, by his servant Job, has acquitted you of the charge. Did you, then, ever "delight yourself in the Almighty"? It is a solemn question. Did your heart and soul ever go out after the living God? Did affection, love, and gratitude ever flow out of your bosom into the bosom of the Lord? Did you ever feel as if you could clasp him in the arms of faith, and live and die in his embrace? Now if your soul has ever felt this, you are no hypocrite; and nothing can rise up out of your wretched heart, as an accusing devil, that can prove you to be one. Or if you cannot fully realise this, if you are one that *always* calls upon God, you are no hypocrite. I do not speak of your regular prayers, or any other of your regularities; for I believe that there is often more of God's Spirit, and more craving after God and delighting in him, in your irregularities, than in all the daily regularities which hypocrites delight in. But I mean, is there a sigh or cry by night, as well as by day; a pouring out of the heart into the bosom of God from time to time, as the Lord works it in you, in trouble, in perplexity, in sorrow, and in distress? This is a test and a mark which no hypocrite ever had or ever can have.

July 8

"There is therefore now no condemnation to them which are in Christ Jesus." – Romans 8. 1.

There is not a more blessed declaration than this in the whole word of truth. It is the sweetest note sounded by the gospel trumpet, for it is the very crown of the whole Jubilee. Is not condemnation the bitterest drop in the cup of trembling? the most thrilling, piercing note of that terrible trumpet which sounded so long and so loud from Sinai's blazing top that all the people that were in the camp trembled? (Exod. 19. 13, 16.) Condemnation is the final execution of God's righteous law, and therefore carries with it all that arms death with its sting and the grave with its terror. The apprehension of this; the dread and fear of being banished for ever from the presence of God; of being lost, and that without remedy; of sinking under the blazing indignation of him who is a consuming fire, has filled thousands of hearts with horror. And it must be so as long as the law speaks in its thunders, as long as conscience re-echoes its verdict, and as long as the wrath of God burns to the lowest hell. O the blessed-ness, then, of that word of grace and truth, worthy to be sounded through heaven and earth by the voice of cherubim and seraphim, "There is no condemnation to them which are in Christ Jesus!"

July 9

"What man is he that feareth the Lord? him shall he teach in the way that he shall choose." – Psalm 25. 12.

In all the multiplicity and variety of circumstances that have distressed the children of God, has the Lord ever taken a wrong step? Though he has baffled nature, though he has disconcerted reason, though he has turned our plans upside down, though perhaps he has done the thing that we most feared, and thwarted every natural purpose and inclination of our heart - can we say that he has erred? that he has made a mistake? that he has acted unwisely? that he has not done that which is for our spiritual good? Murmuring, rebellious, unbelieving heart, hold thy peace! Shall man, foolish man, a worm of the earth, a creature of a day, lift up his puny voice and say, that God can mistake? Your path is very dark, very intricate, very perplexed; you cannot see the hand of God in the trial that is now resting upon you; you cannot believe that it will work together for your good. I admit it. I have felt it. I have known it. But the time will come, when this dark path in which you are now walking, shall be seen full of radiance and light, when you will prove the truth of these words, "He brought the blind by a way that they knew not". When we know God to be infinitely wise, that he cannot err, that all his dealings must be stamped with his own eternal wisdom, we are silenced, we hold our peace, we have nothing to say, we are where Aaron was. When Nadab and Abihu were smitten by the Lord, Aaron knew that God could not err; he held his peace (Lev. 10. 3). This is our right spot. If we know anything of the folly of the creature - if we know anything of the wisdom of God - this is our spot. When our dear Nadabs and Abihus are smitten before our face, our spot is to hold our peace, to put our mouth in the dust; for God is still accomplishing his object, in the face, and in spite of nature, sense, and reason.

July 10

"O thou afflicted, tossed with tempest, and not comforted."
- Isaiah 54. 11.

The Lord here compares his suffering Church to a ship at sea, under bare poles, labouring in a heavy storm, driven out of her course by contrary winds, as was Paul's case in the Adriatic, and doubtful whether she will ever reach the harbour; as the hymn says,

"Half a wreck by tempests driven."

What a picture of a tempest-tossed soul! Sun and stars beclouded, compass lost, chart useless, pilot absent, and breakers ahead! Many, very many of the Lord's dear family are thus "tossed with tempest"; some with a tempest of doubts and fears; others with a tempest of lust and corruptions; some with a tempest of rebellion and fretfulness; others with a storm of guilt and despondency, or with gloomy forebodings and dismal apprehensions. Thus they are driven from their course, their sun and stars all obscured; no clear evidences, no bright manifestations; darkness above, and a raging sea beneath; no harbour in sight, and hope of reaching the desired haven almost gone.

But it is further said of Zion, that she is "not comforted;" that is, not comforted by, nor capable of comfort from, any other than God. This I look upon as a very decisive mark of a work of grace upon the soul. When a man is so distressed in his feelings, so cast down in his mind, and so troubled in his conscience, that none but God can comfort him, we seem to be at once in the footsteps of the Spirit. We do not find hypocrites on this ground. False professors can easily take comfort; they can steal what God does not give, and appropriate what he does not apply. But Zion's special mark is that she is "not comforted", that her wounds are too deep for human balsams, her sickness too sore for creature medicines. God has reserved her comfort in his own hands; from his lips alone can consolation be spoken into her soul.

July 11

"Behold, I will lay thy stones with fair colours." – Isaiah 54. 11.

By these "stones," which the Lord has promised to "lay with fair colours," I think we may understand the blessed truths of the gospel which are laid into the soul by the hand of God. The fair colours are deeply ingrained and embedded in the very substance of the stone, not artificially laid on. They are like beautiful marbles, in which every bright hue and vein penetrate into the deepest substance of the material. Such are the truths of God, beautiful throughout, penetrated with grace and glory into their inmost depths. But these colours are hidden from view till brought out and laid into the soul by the hand of God. However fair or beautiful any word of God be in itself, it only experimentally becomes so as inlaid by his own divine hand into the soul. This brings out the fair colours. How often we read the word of God without seeing the least beauty in it! But let the very same portion come home with sweetness and power to the soul, then beauty, inexpressible beauty, is seen in it immediately; it becomes "a stone of fair colours". Salvation full and free, the pardoning love of God, the precious blood of the Lamb, justification by Christ's imputed righteousness, "wine and milk without money and without price", superabounding grace, eternal mercy, ever-lasting life – these are some of the precious stones with fair colours which God the Spirit with his own hand lays into the conscience.

July 12

"I will lay thy foundations with sapphires." – Isaiah 54. 11.

Before we can stand firmly in the things of God we must have a good foundation, something solid for our faith, our hope, our love, our all, to rest upon. This God promises to lay for his afflicted Zion: "I will lay thy foundations with sapphires". "A gift", we read, " is as a precious stone in the eyes of him that hath it." Every testimony, then, that God gives to the soul, every promise brought into the heart, every manifestation of mercy, every visit of love, or application of truth, we may call, in a spiritual sense, a sapphire; for it is indeed a precious stone, radiant with heaven's own hue. When God thus lays his sapphires in the soul, they afford a solid foundation for faith. And as they are laid by the hand of God himself, they must be firm; as they are sapphires, they must be indestructible. These sapphires, it is true, may every one of them be buried in the dust of carnality and worldly-mindedness; the filth and sewage, the mud and slush, of our fallen nature may roll over them flood after flood. But are they injured thereby? is their nature changed, their value impaired, their hue tarnished, their lustre faded and gone? They may be hidden from view, their setting be obscured, and their faces for a while be dimmed, but one ray from the Sun of righteousness will bring them again to light; one touch of the Polisher's hand will restore all their beauty. Grace has no more communion with sin than a diamond with a dunghill.

July 13

"And I will make thy windows of agates, and thy gates of carbuncles, and all thy borders of pleasant stones." – Isaiah 54. 12.

Upon Zion in her time-state "the Sun of righteousness" does not shine in all his brightness; the "windows of agate," whilst she is in the flesh, temper his rays. Her prospects, too, are not fully bright and clear; as the Apostle speaks, "We see through" (or in) "a glass darkly;" we have not those clear views which the saints have in glory, where they see Jesus face to face. We have prospects sometimes, I hope, in our souls, of God, and Christ, and heavenly glory; but still these views are but semi-transparent, streaked and clouded like a window of agate, not bright and clear as a pane of plate glass. But as Daniel opened his windows toward Jerusalem, that he might see by faith what he could not see by sight, so should we aim to look towards the heavenly Jerusalem, that by faith we may there "see him who is invisible."

But the Lord speaks of Zion's *"gates"*. *"And thy gates of carbuncles."* The carbuncle is of a *blood-red* colour; and why should the Lord have chosen that Zion's gates should be of this peculiar hue? May we not, without wresting the figure too closely, believe that there is some mystic allusion here to the blood of the Lamb? As scarlet wool was taken by Moses, when he sprinkled the people, and as Rahab's house was marked by a scarlet thread, may there not be something here significant in the *colour* of the gates? But "gates", or doors, not only give exit, but admission. How does God hear prayer, and answer it too? Only through the "gate of carbuncle". Prayer ascends through Jesus, and answers descend through Jesus; groans through Jesus enter the ears of the God of Sabaoth, and through the same bleeding gate of mercy do answers drop into the soul. Our poor self-righteous hearts can hardly comprehend this; we think we must have a good frame, or bring a good deed, or something good in ourselves, to make our prayers acceptable to God. Perish the thought! It is nothing but the spawn of self-righteousness. The "gates of carbuncle", the open wounds of the Lamb, through these every prayer ascends, through these every answer comes down; and if we set up anything else, or make a gate of human merit, we do despite to the Spirit of God, and pour contempt upon the grace and blood of the Lamb. *"And all thy borders of pleasant stones."* God's *providential* dealings, which often form the outer setting of his inward mercies, are of pleasant stones. North, south, east, west, all Zion's borders are of precious materials. The daily events of life, the circumstances of family, station, employment, success, or the contrary, the ties of domestic affection, with all those varied circumstances which seem rather the borders and outer courts than the inner sanctuary of gracious experience - yet all these are of divine material and workmanship. Viewed by faith, every event and circumstance of life, however apparently grievous, is a pleasant stone; for Zion is a king's daughter, and the meanest of all her courts is made of pleasant stones. For of wisdom, that is, vital godliness, we read, "Her ways are ways of pleasantness, and all her paths are peace."

July 14

"Look unto me, and be ye saved, all the ends of the earth: for I am God, and there is none else." - Isaiah 45. 22.

Till in soul feeling, we are at "the ends of the earth," we have no eyes to see, no ears to hear, no hearts to feel what a glorious Mediator there is at the right hand of the Father. And the more we feel to be at "the ends of the earth," the deeper is our need of him; and as the Spirit unfolds the mystery of the glorious Person of Christ, and reveals his beauty, the more does he become the object of the soul's admiration and adoration. And O, what a Mediator is held out in the word of truth to living faith! What a subject for spiritual faith to look to, for a lively hope to anchor in, and for divine love to embrace! That the Son of God, who lay in the bosom of the Father from all eternity, equal with the Father and the Holy Ghost, the second Person in the glorious Trinity, should condescend to take upon him our nature, that he might groan, suffer, bleed, and die for guilty wretches, who, if permitted, would have ruined their souls a thousand times a day - what a wonder of wonders! But we cannot enter into, nor feel the power of this mystery till we are reduced to such circumstances, that none but such a Saviour can save our souls. Can we do anything to save ourselves? Then we want not help from that mighty One on whom God has laid help; and we secretly reject him. Can we heal ourselves? Then we want not the good Physician. But when our eyes are opened to see our own thorough ruin and helplessness, and to view the glorious Person of the Son of God, faith is drawn out to flee to and rest upon that glorious Object.

July 15

"But we see Jesus." – Hebrews 2. 9.

Did your eyes ever see him? Do look into conscience – did your eyes ever see Jesus? I do not mean your natural, your bodily eyes; but the eye of faith, the eye of the soul. I will tell you what you have felt, if you ever saw Jesus. Your heart was softened and melted, your affections drawn heavenward, your soul penetrated with thankfulness and praise, your conscience sprinkled with atoning blood, your mind lifted up above all earthly things to dwell and centre in the bosom of the blessed Immanuel. Do you think, then, you have seen Jesus by the eye of faith? Then you have seen the perfection of beauty, the consummation of pure loveliness; you have seen the image of the invisible God; you have seen all the perfections and glorious character of the Godhead shining forth in him that was nailed to Calvary's tree. I am sure such a sight as that must melt the most obdurate heart, and draw tears from the most flinty eyes; such a sight by faith of the beauty and glory of the only-begotten Son of God must kindle the warmest, holiest stream of tender affection. It might not have lasted long. These feelings are often very transitory. The world, sin, temptation, and unbelief soon work; infidelity soon assails all; the things of time and sense soon draw aside; but whilst it lasted, such, in a greater or less degree, were the sensations produced. Now, if you have ever seen Jesus by the eye of faith, and ever had a tender affection going out toward him, you will see him in glory. But you will never see him in glory, if you have not seen him in grace; you will never see him eye to eye in the open vision of eternal bliss, unless you have seen him now upon earth by the faith of God's elect in your heart.

July 16

"For there is one God, and one mediator between God and men, the man Christ Jesus." – 1 Timothy 2. 5.

That *he is God,* is the very foundation of his salvation; for it is his eternal Godhead that gives virtue, efficacy, and dignity to all that as man he did and suffered for his chosen people. If he were not God, God and man in one glorious Person, what hope would there be for our guilty souls? Could his blood atone for our sins, unless Deity gave it efficacy? Could his righteousness justify our persons, unless Deity imparted merit and value to all the doings and sufferings of his humanity? Could his loving heart sympathise with and deliver us unless, "as God over all", he saw and knew all that passes within us, and had all power, as well as all compassion, to exert on our behalf? We are continually in circumstances where no man can do us the least good, and where we cannot help or deliver ourselves; we are in snares, and cannot break them; we are in temptations, and cannot deliver ourselves out of them; we are in trouble, and cannot comfort ourselves; are wandering sheep, and cannot find the way back to the fold; we are continually roving after idols, and hewing out "broken cisterns," and cannot return to "the fountain of living waters." How suitable, then, and sweet it is, to those who are thus exercised, to see that there is a gracious Immanuel at the right hand of the Father, whose heart is filled with love, and whose bowels move with compassion; who has shed his own precious blood that they might live; who has wrought out a glorious righteousness, and "is able to save them to the uttermost that come unto God by him."

July 17

"Though he were a Son, yet learned he obedience by the things which he suffered." – Hebrews 5. 8.

Our gracious Lord had to learn obedience to the will of God by a personal experience of suffering, and especially by an implicit submission to his heavenly Father's will. And what was this will? That he should take upon himself the huge debt which his bride had incurred by original and actual transgression; that he should offer himself as a ransom price to discharge and put it away; that he should bear our sins in his own body on the tree, with everything which was involved in being made a curse for us; that he should by death overcome Satan, who had the power of death, and deliver them who all their life, through fear of death, were subject to bondage; and that, whatever sorrows and sufferings should lie in his path, he should bear them all, and learn, in and by them, implicit sub-mission to the will of God. This was the will of God, for he was determined that his law should be magnified, his justice glorified, his infinite purity and holiness revealed and established; and yet, amidst all and through all his displeasure against sin, that his infinite wisdom, tender pity, everlasting love, and sovereign grace might shine and reign in the happiness of millions through a glorious eternity. This, too, was the joy that was set before Christ, for which he endured the cross, despising the shame, and is now set down at the right hand of the throne of God.

July 18

"Who art thou, O great mountain? before Zerubbabel thou shall become a plain: and he shall bring forth the headstone thereof with shoutings, crying, Grace, grace unto it." – Zechariah 4. 7.

If the literal temple had been built up without any trouble whatever; if all had gone on smooth and easy, there would not have been any shouting of "Grace, grace," when it was finished. But when it was seen how the Lord had brought a few feeble exiles from Babylon; how he had supported them amidst and carried them through all their troubles; and how he that laid the foundation had brought forth the head-stone, all that stood by could say, "Grace, grace unto it." It was these very perplexities and trials that made them join so cheerily in the shout, and made the heart and soul to leap with the lips, when they burst forth with " Grace, grace unto it." And who will shout the loudest hereafter? He that has known and felt the most of the aboundings of sin to sink his soul down into grief and sorrow, and most of the superaboundings of grace over sin to make him triumph and rejoice. Who will have most reason to sing, "Grace, grace"? The lost and ruined wretch, who has feared that he should go to hell a thousand times over, and yet has been delivered thence by sovereign grace, and brought to the glory and joy of heaven. No other person is fit to join in that song; and I am sure no other will join in it but he who has known painfully and experimentally the bitterness of sin and the evil of a depraved heart; and yet has seen and felt that grace has triumphed over all, in spite of the devil, in spite of the world, and in spite of himself, and brought him to that blessed place where many times he was afraid he should never come.

July 19

"The poor have the gospel preached to them." – Matthew 11. 5.

What is the gospel? Is not the gospel a proclamation of pure mercy, of superabounding grace? Does it not declare the lovingkindness of God in sending his only-begotten Son to bleed and die, and, by his obedience, blood, and merit, to bring in a salvation without money and without price? Is not this the gospel? Not clogged by conditions, nor crippled by anything that the creature has to perform; but flowing freely forth as the air in the skies? The poor to whom the gospel is preached, value it; it is suitable to them; it is sweet and precious when the heart is brought down. But if I stand up in religious pride, if I rest upon my own righteousness, if I am not stripped of everything in the creature, what is the gospel to me? I have no heart to receive it; there is no place in my soul for a gospel without money and without price. But when I sink into the depth of creature poverty, when I am nothing and have nothing but a mass of sin and guilt, then the blessed gospel, pardoning my sins, covering my naked soul, shedding abroad the love of God, guiding me into everything good, and leading me up into enjoyment with a Three-One God, becomes prized. When such a pure, such a blessed gospel comes into my heart and conscience, has not my previous poverty of spirit prepared me for it? Has not my previous beggary and necessity made a way for it, made it suitable to me, and when it comes, makes it precious to me? We must, then, sink into poverty of spirit, that painful place, in order to feel the preciousness, and drink into the sweetness and blessedness of the gospel of the grace of God.

July 20

"For if, when we were enemies, we were reconciled to God by the death of his Son, much more, being reconciled, we shall be saved by his life." – Romans 5. 10.

What a fearful spot it is to be in – to feel and fear oneself an enemy to God! I think it is one of the most painful feelings that ever passed through my breast, to fear I was an enemy to God. For what must be the consequence, if a man live and die having God for his enemy? In that warfare he must perish. If God be his enemy, who can be his friend? Such sensations in the bosom are well-nigh akin to despair. Let a man fully feel that he is God's enemy, where can he hide his head? Hell itself seems to afford him no refuge. But he must be exercised with something of this before he can prize reconciliation. He must see himself to be an enemy of God by birth – that he was born in what our Reformers called "birth sin"; and that his carnal mind is enmity against God. O the painful sensations of the carnal mind being enmity against God! It is bad enough to be God's enemy; but that every fibre of our nature should be steeped in enmity against God, that holy and blessed Being to whom we owe so much, and to whom we desire to owe everything; that our carnal heart in all its constitution, in its very blood, should be one unmitigated mass of enmity to God, O it is an awful thought! If you are made to experience that enmity in your bosom, and to feel more or less of its upheavings and risings – that will cut to pieces all the sinews of creature righteousness; that will mar all your comeliness, and turn it into corruption.

Now, when a man is thus exercised, it will make him look out, if he has any root of spiritual feeling, for a remedy. God has provided such in the sacrifice of his dear Son, in the blood of the Lamb; in the sufferings, obedience, death, and resurrection of the blessed Jesus. Now when this is opened up in our soul by the Spirit of God; when faith is given to receive it; when the Holy Ghost applies it; when it is received into the heart (for the Apostle says, "We have received the atonement"), then a *felt* reconciliation takes place; we are then reconciled to God; love takes the place of enmity, praise of sighing, and blessing his name instead of writing bitter things against ourselves.

July 21

"Awake, O sword, against my shepherd, and against the man that is my fellow, saith the Lord of hosts." – Zechariah 13. 7.

Would we see, feel, and realise the exceeding sinfulness of sin, it is not by viewing the lightnings and hearing the thunders of Sinai's fiery top, but in seeing the agony and bloody sweat, and hearing the groans and cries of the suffering Son of God, as made sin for us, in the garden and upon the cross. To look upon him whom we have pierced will fill heart and eyes with godly sorrow for sin, and a holy mourning for and over a martyred, injured Lord. To see, by the eye of faith, as revealed to the soul by the power of God, the darling Son of God bound, scourged, buffeted, spit upon, mocked, and then, as the climax of cruel scorn and infernal cruelty, crucified between two thieves, - this believing sight, this fellowship of the sufferings of Christ, will melt the hardest heart into contrition and compunction. But when we see, by the eye of faith, that this was the smallest part of his sufferings, that there were depths of soul trouble and of intolerable distress and agony from the hand of God as a consuming fire, as of inflexible justice and righteous indignation against sin wherever and in whomever found, and that our blessed Lord had to endure the wrath of God till he was poured out like water, and his soft, tender heart in the flames of indignation became like wax, melted in the midst of his bowels (Psalm 22. 14), – then we can in some measure conceive what he undertook in becoming a sin offering. For as all the sins of his people were put upon him, the wrath of God due to them fell upon him. Separation from God, under a sense of his terrible displeasure, and that on account of sin, that abominable thing which his holy soul hates, – is not this *hell?* This, then, was the hell experienced by the suffering Redeemer when the Lord laid on him the iniquities of us all (Isaiah 53. 6).

July 22

"Our fathers trusted in thee: they trusted, and thou didst deliver them. They cried unto thee, and were delivered: they trusted in thee, and were not confounded." – Psalm 22. 4, 5.

O what a blessed thing it is to have in one's own bosom a secret trust in Jesus – that whilst so many are looking to something in themselves or in one another, resting their eternal salvation on works that really are but the sports of a child, the saint of God is reposing upon the Lord of life and glory! On him he hangs his hope, and in him he puts his trust. These the Lord will honour; nor will he ever disappoint their hope or put their confidence to shame. Whoever trusted in the Lord and was confounded? If you are enabled to trust in him, to believe his faithful word, to discard all creature confidence and to hang the weight of your soul – and O what a weight is that! – upon a faithful, covenant-keeping God, he will never leave, fail, or forsake you. You may find it hard to trust in him at all times or indeed at any time. You may feel a want of something sensible – something to see or hear, distinct from faith. Look not for this. We walk by faith, not by sight. It must be a naked trust in an invisible God. "Some trust in chariots, and some in horses: but we will remember the name of the Lord our God." And if you are enabled so to trust, he will make it manifest sooner or later in your own conscience that you are one of the righteous; light will beam upon your path; glory will dawn upon your heart, and you will have the end of your faith, even the salvation of your soul.

July 23

"That the God of our Lord Jesus Christ, the Father of glory, may give unto you the spirit of wisdom and revelation in the knowledge of him." – Ephesians 1. 17.

Revelation means literally an uncovering or unveiling of a concealed or covered-up object. It is used, therefore, sometimes in the sense of manifesting, making known, or bringing to light, what had before been hidden in darkness and obscurity. This revelation is, therefore, either outward in the word, or inward in the soul, and the two strictly correspond to and are counterparts of each other. Immediately that, by the power of divine grace, a poor Gentile sinner turns to the Lord, the Spirit of revelation removes the veil off the Scriptures, and off his heart. Have we not found it so? What a sealed book was the word of God once to us! How we read or heard it without one real ray of light to illuminate the dark page; and what a thick veil was there of ignorance, unbelief, prejudice, self-righteousness, and impenitence on our heart. But the gracious Spirit of revelation took this double veil away, and by giving us the light of life, made the word of God a new book, and gave us a new heart; and ever since the day when the entrance of his word gave us light, God's word has been a lamp unto our feet, and a light unto our path. But the Spirit of revelation is chiefly given to lead us into a spiritual, experimental, and saving knowledge of Christ. Without this blessed Spirit of revelation Christ cannot be effectually or savingly known. When, therefore, Peter made that noble confession of his faith in Christ as "the Son of the living God," our Lord said to him: "Blessed art thou, Simon Bar-jona: for flesh and blood hath not revealed it unto thee, but my Father which is in heaven."

July 24

"Nevertheless my lovingkindness will I not utterly take from him, nor suffer my faithfulness to fail. My covenant will I not break, nor alter the thing that is gone out of my lips." – Psalm 89. 33, 34.

We live in a changeable, ever-changing world. All without us is stamped with mutation, death, and decay; and as regards ourselves everything within us tells us how frail, weak, and mutable we are. Thus, as viewed by the eye of sense and reason, uncertainty and changeability are ever seen to be deeply stamped, not only on every event of time, but on all we are and have in body and soul; and this experience of what we feel in ourselves and see in all around us often wonderfully tries both our faith and hope, for we are apt to measure God by ourselves, and judge of our state before him, not according to his word, but according to the varying thoughts and exercises of our mind. But when we can look by faith through all these mists and fogs which, as resting on the lower grounds of our soul, so often obscure our view of divine realities, to the fixed purposes of God as manifested in an everlasting covenant, ordered in all things and sure, and have at the same time some testimony of our interest therein, ground is thus afforded both for faith and hope as resting, not on our ever-changing feelings, but on the word and promise of him that cannot lie. It was thus David was comforted on his bed of languishing when the cold damps of death sat upon his brow (2 Samuel 23. 5). It was then in this "everlasting covenant, ordered in all things, and sure," that even before the world was formed, man made, or sin committed, a Saviour was provided, a Redeemer set up, and the persons of the redeemed chosen in him and given to him. How can we think, then, that any changing and changeable events in time can alter and frustrate what was thus absolutely fixed by firm and sovereign decree, or that any mutable circumstances in ourselves or others can defeat and disannul the eternal purposes of God?

July 25

"He that hath received his testimony hath set to his seal that God is true." – John 3. 33.

We can only set to our seal that God is true in any one point of doctrine, experience, or precept when we feel an inward witness that God indeed has declared it. Thus, upon every manifestation of God's goodness to the soul, every application of Christ's blood to the conscience, and every revelation of God's distinguishing grace, it is only as we receive Christ's testimony, experience the inward approbation of it, and feel its sweetness and blessedness that we can set to our seal that God is true. This, we may be well assured, is the only way to know the power and reality of true religion, to understand the Scriptures, and enjoy a convincing testimony that God is our God, Christ our Saviour, the Holy Ghost our Teacher, heaven our eternal home, and that our soul is saved in the Lord Jesus Christ with an everlasting salvation.

And with what divine certainty can such a soul sometimes speak. Sometimes, indeed, we cannot believe anything; it seems as if there were nothing in God's word that we could set our seal to. All seems a mass of confusion, and our ignorance appears so great that we cannot set our seal to any vital truth. But when the blessed Spirit is pleased to testify of the things of God, and we, receiving the testimony of Jesus Christ, walk in the light of that testimony, then there is a holy certainty of and heavenly acquiescence with God's truth. This divine faith will bring us through all our trials and sorrows, and though we may be dragged through a very hell of temptation, yet shall we know God is true.

Here, then, is the grand trial of faith; first to receive Christ's testimony, and then to hang upon that testimony, in spite of all opposition from within and without, from feeling its weight, power, and sweetness.

July 26

"And I will bring the third part through the fire, and will refine them as silver is refined, and will try them as gold is tried: they shall call on my name, and I will hear them: I will say, It is my people: and they shall say, The Lord is my God." – Zechariah 13. 9.

It is a mercy to be in the furnace, and it is a mercy to be brought through it. The Lord's promise to the third part is, that he will bring them through the fire. They must therefore, according to his own word, be put into it, and yet not left in it. It is "through the fire" – right through it from beginning to end, whether it be a long and slow one or short and fierce one. The Lord knows exactly what we can bear, and it is not always the hottest fire which produces the most softening effects. Some metals indeed are so stubborn, and the dross is so deeply ingrained into them, that they seem to require a hotter fire than others. But after the law has done its work, and the dross and tin have been purged away, the Lord does not usually bring again so hot a furnace. It is rather one of trial, temptation, sickness, family affliction, straits in providence, persecution, deep and daily discoveries of the body of sin and death, the hidings of the Lord's face, and denials of his presence which seem to make up that trial which tries every man's faith of what sort it is. By these trials and exercises there is a gradual weaning from the world, a humility, meekness, and brokenness of spirit before the Lord, a greater simplicity and godly sincerity, more willing obedience to the precepts of the gospel, and a greater desire to know the will of God and do it. O that these fruits of the Spirit might abound in us and all the saints and servants of God!

July 27

"That as sin hath reigned unto death, even so might grace reign through righteousness unto eternal life by Jesus Christ our Lord." – Romans 5. 21.

This is the mercy for mourning saints who are sighing and groaning under a body of sin and death, that God has decreed that grace not only *may* reign, but that it *must* reign. Were it left to us, we could no more rescue ourselves from the dominion of sin than the children of Israel could deliver themselves from the house of Egyptian bondage. But they sighed and groaned by reason of the bondage, and their cry came up unto God. He had respect unto his covenant, and looked upon them and delivered them (Exod. 2. 23-25). So God has determined on behalf of his people that sin shall not be their eternal ruin; that it shall not plunge them into crime after crime, until it casts them at last into the gulf of endless woe, but that grace "shall reign through righteousness unto eternal life." But it must reign here as well as hereafter, for by its reign here its eternal triumph is secured. It must then subdue our proud hearts, and never cease to sway its peaceful sceptre over them until it has secured in them absolute and unconditional victory. Now this is what every sincere child of God most earnestly longs to feel and realise. He longs to embrace Jesus and be embraced by him in the arms of love and affection. As the hymn says,

"But now subdued by sovereign grace,
My spirit longs for thy embrace."

He hates sin, though it daily, hourly, momently works in him, and is ever seeking to regain its former mastery; he abhors that cruel tyrant who set him to do his vilest drudgery, deceived and deluded him by a thousand lying promises, dragged him again and again into captivity, and but for sovereign grace would have sealed his eternal destruction. Subdued by the sceptre of mercy, he longs for the dominion of grace over every faculty of his soul and every member of his body. "O," he says, "let grace reign and rule in my breast; let it not suffer any sin to have dominion over me; let it tame every unruly desire, and bring into captivity every thought to the obedience of Christ!" Thus, he who truly fears God looks to grace, and to grace only, not merely to save, but to sanctify; not only to pardon sin, but to subdue it; not only to secure him an inheritance among the saints in light, but to make him meet for it.

July 28

"Howbeit when he, the Spirit of truth, is come, he will guide you into all truth: for he shall not speak of himself; but whatsoever he shall hear, that shall he speak: and he will shew you things to come." – John 16. 13.

There are two grand lessons to be learnt in the school of Christ, and all divine teaching is comprehended and summed up in them. One is, to learn, by the Spirit's teaching, what we are by nature; so as to see and feel the utter ruin and thorough wreck of self, and the complete beggary, weakness, and helplessness of the creature in the things of God. This is the first grand branch of divine teaching. And we have to learn this lesson day by day, "line upon line, line upon line; here a little, and there a little." Through this branch of divine teaching we have almost daily to wade, and sometimes to sink into very painful depths under a sense of our depraved nature. And the other grand branch of divine teaching is, "To know the only true God, and Jesus Christ whom he has sent." To know *who* Jesus is, and to know *what* he is; to know the efficacy of his atoning blood to purge the guilty conscience, the power of his justifying righteousness to acquit and absolve from all sin; the mystery of his dying love to break down the hardness of heart, and raise up a measure of love towards him; and to see, by the eye of faith, his holy walk and suffering image, so as to be in some measure conformed to him, and have his likeness in some measure stamped upon our souls.

July 29

"And Gideon said unto God, Let not thine anger be hot against me, and I will speak but this once: let me prove, I pray thee, but this once with the fleece; let it now be dry only upon the fleece, and upon all the ground let there be dew. And God did so that night: for it was dry upon the fleece only, and there was dew on all the ground." – Judges 6. 39, 40.

Many of the Lord's people labour under doubts and fears, questionings and suspicions as to the reality of the work of grace upon their hearts; whether their convictions were not merely convictions of natural conscience, and whether their joys have been anything else but the joys of the hypocrite. "O," they say, "what would I not give to have a divine testimony that the blessed Spirit was leading me in the right path!" It is through these very doubts that the evidence is obtained. Doubts lead to cries and groans after a divine testimony; and in answer to these cries the heavenly witness is given. A man without doubts is without testimonies. Doubts are to testimonies what the mortise is to the tenon, the lock to the key, the enigma to the solution.

Testimonies are Ebenezers, "stones of help" (1 Sam. 7. 12, *marg.*); but the stone must have a hole dug for it to stand in, and that hole is *doubt.* Doubts of salvation are to manifestations of salvation what hunger is to food, nakedness to clothing, a thunderstorm to a shelter, a gallows to a reprieve, and death to a resurrection. The one of these things precedes, prepares, and opens a way for the other. The first is nothing without the last, nor the last without the first. Thus, next to testimonies, the best thing is spiritual doubts. To know we are right is the best thing; to fear we are wrong is the second best. To enjoy the witness of the Spirit is the most blessed thing this side of the grave; to pant after that enjoyment is the next greatest blessing. I am speaking, mind, only of spiritual doubts; that is, doubts in a spiritual man, for natural doubts are as far from salvation as natural hopes. The path through the valley of Baca is "from strength to strength," that is, according to the eastern mode of travelling, from one halting-place to another, where wells are dug, and "the rain filleth the pools" (Ps. 84. 6, 7). We do not learn either God or ourselves, sin or salvation, in a day. The question is not so much whether you have *much* faith, but whether you have any. It is not quantity, but quality; not whether you have a very great religion, but whether you have any at all. A grain of true faith will save the soul; and I have known many, many seasons when I should have been glad to feel certain that I had the thousandth part of a grain. A grain of mustard seed is the smallest of all seeds; and even faith as small as that can move mountains. Happy is he that has one divine testimony to his eternal interest in the electing love of the Father, in the atoning blood and justifying righteousness of the Son, and in the divine teachings of the Holy Spirit.

July 30

"Him hath God exalted with his right hand to be a Prince and a Saviour, for to give repentance to Israel, and forgiveness of sins." – Acts 5. 31.

Jesus is "exalted to be a Prince and a Saviour to give repentance and remission of sins." The two go together. Whenever he gives repentance, he gives remission; wherever he grants remission, he bestows repentance. It will not do to let repentance go. Every child of God is brought to repent of his sins, and by repentance to forsake them. "But," you say, "have I repented? Considering the nature and magnitude of my sins, were I a repenting sinner, surely I should be mourning and sorrowing over them all the day long." What, then, creates that doubt in your mind? Because you are often hard, dark, dead, cold. Here, then, again, we must distinguish between that godly sorrow for sin which is felt in the spiritual mind, and that hardness and darkness of our carnal mind which is still enmity against God, nor is there faith or love, repentance, or any one good thing in it. But there have been times and seasons when, under a peculiar influence, your heart was softened and melted before God; when sin was truly repented of; when you felt that it was indeed an evil and a bitter thing to sin against so good, so holy, and so great and glorious a God; when the rock melted, the hard heart gave way, the eyes flowed down with tears, and the swelling breast was almost ready to burst with penitential grief for your sins and over the sufferings and sorrows of the Son and Lamb of God, and you could only loathe yourself in dust and ashes before his holy, heart-searching eye.

July 31

"Faith is the substance of things hoped for, the evidence of things not seen." – Hebrews 11. 1.

Wherever there is faith, there is desire; and as faith embraces heavenly realities, desire embraces that of which faith testifies. Now as the soul is wrought upon by a divine power, and faith is drawn forth into blessed exercise upon the promises of which it is persuaded and which it embraces, desire is kindled for their enjoyment. Religion is not a burdensome, painful, melancholy, wearisome, and toilsome task or employment as many think. It has indeed its trials, temptations, afflictions, cutting griefs, and depressing sorrows; but it has its sweetness, its peace, its delights, and its enjoyments. And it is the sweetness that we feel, the enjoyment that we have, and the delighting ourselves in the things of God, which hold our head up and encourage us still to persevere and travel on through the wilderness. It is not all bondage, nor distress of mind, nor sorrow of heart, nor perplexity of soul which the heirs of promise feel. There are sips and tastes, drops and crumbs, and momentary enjoyments, if not long nor lasting, yet sweet when they come, sweet while they last, and sweet in the recollection when they are gone. The Lord gives that which encourages, strengthens, comforts, and delights, and enables us to see that there is that beauty, blessedness, and glory in him which we have tasted, felt, and handled, and which we would not part with for a thousand worlds.

August 1

"For the law of the Spirit of life in Christ Jesus hath made me free from the law of sin and death." – Romans 8. 2.

We by nature and practice are slaves to sin and Satan. We are the sport of the prince of the power of the air, who takes us captive at his will. We are held down also by many hurtful lusts; or, if free from gross sin, are slaves to pride, covetousness, or self-righteousness. Perhaps some idol is set up in the chambers of imagery which defiles all the inner man; or some snare of Satan entangles our feet, and we are slaves, without power to liberate ourselves from this cruel slavery. We groan under it, as the children of Israel under their burdens, but, like them, cannot deliver ourselves. But sooner or later the truth comes to our aid; the truth as it is in Jesus flies to the rescue of God's oppressed family; the blessed Spirit opens it up and seals it upon the heart with a divine power. As, then, under his gracious influences they believe the truth, and feel its power and savour in their heart, a liberating influence is communicated; their fetters and shackles are loosened; the bondage of sin and Satan, and the power and strength of evil are sensibly broken, and a measure of holy freedom is enjoyed. There is no other way of getting from under the bondage of the law but by the application of the gospel, and by believing what the gospel reveals. As the truth, then, comes to the heart as the very word of the living God, power comes with it to believe; faith is raised up to credit the testimony; and as faith begins to credit the truth of God and receive it in hope and love, there is a sensible loosening of the bonds; and then the chains and fetters drop off of themselves. It is with the soul as it was with Peter in prison: when the angel came, and a light shined in the prison, and the angel's words fell upon his ears, "the chains fell off from his hands." There remained nothing then to bar his exit; for "the iron gate that leadeth unto the city opened to them of its own accord". So whatever chains or fetters may hold the soul, let the angel of mercy come; let the message of salvation be revealed, the chains of unbelief drop off, the iron gate of hardness gives way, and the truth makes the soul blessedly free (John 8. 32).

August 2

"Fight the good fight of faith, lay hold on eternal life." – 1 Timothy 6. 12.

It is through faith that the power whereby God keeps his people acts and is made known, and it is very instructive and encouraging to be able to trace in our own hearts the connection between the power of God and the actings of faith. We are not carried to heaven as passengers are carried by the express train to Holyhead, so that if once in the carriage they may go to sleep, look out of the window, or read the newspaper without fear of losing their way, or not reaching their destination. Though kept by the power of God, we have to fight every step of the way. It is this living, fighting, struggling, and yet eventually conquering faith, which sets the tried and exercised child of God at such a distance from the loose and careless doctrinal professor, who is hardened and emboldened to presume, and even walk in ways of sin and death by holding the doctrine of being kept by the power of God, without knowing anything of the secret way by which this power works and keeps. To such we may adapt the language of James. You believe that the elect of God are kept by his Almighty power unto salvation. "Thou doest well: the devils also believe, and tremble" – which you do not if you be one of these loose professors. But does God keep you? Does he keep you from evil, that it may not grieve you? Does he keep your eye single, your conscience tender, your heart prayerful, your life and walk circumspect, your eye from adultery, your tongue from folly, your hands from covetousness, and your feet from the ways of pride and worldliness? You have no evidence that you are an heir of God and are being kept by his power unto salvation, unless you have some experience *how* he keeps, and that as it is by power on his part, so it is through faith on yours. Whenever we slip, stumble, or go astray, it is through the power of unbelief; and whenever we stand, fight, or prevail, it is by faith.

August 3

"One shall say, I am the Lord's; and another shall call himself by the name of Jacob; and another shall subscribe with his hand unto the Lord, and surname himself by the name of Israel." – Isaiah 44. 5.

Another *shall call himself by the name of Jacob.* Jacob was a wrestler, for he wrestled all night with the angel; and by wrestling he obtained the blessing. So at present you may be a wrestling Jacob, but have not yet come off a prevailing Israel. You may not be without a sense of guilt and bondage at times in your conscience, and may often doubt and fear whether the root of the matter be in you, because you cannot use the language of assurance and say, "I am the Lord's." Still you may be a wrestling Jacob. The Lord may have put his Spirit in you to enable you to wrestle with him for the blessing, and yet he may not have given you that appropriating faith whereby you can believe that he is yours, and can call him such. How full was the patriarch Jacob of doubt and fear when his own life, and that of his wife and children, lay in the very hands of the injured Esau! But it was this very fear which made him wrestle all the harder, and more fervently cry out, "I will not let thee go, except thou bless me." Can you not say, "I am seeking for a blessing of this kind with all my heart; I am wrestling with God for it by prayer and supplication, and nothing less can satisfy me?" If this be your experience, you certainly may "call yourself by the name of Jacob". *"And shall surname himself by the name of Israel."* As Jacob represents a wrestler in the court of grace, so Israel is the emblem of one who has obtained the blessing. When, therefore, any wrestling Jacob has prevailed with God by strength of arm, he may surname himself by the name of Israel. He can then say, "I have wrestled with God for the promised blessing, and have obtained it. I have cried unto the Lord, and he has heard my cry. I have spread my petition before him, and he has at last granted it." So wrestled and so prevailed Hannah, David, Hezekiah, and many a saint both dead and living.

August 4

"And they that know thy name will put their trust in thee." – Psalm 9. 10.

There is a knowing of God's name. By the "name of God" are to be understood the revealed perfections of the Almighty – all that he has revealed concerning himself in the Scriptures of truth. Every attribute, every perfection, everything that God has said of himself, is summed up in the "name of God". But especially does the "name of God" signify the Son of his love, who is "the brightness of his glory, and the express image of his Person"; as he said to Moses, "Behold, I send an Angel before thee, to keep thee in the way, and to bring thee into the place which I have prepared. Beware of him, and obey his voice, provoke him not; for he will not pardon your transgressions: for *my name is in him"*; that is, all my revealed perfections, all my glorious character, all my divine attributes are in him; "for in him dwelleth all the fulness of the Godhead bodily." Now, there is a *knowing* this name of God; that is, there is such a thing as an experimental acquaintance in the soul with the perfections of God as revealed in the Scriptures. His name is therefore known when the perfections of God are revealed in the heart and conscience by the power of the Spirit. And this is by virtue of living faith in the soul. By faith we see God. By faith we know God. When we receive into our hearts the truth as it is in Jesus, and when we believe by living faith what God has said of himself in the word, then we know the name of God; and every manifestation of God's mercy, every token of God's favour, and every shining in of God's perfections, is a discovery in our hearts, a raising up in our souls of the knowledge of God's name.

August 5

"He shall send from heaven, and save me from the reproach of him that would swallow me up. Selah. God shall send forth his mercy and his truth." – Psalm 57. 3.

And where is God's mercy revealed? Outwardly in the word of God; inwardly in the heart. And it is by sending his mercy into the conscience, shedding abroad his love in the soul, manifesting his pardoning favour within, that God "saves from the reproach of him that would swallow us up." Man may say, 'I do not doubt your religion; surely you have marks and testimonies of being a child of God!' Ministers may come and endeavour to soothe you, and often by their soothing make more mischief than they mend: 'O, no doubt, if you are exercised with these things you are a child of God;' as though a man could be satisfied with exercises, and because he is hungering and thirsting after the Lord, could be contented with his famine and his drought. No; these things do not touch the secret malady, do not go far enough, nor deep enough, nor come with divine power as from the mouth of the Lord himself. All short of this leaves the poor patient afflicted, desolate, and dejected; and does not remove that under which his soul labours. But mercy, sweet mercy, sent from heaven, and dropped from above into his spirit, applied to his conscience, revealed to his heart, and brought warm into his very soul by the Spirit of God – *that* saves him from the reproach of every enemy that would swallow him up. For if he can lean, confidently lean upon the arms of mercy, what can man do, what can Satan do, what can sin do, what can death do, what can hell itself do to hurt him? If the mercy of God is on his side, revealed to his heart, and sent from heaven into his soul, who or what shall swallow him up?

August 6

"For there are three that bear record in heaven, the Father, the Word, and the Holy Ghost: and these three are one." – 1 John 5. 7.

A spiritual knowledge of the Trinity lies at the foundation of all vital godliness. To know Father, Son, and Holy Ghost by special teaching and divine revelation, is the sum and substance of spiritual religion, and is eternal life; according to the Lord's own testimony, John 17. 3, "And this is life eternal, that they might know thee the only true God, and Jesus Christ, whom thou hast sent." Thus, sooner or later, the Lord leads all his people into a feeling acquaintance with, and divine reception of this glorious mystery; and thus they come to know the Father's electing love, the Son's redeeming work, and the Spirit's inward testimony; and that these Three are One. But how opposed to nature, sense, and reason is this glorious mystery; and how they all rise up in rebellion against it! How can Three be One or One be Three? nature asks and reason argues. And yet the babes receive and believe it. For take away the doctrine of the Trinity, and all their hope is gone in a moment. How can we rest upon Christ's atoning blood, if it is not the blood of the Son of God? or upon his justifying righteousness, if not the righteousness of God? or how could we be kept, led, taught, and guided by the Holy Ghost, if he too was not a divine Person in the Godhead? Thus we come to know the mystery of Three Persons in the Godhead, by feelingly receiving into our hearts the work of each with power; and yet we know that these Three are but one God. It is this inward reception of the truth in the love of it which holds up the soul in a storm. We are often tossed about, and ready to say, "How can these things be?" But we are brought up by this deep-rooted feeling, as the anchor brings up the ship in the gale, that we are undone without it. If this mystery be removed, our hope must be removed with it; for there is no pardon, peace, nor salvation, but what stands in, and flows out of, an experimental knowledge of the Three-One God.

August 7

"And what is the exceeding greatness of his power to us-ward who believe, according to the working of his mighty power, which he wrought in Christ, when he raised him from the dead, and set him at his own right hand in the heavenly places." – Ephesians 1. 19, 20.

It is no great mystery that the Son of God should be exalted to the throne of power. It is but a step from the bosom of the Father to his right hand. But that one in our nature should be exalted to that seat of pre-eminence and power; that the Mediator between God and man should be *the man* Christ Jesus; that the hands which once were nailed to the cross should now hold the sceptre, and that the feet which once walked on Lake Gennesaret, which were weary and dust-soiled at Jacob's well, which were washed with a sinful woman's tears and kissed in penitential grief and love with polluted lips – that these very feet should now have all things put under them both in heaven and earth, *there* is the mystery. And yet what food for faith. The living family of God want a living Saviour, one who can hear and answer prayer, deliver out of soul-trouble, speak a word with power to the heart when bowed down with grief and sorrow, sympathise with them under powerful temptations, support them under the trials and afflictions of the way, maintain under a thousand discouragements his own life in their soul, sustain under bereavements the mourning widow, and be a father to her fatherless children; appear again and again in providence as a friend that loveth at all times and a brother born for adversity, smile upon them in death, and comforting them with his rod and staff as they walk through the valley of its dark shadow, land them at last safely in a happy eternity.

August 8

"Have mercy upon me, O God, according to thy lovingkindness: according unto the multitude of thy tender mercies blot out my transgressions." – Psalm 51. 1.

This psalm is very suitable to the wants and feelings of every sensible sinner, for it is not necessary to have committed David's sin to have a measure of David's repentance and confessions, and of David's desires, breathings, and supplications. "Have mercy upon me, O God," he says, "according to thy loving-kindness." To ask God to have mercy upon us is one of the first cries that a convinced sinner puts up to God. It was so with the publican in the temple; and where it is sincere, God will certainly hear it "according to his loving-kindness," for he is full of love and kindness to poor, mourning sinners. How the psalmist also begs of the Lord to "blot out his transgressions according unto the multitude of his tender mercies." As our sins in thought, word, and deed are a countless multitude, of which every one deserves hell, we need "the multitude of his most tender mercies" to blot them out. We may see the stars in the sky, the sands on the sea-shore, the drops of dew on the grass, the waves rolling in upon the beach; but both our sins and God's tender mercies exceed them all. How he showed these tender mercies in giving his dear Son to suffer, bleed, and die for miserable sinners; and how we need all these tender mercies to pity and pardon us and our transgressions. And how earnestly David begged, "Wash me *throughly* from mine iniquity, and cleanse me from my sin." It is only the washing of God himself that can wash us *throughly*. If we could shed an ocean of tears it would not wash away one sin; but the blood of Christ cleanseth from all sin. In order to make us know this, the Lord shews us and makes us feel the guilt and burden of sin, and that we can do nothing to put it away. Pardon must be his own free gift, and that every sensible sinner is made to feel.

August 9

"Godliness is profitable unto all things." – 1 Timothy 4. 8.

What is "profitable"? I may define it in one short sentence – that which does the soul good. Now "godliness" is profitable unto all things, as doing the soul good in all circumstances. Here it stands apart and separate from everything of a worldly nature. Here it is distinguished from the "bodily exercise that profiteth little". It is "profitable unto all things." In sickness, in health; in sunshine, in storm; upon the mount, in the valley; under whatever circumstances the child of God may be, "godliness" or rather the "exercise" of godliness is profitable. And it is drawn out by these circumstances. It lives in the face of trials; it is strengthened by opposition; it becomes victorious through defeat; it gains the day in spite of every foe:

> "Stands every storm, and lives at last."

It does not die away like "bodily exercise"; it does not bloom and fade away in an hour; it is not like Jonah's gourd that grew and withered in a night; it does not leave the soul in the horrors of despair when it most needs comfort; it is not a fickle, false friend that turns its back in the dark and cloudy days of adversity. It is "a friend that loveth at all times", for the Author of it "sticketh closer than a brother". It can come to a bed of sickness when the body is racked with pain; it can enter a dungeon, as with Paul and Silas when their feet were in the stocks; it can go, and has gone with martyrs to the stake; it soothes the pillow of death; it takes the soul into eternity; and therefore it is "profitable unto all things". It is a firm friend; a blessed companion; the life of the soul; the health of the heart; yea, "Christ himself in you, the hope of glory". It is God's own work, God's own grace, God's own Spirit, God's own life, God's own power, God's own dealings, which end in God's own happiness; and therefore it is "profitable unto all things".

August 10

"Having promise of the life that now is, and of that which is to come." – 1 Timothy 4. 8.

True religion lies deep; it is not a balloon hovering over us miles up in the air. It is like truth – it lies at the bottom of the well. We must go down, then, into religion, if we are to have it really in our hearts. The Lord Jesus Christ was "a man of sorrows, and acquainted with grief". He took the lowest, last, and least place. He was always down; so that if we are to be companions with the Lord Jesus Christ, we must go down with him – down into the valley, down into suffering, down into humiliation, down into trial, down into sorrow. When we get puffed up by worldly joy, or elated by carnal excitement, we do not sympathise with the Lord Jesus Christ in his suffering manhood; we do not go with him then into the garden of Gethsemane, nor behold him as "the Lamb of God" on the accursed tree. We can do without Jesus very well when the world smiles, and carnal things are uppermost in our heart. But let affliction come, a heavy cross, a burden to weigh us down, then we drop into the place where the Lord Jesus is only to be found. We find, *then,* if the Lord is pleased to bring a little godliness into the soul, and to draw forth this godliness into vital exercise, that it has "the promise of the life that now is". There are promises connected with it of support and strength, comfort, consolation, and peace, that the world knows nothing of; there is a truth in it, a power, a reality, a blessedness in it, that tongue can never express. And when the soul gets pressed down into the vale of affliction, and the Lord is pleased to meet with it there, and visit it then, and draw forth godliness in its actings and exercises, then it is found to have "the promise of the life that now is". Faith, hope, love, repentance, prayerfulness, humility, contrition, long-suffering, and peace - all these gifts and graces of the Spirit are exercised chiefly when the soul is down in affliction. Here is "the promise of the life that now is" in the drawing forth of these heavenly graces in the heart.

And godliness hath the promise also of "the life which is to come." It supports in life and in death; and takes the soul into a happy and blessed eternity. Grace will end in glory; faith in sight; hope in fruition. The soul taught of God will see Jesus as he is. Thus godliness has "the promise of the life which is to come", when eternal peace shall abound, tears be wiped from off all faces, and grace consummated in endless bliss.

August 11

"That by two immutable things, in which it was impossible for God to lie, we might have a strong consolation, who have fled for refuge to lay hold upon the hope set before us." - Hebrews 6. 18.

If ever there was in your experience a season never to be forgotten of alarm, of fear, of terror, of guilt, of apprehension; and then when you scarcely knew what to do, think or say, there was a view opened up to you of a refuge in the Person and work, blood and righteousness of the Lord the Lamb; if as driven or drawn you fled to it, were kindly received, and found safe harbourage from guilt and doubt and fear, then you surely know what it is to have fled for refuge to lay hold upon the hope set before you. It is these, and these only, who are heirs of promise; and therefore how important it is to have had some personal experience of these things. How are we to know whether we possess the life of God in our soul, the grace of God in our heart, unless there has been some such fleeing and some such laying hold? Do see, then, if you can trace these two things in your breast: first, if there ever was a season with you when you feared, and trembled at the wrath to come, and were compelled to flee for refuge from it. But, secondly, finding no refuge in self, and that all your own righteousness was a bed too short and a covering too narrow, you fled to Jesus as your only hope; and as there was a sweet opening up to the eye of your faith of a refuge provided in the Lord the Lamb, you were enabled to take hold of him in his covenant characters and blessed relationships, and found in him rest and peace. If, then, you can find these two features of divine life in your soul, you are one of the characters of whom our text speaks; you have fled for refuge to lay hold upon the hope set before you in the everlasting gospel.

August 12

"My soul fainteth for thy salvation: but I hope in thy word." – Psalm 119. 81.

How difficult, for the most part, it is, and we may add, how rare to be able to realise for ourselves, with any degree of abiding permanency, a sweet experimental sense of, and an assured interest in those spiritual blessings with which, so far as we are believers in the Son of God, we are blessed in heavenly places in Christ Jesus. Glimpses, glances, transient views, sips and tastes, drops and crumbs sweet beyond expression whilst they last, but rarely given and soon gone, are, generally speaking, all we seem to get after much hard labour, many cries, earnest entreaties, and vehement longings before the Lord, as he presents himself to our faith, seated on the throne of his grace. How many there are who are daily and sometimes almost hourly crying out, if not in the exact words, yet in the substance of them:

> "O come, thou much-expected Guest!
> Lord Jesus, quickly come!"

And yet how long he seems to delay his coming! How continually are they looking upward till eyes and heart seem alike to fail, waiting for his appearing more than they that watch for the morning; how willing to make any sacrifice, to do anything, be anything, or bear anything, if he would but manifest himself to their souls. How often are they searching and examining their hearts, lips, and lives, to see if there be any evil way in them which makes him hide his lovely face, and not drop one word into their longing breasts, whereby they might hold sweet communion with him! How they desire to be blessed with real contrition of heart, and godly sorrow for their sins, and be melted and dissolved at his feet, under a sight and sense of his bleeding, dying love!

But whence spring all these longing looks and waiting expectations? Do not all those earnest desires and vehement longings show that those in whom they so continually are found are begotten again to a lively hope, by the resurrection of Jesus Christ from the dead? It is divine life in their souls which is the spring and source of these inward breathings, lookings, and longings; and this divine life arises out of a new and spiritual birth, which is itself the fruit of the resurrection of Jesus Christ from the dead. It is not the still-born child that cries; it is the cry of the living child which so goes to the heart of the mother.

Thus the cries of which we have spoken show that there is life. But with life there is hope; for why should a man be ever crying after, waiting for, and anxiously expecting a blessing which he has no hope ever to obtain? If, then, these had no living hope, would they cry? There are no cries in a dead hope. It is because the grace of hope in their breasts is, like every other grace of the Spirit, alive unto God, that it acts in union with faith and love, to bring them and keep them earnest, sincere, and unwearied before the throne, expecting and anticipating what God has promised to bestow on those who wait upon him.

August 13

"The Spirit itself beareth witness with our spirit, that we are the children of God." – Romans 8. 16.

You may not perhaps, for the most part, enjoy a strong or clear assurance of your interest in Christ; you may be frequently much exercised whether you are a child of God; and yet you may at times have had a sweet testimony that grace is in your heart. You may have heard the servants of God so describe the feelings of your soul, so enter into your exercises, and bring forward such evidences of grace, that, in spite of all your unbelief, you were convinced that if these men spake agreeably to the mind of God, which you could not well doubt from the power which accompanied it, you were one of his children; and as you felt this inward witness, your heart was softened and moved within you, and you could not help lifting up your soul in praise and adoration to the God of all your mercies. You might sink again almost as low as before; but whilst that heavenly feeling lasted, you had a testimony in your conscience that you were a child of God, and could then and there believe that he was your Father and heavenly friend. This text does not, therefore, cut off those who have not reached the full assurance of faith; it does not imply, much less say, that everybody shall be cut off and sent into everlasting perdition who cannot clearly and boldly declare that the Spirit itself beareth witness with their spirit that they are the children of God. On the contrary, it opens its benign arms to everyone who has in any degree or at any time received any deliverance, felt any measure of spiritual consolation, or been favoured with any testimony of his acceptance in the Beloved. It does not come as a two-edged sword to kill all who do not enjoy the full assurance of faith, but still have felt the power of the truth in their hearts. It does not say to such, "You have neither part nor lot in the matter." It would rather draw them forward into the sheltering arms of eternal mercy, and encourage them to press on to know more and more of that inward witness which alone can cheer them in hours of darkness and distress, support them upon a dying bed, and enable them to walk without doubt and fear through the gloomy valley of the shadow of death.

August 14

"And if children, then heirs; heirs of God and joint-heirs with Christ; if so be that we suffer with him, that we may be also glorified together." – Romans 8. 17.

O the blessedness of being a child of God! Can heart conceive or tongue express the heights and depths of grace and glory, the safety, the happiness, the honour, the bliss, the delight of being an heir of God and a joint-heir with Christ? We soon shall have to put off our mortal bodies – soon have to lie down with the worms of the grave and the clods of the valley – soon have to enter into the invisible world. Well may we then ask ourselves what are our prospects of eternity? Where then will be our inheritance? Will it be one of eternal misery and woe, of weeping and wailing and gnashing of teeth, or of the pleasures which are at God's right hand for evermore? Have we any evidence or testimony that we are the children of God? Has the Spirit ever borne any direct or indirect witness to our adoption into his family – to our sonship and to our heirship? When we review our past experience, can we find any marks that we can look upon with a good measure of faith and hope as sound, scriptural evidences that we are heirs of God and joint-heirs with Christ? Can you look back upon that memorable season when the Lord was first pleased to work upon your conscience and convince you of your sins? – to that time of love when Christ was first revealed to your heart? – to that day of affliction and trouble when a sweet promise of interest in his love and blood was sealed with divine power upon your soul? Can you find any solid, substantial marks or tokens that you are a partaker of saving and sanctifying grace, born of God, separated from the world as a pilgrim and a stranger, and pressing onward through a thousand foes and fears to a heavenly country? It is of no use leaning upon the testimony of man, or upon any vain hopes or presumptuous confidence that may spring up in a self-righteous, deceitful heart. It is the witness of the Spirit with our spirit, more or less clear – the shining in of the light of the Lord's countenance – the manifestations of his presence and love, which alone can really satisfy a child of God of his being a partaker of grace and of the glory that is to be revealed at the coming of the Lord Jesus.

August 15

"O that I knew where I might find him! that I might come even to his seat! I would order my cause before him, and fill my mouth with arguments." – Job 23. 3, 4.

Was not Job in the same spot where we often are? If this aged patriarch had not known what it was to be shut up in his mind, harassed and distressed, and well-nigh overwhelmed with the attacks of the wicked one, he would not have said, "O that I knew where I might find him! that I might come even to his seat! I would order my cause before him, and fill my mouth with arguments." Has that ever been, is it now, the genuine feeling, the real experience of your soul? Do look into your heart, you that fear God. Do look for a moment, if you have never looked before, at the work of grace (and where are you, if you have never looked at it?) and consider if you know anything of these matters. Did you ever, in a feeling of darkness, gloom, bondage, and distress of soul, cry (I do not say the words, it is the feelings we want, let the words go), "'O that I knew where I might find him!' Lord, I do want to find thee; my soul longs after thee; I want a taste of thy blessed presence; I want to embrace thee in the arms of my faith; I want the sweet testimonies of thy gracious lips; 'O that I knew where I might find thee!' I would not care what I went through." If so, then these very things show that you have the fear of God in your souls, and the teaching of the Spirit in your hearts. You are where Job was, and if you know something of what Job speaks here, "O that I knew where I might find him! that I might come even to his seat!" – if that is the desire of your soul, you have Job's religion, you have Job's experience, you have Job's affliction in this matter, and you will have Job's deliverance, Job's joy, Job's peace, and Job's salvation. Job's God is your God, and you will be where Job now is, bathing your ransomed soul in all the glory of the Lamb.

August 16

"Thou hast ascended on high, thou hast led captivity captive: thou hast received gifts for men; yea, for the rebellious also, that the Lord God might dwell among them." Psalm 68. 18.

What a painful thing it is to be rebellious! There is hardly any feeling worse than rebellion to a man whose conscience is made tender in God's fear. To have rebellion against a holy and wise God; rebellion against his dealings with us in providence; against his teachings in grace; because we have not more of the light of his countenance; because we have not more and clearer testimonies and manifestations! We know in our judgment that God cannot err in any of his dealings, and yet to find at times such awful rebellion against God, O how painful it is! The least trifle can work up rebellion. It does not want a storm or a gale to lift up its proud waves. The slightest breath, the faintest breeze that blows, will at times stir up the billows of the rebellious heart, and make it swell with tumultuous heavings. But what a mercy it is to the poor souls that groan and grieve under a rebellious heart, that this ascended Mediator has received gifts for them! It is not your patience, meekness, and good temper, nor your gentle and quiet disposition, that bring down grace into your hearts; but God the Father has lodged all the graces and gifts of the Spirit in his dear Son, and they are given to you because you have an interest in his blood and righteousness. The Lord teaches us this. If we were always patient, meek, holy, submissive, never harassed by the devil, and never felt the workings of corruption, we should begin to think we had some power to please God in ourselves, and should slight and neglect a precious Saviour.

But when taught by painful experience what a depraved nature and rebellious heart we carry in our bosom, when the Lord lets down a little mercy and grace into our soul, we then know the blessed quarter whence it comes, and learn to abhor ourselves and bless his holy name.

August 17

"If a man also strive for masteries, yet is he not crowned, except he strive lawfully." – 2 Timothy 2. 5.

In other words, it is not a bare striving, but a striving according to certain rules. But these rules are spiritual rules; and being spiritual rules, exclude everything of sense, reason, and nature. Now man, in an unregenerate condition, whether he be in a state of profanity, or in a state of profession, has no spiritual knowledge of the way by which to overcome. He may strive against his lusts; he may endeavour to overcome those things that conscience bears testimony against; but he is not crowned, because he strives not lawfully. He strives in his own strength; contends in his own wisdom; and trusts in his own righteousness. Such strugglers and such overcomers (if overcomers they ever are) are not crowned, because they strive not according to the rules laid down in God's word. This at once excludes all creature righteousness, human wisdom, and natural strength. This takes the crown completely off the creature, and puts it on the head of the Redeemer.

There are certain rules then laid down in the Scripture, according to which we are to fight and to overcome. For instance, the Lord of life and glory is held out in the word as our pattern: "He hath left us an example, that we should follow his steps." He fought the battle before us; and he gained the victory, not for himself only, but for his people; and he has left us here below to walk in his footsteps, and to overcome in the same way as he did; as we read, "To him that overcometh will I grant to sit with me in my throne, even as I also overcame, and am set down with my Father in his throne." All striving then, and all overcoming, which is not in the steps of Christ, and precisely (in a measure) in the same way in which Jesus strove and overcame, is not the overcoming which is crowned with God's approbation.

August 18

"And this is the record, that God hath given to us eternal life, and this life is in his Son." – 1 John 5. 11.

How often we are looking and looking in vain for life in ourselves. True it is that if God has quickened our souls we are partakers of life divine, of life spiritual, of life eternal, of the life that is in Christ and comes from Christ; and yet how often we vainly seek to find it warm and glowing in our breasts. If once given it never dies; but it is often hidden beneath the ashes, and thus though it slowly burns and dimly glows, yet the ashes hide it from view, and we only know it is there by some remains of warmth. "Your life is hid with Christ in God" (Col. 3. 3); and therefore not only hidden as treasured and stored up safely in God, but hidden from the world, and even hidden from the eyes of its possessor. Christ is our life. There is no other. To look, then, for life in ourselves independent of and distinct from the fountain of life is to look for that in the creature which is lodged in the divine Creator, is to look for that in man which dwells in the God-man; to look for that in self which is out of self, embosomed in the fulness of the Son of God. And it is not merely that life is in him, but he is the life itself. As the sun not only has light and heat, but is light itself and heat itself, so the blessed Lord not only grants life, but he himself is what he grants. As a fountain not only gives water, but is itself all water, so Christ not only gives what he is, but is all that he gives. Not only, therefore, is he the "resurrection", centring in himself everything, both for time and eternity, which resurrection contains and resurrection implies, but he is "the life", being in himself a fountain of life, out of which he gives from his own fulness to the members of his mystical body.

August 19

"The Lord is merciful and gracious, slow to anger, and plenteous in mercy. He will not always chide: neither will he keep his anger for ever." – Psalm 103. 8, 9.

God is angry and justly angry with the sins of his people. He hates sin with a perfect hatred. He cannot but entertain unceasing wrath against it. It is so contrary to the purity and perfection of his holy nature, that wherever he meets with sin his indignation flashes out against it. And till we have some discovery and manifestation of Christ to assure us of an interest in his precious blood and finished work, we cannot separate the anger of God against our sins from the anger of God against our persons. But when the Lord is pleased to reveal a sense of his goodness and mercy in the Person and work of his dear Son, then we can see by the eye of faith that though he is angry with our sins, he is not angry with our persons, but accepts us in the Beloved, having chosen us in him before the foundation of the world, that we should be holy and without blame before him in love. Thus he retains not his anger for ever. And why? Because it is propitiated, put away, not retained so as to burn to the lowest hell. The blessed Lord has offered a sacrifice for sin; put away the punishment and penalty due to transgression, propitiated and appeased, and thus put away his indignation and fiery displeasure against the sins of his people; for all the anger of God due to their sins and to their persons was discharged upon the Person of Jesus as he stood our representative and hung upon the cross a bleeding sacrifice, putting away sin by the offering of himself. This is the reason why he retaineth not his anger for ever, it being appeased and put away through the propitiation of our blessed Lord, that it should not burn against the persons of the people of God, nor consume them with the fiery indignation that shall burn up the wicked.

August 20

"And there I will meet with thee, and I will commune with thee from above the mercy seat, from between the two cherubims which are upon the ark of the testimony, of all things which I will give thee in commandment unto the children of Israel." – Exodus 25. 22.

What heart can conceive or tongue describe the blessedness of this heavenly truth that at all times, under all circumstances, and in all places there is provided a mercy seat, a throne of grace, at which the God of all grace and a sensible sinner may freely meet without let or hindrance, if indeed there be any spirit of prayer in the petitioner's breast? As no place, so no circumstance is too dark for his eye not to see; as no covering is too thick, so no circumstance is too obscure for his sight not to pierce through: "Can any hide himself in secret places that I shall not see him? saith the Lord. Do not I fill heaven and earth? saith the Lord." So felt the Psalmist: "If I say, Surely the darkness shall cover me; even the night shall be light about me. Yea, the darkness hideth not from thee; but the night shineth as the day: the darkness and the light are both alike to thee". By night upon our bed; by day in our various occupations; in the crowded streets or in the lonely fields; surrounded by the ungodly or in company with the Lord's people, we may, if the Lord the Spirit enable us, lift up a hearty sigh, utter a confessing word, and pour forth one simple desire. This may not to some seem to be sufficient to warrant the gracious fulfilment of the promise, "There will I meet with thee;" and yet every relief thereby obtained proves that it is so; for wherever or whenever we get any sense of the Lord's presence or of the Lord's power, any intimation that his eye is upon us for good, and his ear listening to our cry, be the prayer short or long, be it uttered on our knees or sighed out on our feet, be it in the quiet room or the bustling street, we have in it that evidence which each believer knows best in the sweet experience of it, that God does fulfil his own gracious word, "There will I meet with thee".

August 21

"O Lord, by these things men live, and in all these things is the life of my spirit." – Isaiah 38. 16.

When Hezekiah said, "by these things men live", he meant that by these trials and deliverances, by these sinkings and risings, strippings and clothings, emptyings and fillings, "by these things men", that is, spiritual men, "live". It is a mystery, but a great truth, that just in proportion as we die to the world, to self, to sense, to nature, and to false religion, the more the life of God is strengthened in our conscience. The Lord, perhaps, has taught some of you this truth through great afflictions. But when these trials came upon you at the first, it seemed as though they would entirely overwhelm you; they took away your standing, and it appeared as though they had destroyed your faith and hope. But though these floods of temptation passed over the soul, they swept away nothing but rubbish, which till then was mistaken for the inward teachings of God the Spirit. So far then from these afflictions overwhelming your faith, you found that faith was secretly strengthened by the very flood that threatened at first to drown it. True faith is no more destroyed by sharp trials, than the oak is destroyed by cutting away the ivy, or by a storm blowing down some of its rotten branches. And thus, as the oak, the more the winds blow upon it, takes a firmer root in the soil; so the storms and tempests that blow upon the soul, only cause it to take a firmer hold of the truth, and to strike its fibres more deeply into the Person, love, work, and blood of Jesus. So that, "by these things men live", for through them, the life of God is maintained and kept up in the soul, the Holy Ghost secretly strengthening it by the very things that seemed to threaten it with destruction.

August 22

"Continue thou in the things which thou hast learned and hast been assured of." – 2 Timothy 3. 14.

Various hindrances meet the child of God in his path heavenwards. And their tendency is such, that but for the grace of God, they would effectually succeed in driving him from the faith. When, then, he has to meet a head wind blowing right in his teeth, when the storm and hail beat roughly upon him, when the waves rise high and the stream runs strong, there seems no getting on; and he fears that he shall be like "the children of Ephraim, who, being armed, and carrying bows, turned back in the day of battle." And yet there is that grace implanted in his heart, there is that faith which God the Spirit first created and still keeps alive in his soul, that though he may for a moment be driven aside, he yet never turns his back upon the truth; though retarded for a moment, his face is still Zion-wards. I can say for myself, that all the trials I have passed through, all the temptations I have been in, and all the persecutions I have had to endure, from sinner and from saint, have only served to rivet the truth of God more firmly in my heart. I find the trials, sufferings, exercises from without and from within, instead of driving faith out of the soul, having that effect which Satan would produce by them, and driving the heart from truth into error, from the Church of God into the world, – I can say, from feeling experience, that these inward and outward trials only rivet the truth, and the love of the truth, more deeply in my heart; and instead of driving out faith, they have only tended to strengthen, encourage, and confirm it.

August 23

"But we are bound to give thanks alway to God for you, brethren beloved of the Lord, because God hath from the beginning chosen you to salvation through sanctification of the Spirit and belief of the truth: whereunto he called you by our gospel, to the obtaining of the glory of our Lord Jesus Christ." – 2 Thessalonians 2. 13, 14.

The first work of grace is to kill rather than to make alive; to wound rather than to heal; to bring down rather than to lift up; to reveal the law rather than the gospel. For "balm is useless to the unfeeling." Salvation with all its superabounding grace is but an empty sound to those who have never felt themselves cut off from all help or all hope. So, in a sense, there is a calling under and through, if not by the law, in the first teaching and operations of the Spirit of God, bringing the soul under its condemnation as a ministration of death. But when the law has done its office, and the sinner is slain by its killing power, then there comes to his aid and deliverance, what the Apostle speaks of here, the calling by the gospel. When the gospel utters its melodious voice; when pardon is proclaimed through the sacrifice of Jesus; when peace reaches the heart through atoning blood revealed to the conscience; when the glad tidings of salvation by grace are no longer a mere sound in the letter, but are made the power of God unto salvation to every one that believeth; when heavenly light shines into the mind; when divine power attends the word to the soul; when faith is raised up, hope casts its anchor within the veil, and the love of God is shed abroad, then and there is the calling of which the Apostle here speaks – a calling by the gospel. The sound of the gospel trumpet, like the silver trumpet on the great day of Jubilee, reaches the ear and heart of the captive exile and he hasteneth that he may be loosed (Isa. 51. 14). The scene now changes; the storms of God's wrath blow over; the day-star appears in the dawning morn of the gospel day, "a morning without clouds" (2 Sam. 23. 4), until the Sun of righteousness in due time rises with healing in his wings. As, then, the gospel is thus made the power of God unto salvation, the soul is enabled to listen to, and embrace it as a joyful sound. Now just in proportion as faith receives it, hope anchors in it, and love embraces it, is evidence given of our being from the beginning chosen unto salvation.

August 24

"If thou knewest the gift of God, and who it is that saith to thee, Give me to drink; thou wouldest have asked of him, and he would have given thee living water." – John 4. 10.

We cannot know the *nature,* though we may know the *necessity,* of the gift of God, till we experience its power as revealed and shed abroad in our soul. *Then* we know some measure of the gift of God when we feel eternal life flowing through our spiritual veins. How do I know I live naturally? Is not my participation of natural life known to me by an internal consciousness that I possess it? I know I live, because I feel that I live. And so, if we have spiritual life, there will be, at times and seasons, an internal consciousness that we have it; we shall feel the spiritual heart beat, and the spiritual lungs breathe, and the spiritual eyes see, and the spiritual ears hear: in a word, we shall be internally conscious of those emotions and sensations which are peculiar to the life of God in the soul. Spiritual life will be seen in its own light, felt in its own power, and shine forth in its own testimony. The little that we do know (and it is indeed for the most part but a little) makes us long for more of it. If ever we have received "the gift of God" into our conscience; if ever we have felt the mysterious operation of divine life in our hearts; if ever we have known the sweet emotions and peculiar sensations by which it manifests itself, it has killed us to all other religions; and as a measure of divine life has flowed into the heart out of the fulness of the Son of God, we want no other religion but that which stands in the power of God; by that alone we can live, and by that alone we feel that we can die.

August 25

"Receiving the end of your faith, even the salvation of your souls." – 1 Peter 1. 9.

What a blessed, what a glorious end is this; what a prize to win, what a victory to gain, what a crowning consummation of all that faith has believed, hope expected or love embraced! Whatever doubts and fears may have harassed the mind, whatever sore temptations may have distressed the soul, whatever deep afflictions, painful trials, heavy guilt, and hard bondage may have sunk it low, so low sometimes, as if it never would get over them or rise out of them, still that faith, which is God's gift and work, lives through all, and there is a blessed end in store for it – the salvation of the soul. And O, what does this not comprehend and imply? Think of what salvation is from; think of what salvation is unto. Neither the one nor the other can be fully known on this side of eternity. You may have had some glimpses of hell, you may have had some glimpses of heaven; some taste of the wrath to come, some taste of the glory that shall be revealed. But you have had only a small taste of either. The wrath of God, the horrors of a guilty conscience, the terrors of despair, the falling into his hands who is a consuming fire you may have, in some small measure, felt or feared; but you have never known, for nature could not bear it, the full and terrible extent of those dreadful realities. And so you may have had glimpses and glances, earnests and foretastes of the glory that shall be revealed; but you have never enjoyed, for nature could not bear it, what saints enjoy in the immediate presence of God. But if you have seen, tasted, handled, felt, and enjoyed a little of what you are saved from, and a little of what you are saved unto, it will make you bless God for having given you even a grain of that true and living faith, the end of which will be the salvation of your soul.

August 26

"If any man among you seemeth to be wise in this world, let him become a fool, that he may be wise." – 1 Corinthians 3. 18.

The fruit and effect of divine teaching is, *to cut in pieces, and root up all our fleshly wisdom, strength, and righteousness.* God never means to patch a new piece upon an old garment; he never intends to let *our* wisdom, *our* strength, *our* righteousness have any union with *his;* it must all be torn to pieces, it must all be plucked up by the roots, that a *new* wisdom, a *new* strength, and a *new* righteousness may arise upon its ruins. But till the Lord is pleased to teach us, we never can part with our own righteousness, never give up our own wisdom, never abandon our own strength. These things are a part and parcel of ourselves, so ingrained within us, so innate in us, so growing with our growth, that we cannot willingly part with an atom of them till the Lord himself breaks them up, and plucks them away. Then, as he brings into our souls some spiritual knowledge of our own dreadful corruptions and horrible wickedness, our righteousness crumbles away at the divine touch; as he leads us to see and feel our ignorance and folly in a thousand instances, and how unable we are to understand anything aright but by divine teaching, our wisdom fades away; and as he shows us our inability to resist temptation and overcome sin, by any exertion of our own, our strength gradually departs, and we become like Samson, when his locks were cut off. Upon the ruins, then, of our own wisdom, righteousness, and strength, does God build up Christ's wisdom, Christ's righteousness, and Christ's strength: as Jesus said to his servant Paul, "My strength is made perfect in weakness"; and this brought him to that wonderful conclusion, "Most gladly therefore will I rather glory in my infirmities, that the power of Christ may rest upon me" (2 Cor. 12. 9). But only so far as we are favoured with this special teaching are we brought to pass a solemn sentence of condemnation upon our own wisdom, strength, and righteousness, and feelingly seek after the Lord's.

August 27

"The desire of our soul is to thy name, and to the remembrance of thee." – Isaiah 26. 8.

How sweet and expressive is the phrase, "*The desire of our soul!*" How it seems to carry our feelings with it! How it seems to describe the longings and utterings of a soul into which God has breathed the spirit of grace and mercy! "The desire of our soul", – the breathing of our heart, the longing of our inmost being; the cry, the sigh, the panting of our new nature; the heavings, gaspings, lookings, longings, pantings, hungerings, thirstings, and ventings forth of the new man of grace – all are expressed in these sweet and blessed words, "The desire of our soul!" And what a mercy it is, that there should ever be in us "the desire" of a living soul; that though the righteous dealings of God are painful and severe, running contrary to everything nature loves; yet that with all these, there should be dropped into the heart that mercy, love, and grace, which draw forth the desire of the soul toward the Name of God. This is expressed in the words that follow, "With my soul have I desired thee in the night!" If you can say no more about the work of grace upon your heart than *that* – can you really use these words as descriptive of feelings experienced within, " With my soul have I desired thee in the night"? Is your soul longing after the Lord Jesus Christ? Is it ever in the night season panting after the manifestation of his presence? hungering and thirsting after the dropping-in of some word from his lips, some sweet whisper of his love to your soul? These are marks of grace. The carnal, the unregenerate, the ungodly, have no such desires and feelings as these; there is nothing in their heart corresponding with "the desire of the soul unto the Name of God". But it is the case with all the righteous; for "the desire of the righteous shall be granted."

August 28

"And stablish you in every good word and work." – 2 Thessalonians 2. 17.

The living family of God need to be established in the truth, so as not ever to be "children tossed to and fro with every wind of doctrine". It is not sufficient for a building to be reared: it must be established before we can know whether it will stand. The most anxious moment of the builder is to see how it will settle; how the walls will bear the roof, and every part stand firm and good without bulging or slipping. When the centring is taken away from a newly-built arch, how the architect looks to see whether it will settle well and the extent of the drop, if there be any. So in grace. It is not merely making a profession that will serve. Many a building stands well as long as the scaffolding remains; many an arch looks firm whilst the centring supports it. So many seem to stand well in early days, when upheld by zeal and earnestness, or strengthened by the support of others. But how will the soul stand when helps are removed? Will it be stablished in the faith, or fall into some error or some gross evil, and thus, like an arch badly built, drop into ruin when the centring is taken away. How we continually see those who once seemed firm in the truth now greedily drinking down some deadly error presented to their lips under the charm of a plausible novelty; and others fall headlong into some open sin, or get entangled in some delusion. O that the Lord would stablish you, me, and all who desire to fear his name firmly and deeply in his precious truth, that we may never fall a prey to evil or error, but may have a religion of his own maintaining; that the work upon our heart may be the genuine work of God first and last; a building of his own raising and his own establishing, that it may stand firm amidst the storms of time, and endure for all eternity!

August 29

"He sent his word, and healed them, and delivered them from their destructions." – Psalm 107. 20.

What an effect a word from God can produce! Be it in reading; in hearing; on the knees; or in secret meditation; when a word drops from the Lord's mouth with any divine power into the soul, what a change it produces! And nothing but this divine power can ever bring a poor sinner out of his miserable condition. When this comes, it does the work in a moment; it heals all the wounds which sin has made, and repairs all the breaches in the conscience that folly has produced. One word from God heals them all. The Lord does not come as it were with plasters to heal first one sore and then another. He heals now as in the days of his flesh. When he healed then, he healed fully, at once, completely. The earthly doctor heals by degrees; he puts a plaster on one sore, and a liniment on another; and heals one by one. But when the Lord heals, it is all done in a moment. The balm of Gilead flows over all the wounds, heals them up, and makes them perfectly whole. It is then with the soul as with the woman with the issue of blood, "she felt in her body that she was healed of that plague." And this is healing! Any testimony from God, really from God, does it in a moment. If you can get but one word from God into your soul to make you believe you are a child of God, and interested in his pardoning love and mercy, every wound, though there be a million, yes, every wound will be healed instantaneously. This is the only healing worth having. To be healed by evidences is like being healed by plasters. You want an evidence here, and an evidence there, as a man that has his body full of sores wants a plaster upon every wound. One word from God is the real panacea, the true, the only "heal-all"; and Jesus (Jehovah-rophi, "the Lord my healer") the only true infallible Physician. Would you be healed completely, you must look to the Lord, and not to man; be a Hezekiah, not an Asa.

August 30

"As obedient children, not fashioning yourselves according to the former lusts in your ignorance: but as he which hath called you is holy, so be ye holy in all manner of conversation; because it is written, Be ye holy; for I am holy." – 1 Peter 1. 14-16.

Grace lays us under the greatest of all obligations to its free and bountiful Giver, and especially to render a believing obedience to his revealed will and word. It is his free, sovereign, and distinguishing grace alone which makes and manifests us to be his children, and therefore it demands of us, as a feeble and most insufficient tribute of grateful praise, that we should walk worthy of the vocation wherewith we are called, and glorify him in our body and spirit which are his. He that has never known and felt this knows nothing of the riches of God's grace in the manifestation of mercy and love to his soul. Such a one knows, that do what he can, he can never do enough to show forth the praises of him who hath called him out of darkness into his marvellous light, and his grief and burden ever are that, through the power of indwelling sin, he cannot do the things that he would, but is always falling short, always sinning against bleeding, dying love. To such a one, therefore, the precepts of the gospel are as dear as the promises, and he sees that they are set in the word of truth as "a lamp to his feet and a light to his path", a guiding rule by which, if he could but direct his steps, he would glorify God, walk in peace and love with his people, preserve a good conscience, and adorn the doctrine which he professes in all things. Obedience, therefore, to him is a sweet word, and is viewed by him as a precious portion of that free and everlasting gospel which, in restoring fallen man to God's favour, restores him also to an obedience acceptable in his sight.

August 31

"For I reckon that the sufferings of this present time are not worthy to be compared with the glory which shall be revealed in us." – Romans 8. 18.

What is to be compared with the salvation of the soul? What are riches, honours, health, long life? What are all the pleasures which the world can offer, sin promise, or the flesh enjoy? What is all that men call good or great? What is everything which the outward eye hath seen, or natural ear heard, or hath entered into the carnal heart of man, put side by side with being saved in the Lord Jesus Christ with an everlasting salvation? For consider what we are saved *from,* as well as what we are saved *unto.* From a burning hell to a blissful heaven; from endless wrath to eternal glory; from the dreadful company of devils and damned spirits, mutually tormenting and tormented, to the blessed companionship of the glorified saints, all perfectly conformed in body and soul to the image of Christ, with thousands and tens of thousands of holy angels, and, above all, to seeing the glorious Son of God as he is, in all the perfection of his beauty, and all the ravishments of his presence and love. To have done for ever with all the sorrows, troubles, and afflictions of this life; all the pains and aches of the present clay tabernacle; all the darkness, bondage and misery of the body of sin and death; to be perfectly holy in body and soul, being in both without spot, or blemish, or any such thing, and ever to enjoy uninterrupted union and communion with the Father, Son, and blessed Spirit - O what a heaven lies before the believing saints of God as the end of their faith in the salvation of their souls!

September 1

"This is his name whereby he shall be called, THE LORD OUR RIGHTEOUSNESS" - Jeremiah 23. 6.

What a sweet view does this give of Jesus! We look sometimes at Christ's righteousness as distinct from Christ. Shall I use a figure? We look at the garment as distinct from the maker and wearer of the garment. We look at the righteousness so much, that we scarcely look at him who wrought out that righteousness. Now, we must not separate Jesus from his righteousness. We must not look merely at the garment, the imputed robe, and forget him that wrought it out, that puts it on, and that keeps it to this day in firm possession. But when we can see, that not only the obedience of Christ, but Christ himself - all that Jesus is - all that Jesus has, as head of his Church, as the risen Mediator, as the great High Priest over the house of God - when we can see that this God-man, Immanuel, is made unto his people righteousness, how it expands the prospect! Then we look, not merely at the robe itself, beautiful, comely, and glorious; we look farther - we look at him that made it. We do not look merely at the robe as distinct from him. We look at him who made that robe what it is - Jesus, who ever lives at the right hand of the Father to make intercession for us. This, to my mind, is a sweet view. If I sink down into creature sinfulness, shame, and guilt, and see Jesus made of God unto me righteousness, what need I more? Has God made him so? Who can unmake him so? Has God made the Son of his love righteousness to my soul, that I may stand in him without spot, speck, or blemish? Who is to alter it? Can sin alter it? That is atoned for. Can the devil alter it? He is chained down unto the judgment of the great day. Can the world alter it? They cannot stretch forth their finger to touch one thread of that robe, to touch one lineament of the Redeemer's countenance. If he is made unto me righteousness, what more do I want? If I can find a shield, a shelter, and a refuge in him as my righteousness, what more can I want to preserve me from the charge of men or devils?

September 2

"Therefore let us not sleep, as do others; but let us watch and be sober." - 1 Thessalonians 5. 6.

Here sobriety is opposed to sleepiness, and is connected with walking in the light and in the day, as sleepiness and its frequent cause, drunkenness, are connected with darkness and night. One of the greatest curses God can send on a people and its rulers, its prophets and seers, is a spirit of deep sleep, as the prophet speaks: "For the Lord hath poured out upon you the spirit of deep sleep, and hath closed your eyes: the prophets and your rulers, the seers hath he covered." But to be sober is to be awaked out of this sleep, and, as a consequence, to walk not only wake-fully but watchfully.

It implies, therefore, that careful, circumspect walking, that daily living, moving, speaking, and acting in the fear of God, whereby alone we can be kept from the snares spread for our feet at every step of the way. How many have fallen into outward evil and open disgrace from want of walking watchfully and circumspectly, and taking heed to their steps. Instead of watching the first movements of sin and against, as the Lord speaks, "the entering into temptation", they rather dally with it until they are drawn away and enticed of their own lust which, if unchecked, goes on to conceive and bring forth sin, which, when it is finished or carried out and accomplished in positive action, bringeth forth death.

September 3

"Because thine heart was tender, and thou hast humbled thyself before the Lord,... I also have heard thee." – 2 Kings 22. 19.

This tenderness of heart was a mark in Josiah, on which the Lord, so to speak, put his finger; it was a special token for good which God selected from all the rest, as a testimony in his favour. The heart is always tender which God has touched with his finger; this tenderness being the fruit of the impression of the Lord's hand upon the conscience. You may know the difference between a natural conscience and a heart tender in God's fear by this, that the natural con-science is always superstitious and uncertain; as the Lord says, it "strains at a gnat, and swallows a camel." It is exceedingly observant of self-inflicted austerities, and very fearful of breaking through self-imposed rules; and whilst it will commit sin which a man who has the fear of God in his heart would not do for the world, it will stumble at mere unimportant trifles at which an enlightened soul would not feel the least scruple. But here is the mark of a heart tender in God's fear; it moves as God the Spirit works upon it. It is like the mariner's compass, which having been once touched by the magnet, always turns toward the north; it may indeed oscillate and tremble backwards and forwards, but still it will return to the pole, and ultimately remain fixed at the point whence it was temporarily disturbed. So when the heart has been touched by the Spirit, and has been made tender in God's fear, it may for a time waver to the right hand or to the left, but it is always trembling and fluctuating till it points towards God, as the only and eternal centre of its happiness and holiness.

September 4

"I will make darkness light before them, and crooked things straight.' – Isaiah 42. 16.

What is the mind of man – of any man – of your mind, my mind, under affliction? Let him be tried with pain of body, poverty of circumstances, sickness in his family, guilt of conscience, hard bondage in his own soul, without any beam of divine light upon his path, and what is he? A murmuring, rebellious wretch, without a grain of resignation, without a particle of contentment or submission to the will of God. But let the glory of the Lord be revealed; let him have a view by faith of a suffering Jesus; let some ray of light shine upon his path; let there be some breaking in of the exceeding weight of glory that is to be manifested at Christ's appearing; where are all his crooked things now? All made straight. But how? By his crooked will – crooked because it did not lie level with the Lord's – being made to harmonise with the promise and precept, the footsteps and example of the blessed Jesus. The crook is not taken out of the lot, but straightened in the lot; the cross is not removed from the shoulder, but strength – that strength which is "made perfect in weakness" – is given to bear it. So it was with Christ himself in the garden and on the cross; so it is with the believing followers of the crucified One.

September 5

"Bow down thine ear, O Lord, hear me: for I am poor and needy." – Psalm 86. 1.

Whatever deliverance a man may have experienced, let him have been delivered from the lowest hell, and have had his feet placed upon a rock, yet all his life long he will have this experience wrought in him by the Holy Ghost, – to be "poor and needy". And only so far as he is poor and needy, will he want to know anything experimentally of the riches of Jesus Christ, or to taste the consolations which the Spirit of God alone can communicate to the parched and thirsty soul. How many we find in our day, who are "rich and increased with goods and have need of nothing", and yet they are always speaking and boasting of the riches of Christ. But what can they know of Christ's riches? His riches are for "the poor and needy"; his blood is for the guilty; his righteousness is for the naked; his perfect work and finished salvation is for those who continually stand in need of his powerful arm to save them from the lowest hell. And, therefore, whatever notions men may have about Christ's riches, and Christ's blood and righteousness, and Christ's glorious salvation; there are none that prize it, that pant with unutterable longings after it, that really desire to live upon it as the very food of their heart, that are crying unto God continually for the sweet manifestations of it, that are restless and uneasy and dissatisfied without the sweet enjoyment of it, – there are none that thus breathe and thus feel, except those who are spiritually "poor and needy," being stripped and emptied and despoiled of everything that the flesh can boast of, and everything that nature can exalt itself with.

September 6

"Exercise thyself unto godliness." – 1 Timothy 4. 7.

The Lord trieth the righteous (Ps. 11. 5). In fact, a righteous life is for the most part a tried life. There is not a child of God, whose graces are lively and active, that is not tried in his soul. I have no more belief that the soul can live without exercise than that the body can. The more the soul is exercised, the healthier it will be. Trial is one main source of exercise. If you are tried as to your standing; tried as to your state; tried as to the reality of the work of grace upon your soul; tried as to your experience; tried as to your manifestations, deliverances, and evidences; tried by your sins; tried by Satan; tried by professors; tried by profane; and above all tried by your own heart, and that continually – it will keep your soul in exercise. And this is "exercise *unto* godliness." If these exercises are *unto* godliness, they lead to godliness, they take you on your way to godliness, they bring you near to godliness, they bring you into godliness; and, above all things, they bring godliness into your soul. And thus, there is an exercise of the soul *unto* godliness. Does not your heart at times seem without a grain of it? You see what godliness is in its nature, in its branches, in its fruits, in its graces, in what a Christian should be, practically, experimentally, and really – outwardly and inwardly – in the church, and in the world. You say, "I a Christian! I a godly man or woman! Let me compare myself with godliness. Am I godly? Is there grace in my heart? Do I live? do I speak? do I think? do I act? do I walk? do I suffer as becomes a Christian? Is my life, my profession, my conduct – in the family, in the world – in the business, in the church – at home, abroad – openly, secretly – privately, publicly – is it such that I can take it and lay it down, step by step, with vital, real, experimental, scriptural godliness? O," say you, "I shrink back from the test. There are many things in me, inwardly and outwardly, which will not bear to be weighed up with godliness as revealed in the Scriptures of truth." Well, your mind is exercised, I suppose, when you have these workings. Now, what is the result? It is an "exercise unto godliness". You want it; you strive for it; you cry for it; you press after it; you know that none but the Lord can work it in your soul; you feel needy, naked, and destitute; you know that without it you can neither happily live nor die; yet have it you must, or perish body and soul for ever.

September 7

"The grace of our Lord Jesus Christ be with your spirit." – Philemon 25.

It is the regenerating breath of the Lord Jesus Christ which makes the soul alive unto himself. This is manifest from his own language: "It is the Spirit that quickeneth; the flesh profiteth nothing: the words that I speak unto you, they are spirit, and they are life" (John 6. 63). Then for the first time "the grace of our Lord Jesus Christ is with our spirit." For you will observe that the grace of our Lord Jesus Christ is not with our carnal mind: *that* ever remains the same, a body of sin and death, flesh, corrupt flesh, "in which dwelleth no good thing", and therefore not the grace of our Lord Jesus Christ. His grace is with our spirit, that "new man" of which we read that "it is after God, [that is, after the image of God] created in righteousness and true holiness." This is called our "spirit", because it is born of the Spirit, as the Lord himself unfolded the solemn mystery to Nicodemus: "That which is born of the flesh is flesh; and that which is born of the Spirit is spirit." This is no subtle, wire-drawn distinction, but a very important truth; for unless we see the difference between the two natures, the spirit and the flesh, the law in the members and the law of the mind, we shall always be in bondage, as looking for holiness in the flesh. The grace of our Lord Jesus Christ being thus with our spirit, it breathes from time to time upon that spirit, moves and acts in it and upon it; for there is what I may call a gracious or spiritual union between the two. Thus we can no more live without the grace of the Lord Jesus Christ than the earth can live without the sun. He must shine, or we have no light; he must revive, or we have no warmth; and he must fertilise, or we bring forth no fruit. Thence time after time there is an outgoing of the single desire of the soul to the Lord Jesus Christ that his grace would be with our spirit; that his grace may be ever flowing forth into us, so as to make us new creatures, dispel all doubt and fear, break to pieces all bonds and fetters, fill us with love and humility, conform us to his suffering image, produce in us every fruit that shall redound to his praise, be with us in life and death, and land us safe in eternity.

September 8

"For it became him, for whom are all things, and by whom are all things, in bringing many sons unto glory, to make the captain of their salvation perfect through sufferings." – Hebrews 2. 10.

When, with believing eyes, we can view God the Son as the eternal salvation of all whom the Father gave unto him; when we can see him, by the eye of faith, coming down into this lower world, taking our nature into union with his own Divine Person; when, by faith, we can accompany the Man of Sorrows into the gloomy garden of Gethsemane, or behold him groaning, bleeding, and dying on the cross, an object of ignominy and shame, and believe that in this way, and this alone, salvation could be wrought out, O, what a view it gives us of the demerit and awful nature of sin, that nothing short of the incarnation of God's only begotten Son, nothing short of such a tremendous sacrifice could put away sin, and bring the elect back unto God! On the one hand, as we take a glance at the suffering and dying Lamb of God, how it shews us the awful and abominable nature of sin; and, on the other hand, when we can see by the eye of faith what that work is, by whom that work was wrought out, and how glorious and efficacious that work must be which the Son of God, equal with the Father in glory and majesty, undertook and went through to the uttermost, – how it exalts salvation in our eyes! Thus a believing sight of the Lord Jesus hanging upon Calvary's tree, not only, on the one hand, shows us the awful nature of sin, but, on the other, how full, how complete, how glorious, and how effectual must that salvation be, of which the expiring Son of God could say, "It is finished!"

September 9

"For I will pour water upon him that is thirsty." – Isaiah 44. 3.

Thirst, as a feeling of the soul, in a spiritual sense, is certainly indicative of divine life. It is as impossible, spiritually viewed, for a man dead in sin to thirst after a living God, as for a corpse in the graveyard to thirst after a draught of cold water from the well. I know for myself that such a feeling as thirsting after God had no place in my bosom until the Lord was pleased to quicken my soul into spiritual life. I had heard of God by the hearing of the ear; I had seen him in creation, in the starry sky, in the roaring sea, in the teeming earth; I had read of him in the Bible; I had learnt his existence by education and tradition; and I had some apprehensions of his holiness in my natural conscience; but as to any spiritual thirsting after him, any earnest desire to fear him, know him, believe in him, or love him, – no such experience or feeling, I can say for myself, ever dwelt in my bosom. I loved the world too dearly to look to him who made it, and myself too warmly and affectionately to seek him who would bid me crucify and mortify it. A man, therefore, I am well convinced, must be made alive unto God by spiritual regeneration before he can experience any such sensation as is here conveyed by the figure "thirst," or know anything of the Psalmist's feelings when he cried, "As the hart panteth after the water-brooks, so panteth my soul after thee, O God. My soul thirsteth for God, for the living God" (Ps. 42. 1, 2). Now wherever God has raised up in the soul this spiritual thirst after himself, he certainly will answer that desire, "the desire of the righteous shall be granted" (Prov. 10. 24). His own invitation is, "Ho, every one that thirsteth, come ye to the waters" (Isa. 55. 1); and Jesus himself says with his own blessed lips, "If any man thirst, let him come unto me, and drink" (John 7. 37). Nay, he opened his ministry by pronouncing a blessing on such, "Blessed are they which do hunger and thirst after righteousness: for they shall be filled."

September 10

"And floods upon the dry ground." – Isaiah 44. 3.

How often does the soul, born and taught of God, feel that it is this "dry ground"! It would fain be fruitful in every good word and work; it would be adorned with every grace of the Spirit within, and with every good and godly fruit without. Let no one think that the child of God is careless or indifferent either as to inward or outward fruit. There is nothing too holy, too heavenly, too spiritual, or too gracious which the child of grace would not desire inwardly to experience and outwardly produce. But he feels that he cannot by any exertion of his own produce this fruitfulness after which he sighs. As well might a barren field convert itself into a fruitful garden without being tilled by human hand or without rain from the sky, as a soul that feels and knows its own barrenness produce by its own exertions a crop of the fruits of righteousness. But the Lord that knows the desire of the heart, and its inward mourning over its own barrenness, has given in the text a sweet and gracious promise, "I will pour floods upon the dry ground." A partial shower would not be enough. The dry ground would soon absorb a few drops of summer rain. Floods must come, either from the skies or from the streams of that river which makes glad the city of God, to produce this mighty change. These "floods" are the promises poured into the soul, the love of God shed abroad in the heart, the manifestations of Christ and of his atoning blood, the inflowings of grace as super-abounding over all the aboundings of sin, and the flowing of peace as a river into the contrite spirit.

September 11

"I will pour my spirit upon thy seed, and my blessing upon thine offspring." – Isaiah 44. 3.

In pouring out his Spirit upon Zion's seed, God pours out therewith every spiritual blessing that there is in his heart or hands to bestow. Whatever earthly good you may enjoy, without the blessing of God it will but prove a curse; whatever afflictions fall to your earthly lot, if God bless, they must all eventually be made a blessing. Nor is this blessing niggardly given, for the Lord has here promised that he will *pour* it out! It shall be given as profusely and as abundantly as the Spirit himself. Nor shall Zion doubt either the blessing itself or the source whence it comes, for it carries its own evidence, shines in the light of its own testimony, and manifests itself by its own effects. And does not the contrast between the dry ground and the promised showers of blessing enhance it all the more? Your very barrenness and sterility make the promise all the more suitable, and therefore all the more sweet. If you look into yourself, a barren wilderness meets your view. If you look up, you see the clouds of blessing floating in the pure sky. You see that the Lord has promised to "pour water upon him that is thirsty, and floods upon the dry ground". You beg of him to fulfil that promise to your soul. You have no other plea but his own word of promise, no other recommendation but your own miserable barrenness. He enables you to cry to him. He listens to that cry, and in his own time pours water upon your thirsty soul, and floods upon your dry and parched heart. O may a sense of our poverty and destitution be ever a means, in his sacred hand, of leading us to seek that blessing which he alone can bestow!

September 12

"A prudent man foreseeth the evil, and hideth himself: but the simple pass on, and are punished." – Proverbs 22. 3.

Noah, warned of God, prepared an ark to the saving of his house. Lot, admonished by the angels, fled out of Sodom. So there is a fleeing from the wrath to come. How careless, how secure, and unconcerned are we till quickened with spiritual life! Solomon speaks of those who sleep on the top of a mast, where one jerk of the wave, or one turn of the sleeper may precipitate him into the boiling ocean. God's anger is gathering against a wicked world. Who will escape this fearful storm of eternal, unmitigated wrath? Those who flee to Jesus. Who flee to Jesus? Those only who feel their need of him. How are they made to feel their need of him? By the flashes of God's anger. Whence issue these flashes? Out of the thunder-cloud of God's holy law – the revelation which he has made of his anger against transgressors. How necessary then to feel the application of the law to the conscience, to experience what Job calls, "the terrors of God", that Jesus Christ, who is a "covert from the tempest", may be seen and fled unto! It is like the warning given in Egypt of the grievous hail: "He that feared the word of the Lord among the servants of Pharaoh made his servants and his cattle flee into the houses: and he that regarded not the word of the Lord left his servants and his cattle in the field" (Exod. 9. 20, 21). Faith credits what unbelief derides. As is their nature and operation, so is their end. Faith ends in salvation; unbelief in perdition.

September 13

"For our gospel came not unto you in word only, but also in power, and in the Holy Ghost, and in much assurance." – 1 Thessalonians 1. 5.

The Holy Ghost never comes into any poor sinner's soul, except through the medium of the gospel of the grace of God. Have you ever considered that point? You are praying, perhaps, that the Holy Spirit would teach you, and be in you a Spirit of revelation, a Remembrancer, a Comforter, Instructor and Teacher. You pray for his gifts, and graces, and sanctifying operations; but have you ever viewed these graces in connection with the gospel of Jesus Christ? Now, if you want the Holy Spirit to come into your soul, you must keep firm hold of the gospel; you must not run away from it to the law or to self; but keep firm, fast hold of it, so far as you have felt its power, and have a living faith in it. If, then, you are tried, still hold the gospel. If Satan get you into his sieve, still hold the gospel; if in the furnace of affliction, still hold the gospel; if called on to wade through floods of sorrow, still hold fast the gospel. Let not Satan, if ever you have felt the power and the preciousness of the gospel, baffle you out of it, and drive you from it; but hold to the gospel, for it is your life. Indeed, where else will you find anything to suit your case if you are a poor, tempted, tried sinner? Will you go to the *law,* which can only curse and condemn you? Will you go to *yourself?* What is self? A heap of ruins. Where, then, will you go? After all, you must come to the gospel, if your soul is to be saved and blessed, and if you are to experience the consolations of the Holy Ghost, who alone can bless and comfort you. I want, with God's blessing, to impress this vital truth upon your conscience, that you may not be looking away from the gospel, and as Berridge says, "squint and peep another way", but that you may keep your eyes firmly fixed on the gospel; for if you believe it, it can and will save your soul. Does not the Apostle say it is "the power of God unto salvation to every one that believeth", so that there is neither power nor salvation in anything else? Never, therefore, expect power, salvation, or comfort, but in, and by, and through the Holy Ghost preaching the gospel into your heart.

September 14

"Such as sit in darkness and in the shadow of death." – Psalm 107. 10.

God's people are here represented not as sitting in *death;* were they sitting there, they would be dead altogether; but they are sitting *in the shadow of death.* Observe, death has lost its reality to them; it now can only cast a shadow, often a gloomy shadow, over their souls; but there is no substance. The quickening of the Spirit of God in them has destroyed the substance of death spiritually; and the death and resurrection of Jesus have destroyed the substance of death naturally. Yet, though the gloomy monster, deadness of soul, and that ghastly king of terrors, the death of the body, have been disarmed and destroyed by "Immanuel, God with us"; yet each of them casts at times a gloomy, darkling shadow over the souls of those that fear God. Is not your soul, poor child of God, exercised from time to time with this inward death? Deadness in prayer, deadness in reading the word, deadness in hearing the truth, deadness in desires after the Lord, deadness to everything holy, spiritual, heavenly, and divine? How it benumbs and paralyses every breathing of our soul Godward! Yet it is but a *shadow.* Write not bitter things against yourself, poor, tempted, exercised child of God, because you feel such deathliness and coldness from time to time in your heart. It will not destroy you; nay, it is life in your soul that makes it felt; and the more the life of God has been felt in your conscience, the more painfully the deathliness of your carnal mind is experienced. Do you expect that your carnal mind will ever be lively in the things of God? What is it but a lump of death, a huge mass of ungodliness, which, like some behemoth, upheaves its broad flanks continually in the heart? Yet the people of God are very often troubled in their minds by the gloomy shadow that this death casts over their souls. But this trouble is a mark of life. If I were dead, could I feel it? The worst symptom of the dead in sin is, that they do not feel it. But, whilst we feel it, whilst we sigh on account of it, whilst we hate it, and hate ourselves on account of it, though it may pain and grieve, it never can destroy. It has lost its substance, though it casts its gloomy shadow.

September 15

"Hear counsel, and receive instruction, that thou mayest be wise in thy latter end." – Proverbs 19. 20.

What lessons we need day by day to teach us anything aright, and how it is for the most part "line upon line, line upon line; here a little, and there a little". O what slow learners, what dull, forgetful scholars, what ignoramuses, what stupid blockheads, what stubborn pupils! Surely no scholar at a school, old or young, could learn so little of natural things as we seem to have learnt of spiritual things after so many years' instruction, so many chapters read, so many sermons heard, so many prayers put up, so much talking about religion. How small, how weak is the amount of grace compared with all we have read and heard and talked about. But it is a mercy that the Lord saves whom he will save, and that we are saved by free grace, and free grace alone, through the blood and righteousness of the Son of God. "He of God is made unto us wisdom, and righteousness, and sanctification and redemption"; so that if we have him we have everything, and if we have him not we have nothing. Where these things are felt they will cause exercise of soul, with many prayers and supplications to the God of all our mercies; and all this will strip and empty us of that light, superficial, and flimsy profession which seems so current in our day.

September 16

"For he is our peace, who hath made both one, and hath broken down the middle wall of partition between us." – Ephesians 2. 14.

He is our peace. This necessarily springs from being reconciled and brought nigh by the blood of Christ. Sin has not only made us enemies to God, but made God an enemy to us. What peace, then, can there be between us whilst thus mutual enemies? Peace is between friends, not between foes. During this state of hostility and warfare, as there is no real, so there can be no felt or enjoyed peace. But the removal of the cause of the war brings about peace, first really and then experimentally. Christ has made peace through the blood of his cross (Col. 1. 20). There is now no enmity on the part of God, for it was a law enmity. God always loved his people in Christ; and as he is unchanging and unchangeable, he never could or did hate them. But as a judge is an enemy to a criminal, even were that criminal his own son, so, as Judge and Lawgiver, God was an enemy to his own elect, viewed as law-breakers. But when the law was fulfilled, and all the breaches of it atoned for by the obedience and death of his dear Son, then this law enmity was removed, and the anger of God against sin and the sinner pacified. Sin, therefore, being put away, the whole cause of that law enmity is removed; and when we believe in the Son of God, and receive the atonement by his precious blood, then there is no enmity on our side; for the goodness, mercy, and love of God melt the heart into the sweetest humility, affection, and love to and before him.

September 17

"The secret of the Lord is with them that fear him; and he will shew them his covenant." – Psalm 25. 14.

The secret of the Lord (that is, *present* possession) "*is* with them that fear him; and he *will* shew them" (that is, something *future)* "his covenant." This shows, that while all the people of God, who fear his name, have the secret with them, that is, a measure of the secret, yet all the people of God have not the covenant revealed to them at the same time with the secret. The "secret" is in the present tense; the "showing of the covenant" is in the future. It is very sweet to see how the Holy Ghost has discriminated between these blessings. If, for instance, it had run thus, "The secret of the Lord is with them that fear him, and he shews to them his covenant," some doubting, desponding child of God might say, "How can I be one of those that fear God? for it says, God shows to them his covenant, and he has not shewn it to me yet." But being put in the future tense, "he *will* shew to them his covenant," it takes the form of a promise, and so is just adapted and sweetly suited to their wants. This covenant is the covenant that "stands fast for evermore"; the ever-lasting covenant of grace, which stands in the Person, love, blood, and work of the Son of God; the covenant made by a Triune Jehovah, on behalf of the elect, before the world was. What a suitable foundation for a poor tottering heart! The Lord in showing this covenant unto them that fear him, shows them that it is all of grace, and therefore meets all their unworthiness and superabounds over all the aboundings of their sin; that it is more than a match for their aggravated iniquities, and will land them safe in glory, because God has determined to bring them there. Nothing but a covenant of grace can suit a poor exercised soul, who knows his helplessness and worthlessness; and the Lord shows this to them that fear him.

September 18

"That the man of God may be perfect, throughly furnished unto all good works." – 2 Timothy 3. 17.

What perfection does the Holy Ghost speak of here? Certainly not perfection in the flesh; that is but a wild dream of free-will and Arminianism. But perfection here and elsewhere means a being well-established and grounded in the faith, as we find the Apostle speaking (Heb. 5. 14), "Strong meat belongeth to them that are *of full age*" (literally, as we read in the margin, "perfect"), "even those who by reason of use have their senses exercised to discern both good and evil." Christian perfection does not then consist in perfection in the flesh, but in having arrived at maturity in the divine life, in being what I may call a Christian adult, or what the Apostle terms "a man in Christ." When Paul therefore says, "Let us therefore, as many as *be perfect,*" he means "being no more children, tossed to and fro, and carried about with every wind of doctrine", but favoured with a measure of Christian wisdom and strength. It is this Christian maturity which is called in Scripture, "perfection", and it is only obtained by suffering. It is only in the furnace that the tin and dross of pharisaic righteousness is purged away; and the soul comes out of the furnace "a vessel unto honour, sanctified and meet for the Master's use." The Lord of life and glory was made "perfect by suffering"; and there is no other way whereby his followers are made spiritually perfect. Until a man is led into suffering, he does not know the truth in its sweetness. We are full of free-will, pride, presumption, and self-righteousness. But when the soul is baptised into suffering, it is in a measure established in the truth, strengthened in the things of God, and conformed to the image of Christ.

September 19

"For the Son of man is come to seek and to save that which was lost." – Luke 19. 10.

The *Son of man is come.* What a blessed coming! The Lord Jesus seems to have taken to himself, with the tenderest condescension to our wants, that gracious title, "the Son of man". He was the Son of God, and that from all eternity; but he delights to call himself the Son of man. We want one like ourselves, wearing the same nature; carrying in his bosom the same human heart; one who has been, "in all points, tempted like as we are, yet without sin"; and therefore able to sympathise with and to succour those that are tempted. A sinner like man, when made sensible of his pollution and guilt, cannot draw near unto God in his intrinsic, essential majesty and holiness. Viewed as the great and glorious Being that fills eternity, Jehovah is too great, too transcendently holy, too awfully perfect for him to approach. He must therefore have a Mediator; and that Mediator one who is a Mediator indeed, a God-man, "Immanuel, God with us." The depth of this mystery eternity itself will not fathom. But the tender mercy of God in appointing such a Mediator, and the wondrous condescension of the Son of God in becoming "the Son of man", are matters of faith, not of reason; are to be believed, not understood. When thus received, the humanity of the Son of God becomes a way of access unto the Father. We can talk to, we can approach, we can pour out our hearts before "the Son of man". His tender bosom, his sympathising heart, seem to draw forth the feelings and desires of our own. God, in his wrathful majesty, we dare not approach; he is a "consuming fire"; and the soul trembles before him. But when Jesus appears in the gospel as "the Mediator between God and man," and "a Daysman", as Job speaks, "that might lay his hand upon us both" (Job 9. 33), how this seems to penetrate into the depths of the human heart! How this opens a way for the poor, guilty, filthy, condemned, and ruined sinner to draw near to that great God with whom he has to do! How this, when experimentally realised, draws forth faith to look unto him, hope to anchor in him, and love tenderly and affectionately to embrace him!

September 20

"Be thou in the fear of the Lord all the day long. For surely there is an end; and thine expectation shall not be cut off." – Proverbs 23. 17, 18.

The Lord is here addressing himself to a soul labouring under temptation, and passing through peculiar exercises; and this is the exhortation that he gives it: "Be thou in the fear of the Lord all the day long"; watching his hand, submitting to his will, committing everything into his care and keeping; not hardening your heart against him, but looking up to him, and worshipping him with godly fear; "for surely there is an end". You may be tempted, exercised, and surrounded with difficulties, and see no outlet; but "surely there is an end"; and, when the end comes, it will make all plain and clear. This quiet submission, this watching and waiting, a man can never be brought to unless he has seen an end to all perfection; an end of his own strength, wisdom, and righteousness. To sit still is the hardest thing a man can do. To lie passive at God's footstool when all things seem to be against us; to have a rough path to walk in, to be surrounded with difficulties, and yet to be in the fear of the Lord all the day long, watching his hand, desiring to submit to his will, seeking only that wisdom which cometh from above, and trusting that he will make the way straight; not putting our hand to the work, but leaving it all to the Lord – how strange, how mysterious a path! And yet it is the only one that brings solid peace to a Christian; "for surely there is an end". Whatever sorrows and troubles a man may have to wade through, there will surely be an end of them. If we try to get ourselves out of perplexities, we are like a person trying to unravel a tangled skein of silk by pulling it forcibly; the more it is pulled, the more entangled it gets, and the faster the knots become. So if we are plunged into any trial, providential or spiritual, and we attempt to extricate ourselves by main force, by kicking and rebelling, we only get more entangled. The Lord, then, to encourage us to wait patiently upon him till he shall appear, says, "surely there is an end". This is the universal testimony of the Scripture, that the Lord appears and delivers, when there is none shut up or left; and the experience of the saints agrees with the testimony of the written word: "For I know the thoughts that I think toward you, saith the Lord, thoughts of peace, and not of evil, to give you an expected end."

September 21

"For we are strangers before thee, and sojourners, as were all our fathers: our days on the earth are as a shadow, and there is none abiding." – 1 Chronicles 29. 15.

If you possess the faith of Abraham, Isaac, and Jacob, you, like them, confess that you are a stranger; and your confession springs out of a believing heart and a feeling experience. You feel yourself a stranger in this ungodly world; it is not your element, it is not your home. You are in it during God's appointed time, but you wander up and down this world a stranger to its company, a stranger to its maxims, a stranger to its fashions, a stranger to its principles, a stranger to its motives, a stranger to its lusts, its inclinations, and all in which this world moves as in its native element. Grace has separated you by God's distinguishing power, that though you are in the world, you are not of it. I can tell you plainly, if you are at home in the world; if the things of time and sense be your element; if you feel one with the company of the world, the maxims of the world, the fashions of the world, and the principles of the world, grace has not reached your heart, the faith of God's elect does not dwell in your bosom. The first effect of grace is to separate. It was so in the case of Abraham. He was called by grace to leave the land of his fathers, and go out into a land that God would show him. And so God's own word to his people is now, "Come out from among them, and be ye separate, saith the Lord, and touch not the unclean thing; and I will receive you, and will be a Father unto you, and ye shall be my sons and daughters, saith the Lord Almighty." Separation, separation, separation from the world is the grand distinguishing mark of vital godliness. There may be indeed separation of body where there is no separation of heart. But what I mean is, separation of heart, separation of principle, separation of affection, separation of spirit. And if grace has touched your heart, and you are a partaker of the faith of God's elect, you are a stranger in the world, and will make it manifest by your life and conduct that you are such.

September 22

"The kingdom of God is not in word, but in power." – 1 Corinthians 4. 20.

It is through the word of God in the hands of the Spirit, that this kingdom is set up in the soul. All God's people are agreed on this point, that they have no more religion than they have inward power. And all the living family are sighing, each according to his measure and season, after the manifestation of this divine power in their souls. Those that are under the law, and toiling under heavy burdens, are sighing after relief, and for that relief to come in divine power – power that shall cast all their sins into the depth of the sea. Those who having tasted that the Lord is gracious have lost their first love, are at times breathing out their inmost desire after power to revive their souls. Those who are beset with powerful temptations, and struggling, often ineffectually, with base lusts, are crying after power to deliver their feet from the fowler's snares. Those who are hard, need power to soften; those who are doubting and fearing, need power to give them faith; the backsliding need power to return, and the sinking need power to swim. By power I understand something solid, real, substantial, heavenly, super natural. How do we measure the capabilities of a steam engine? We say that it has so many horse power. But who in his senses would construct a steam engine of two hundred horse power to break sticks and pick up straws? We measure power by its effects. We proportion the one to the other. Now the Holy Ghost, the God of all power and might, would not put forth his mighty and efficacious hand to break sticks and pick up straws in the soul. No. His work is worthy of a God; a "work of faith with power," because springing from a God of power. The God of Israel is not a Baal that is sleeping and needs to be awakened, or gone a journey and therefore too far off to come when needed, but "a very present help in trouble." By this secret power false hopes are swept away, rotten props removed, creature righteousness brought to an end, and the soul is helped and enabled to lean upon the Lord. This power is not noise and rant; but the still small voice of Jesus in the soul. The people of God want no outward voice, but they are seeking after that secret voice of atoning blood in their conscience, that speaketh better things than the blood of Abel. The inward whisper of heavenly love sounding in their soul – not the earthquake of terror, not the fire of divine wrath, but the still small voice of pardon and peace – makes them bow themselves before the Lord, and wrap their faces in their mantle. The Queen of England need not shout aloud in her palace, to give her commands effect. Where the word of a king is, there is power, whether from an earthly monarch or from the King of Zion. We want therefore no noise, bustle, and excitement, no raving and ranting about religion; but we want inward feeling, the very kingdom of God set up in the heart.

September 23

"I am he that liveth, and was dead; and behold, I am alive for evermore, Amen; and have the keys of hell and of death." – Revelation 1. 18.

O what a mercy that he who was dead lives at God's right hand! that he lives as a risen head; that he is not a dead Saviour; but a Saviour that lives for evermore; that can and does bless; that can and does comfort; that can and does bring the soul safely through all. He is not a Saviour that stands as it were upon the brink of a river, and pulls us out when we have swum half way out ourselves; he is not a Saviour that will take us half way to heaven, and then, as Rutherford says, let us "fend" or shift for ourselves. He must take us to heaven throughout. We are nothing, we have nothing without him. He must be, as he is, our "all in all". We value him in his death, nothing but his death could reconcile us to God; we value him in his life, nothing but his life can save. We want salvation now; salvation in the heart; a spiritual salvation revealed in and unto the soul; a salvation worthy of the name, wholly, fully, completely, finally, and everlastingly to the praise of super abounding grace; a salvation that can never be lost; worthy of God, worthy of the God-man; adapted to every want of the soul, coming into every trial of the heart, and able to save the vilest and the worst, "without money and without price."

September 24

"Abide in me, and I in you." – John 15. 4.

The Lord did not use these words as though there were any power in the creature to abide in him. But he was pleased to use them that they might be blessed to his people when the Holy Spirit applied them to the heart; for he adds, *"And I in you."* The one is the key to the other. If we abide in Christ, Christ abides in us. It is by Christ abiding in us, that we are enabled to abide in him. But how does Christ abide in us? By his Spirit. It is by his Spirit that he makes the bodies of his saints his temple; it is by his Spirit that he comes and dwells in them. Though it is instrumentally by faith, as we read, "that Christ may dwell in your hearts by faith;" yet it is through the communication of his Spirit in the soul, and the visits of his most gracious presence. Thus he bids us, encourages us, and influences us to abide in him by his abiding in us. But his abiding in a child of God may be known by certain effects following. If he abide in you, he makes and keeps your *conscience tender.* It is sin that separates between you and him. Therefore, the Lord Jesus Christ, in order that he may abide in you and make you abide in him, makes and keeps your conscience tender in his fear. And this keeps you from those sins which separate between you and him. He may be known, then, to abide in you by the secret checks he gives you when temptation comes before your eyes, and you are all but gone; as one of old said, "My feet were almost gone; my steps had well-nigh slipped." He is pleased to give a secret internal check and admonition; so that your cry is, "How then can I do this great wickedness and sin against God?" And if you go astray and turn from the Lord to your idols, as to our shame and sorrow we often do, he proves that he still abides in you by not giving you up to a reprobate mind, not suffering you to harden your heart against him; but by his reproofs, admonitions, and secret checks in your conscience - by the very lashings and scourgings which he inflicts upon you as a father upon his child, and his secret pleadings with you in the court of conscience - by all these things he makes it manifest that he still abides in you.

September 25

"Through the tender mercy of our God; whereby the day-spring from on high hath visited us." – Luke 1. 78.

By "dayspring" is meant the day-dawn, the herald of the rising sun, the change from darkness to light, the first approach of morn, in a word, the *spring of the day.* But what is this "dayspring" spiritually? It is the intimation of the rising of the Sun of righteousness. It is not the same thing as the Sun of righteousness; but it is the herald of his approach; the beams which the rising sun casts upon the benighted world, announcing the coming of Jesus, "the King in his beauty." This expression was singularly applicable in the mouth of Zacharias. The Lord of life and glory had not then appeared; he was still in the womb of the Virgin Mary. But his forerunner, John, had appeared as the precursor, the herald of his approach, and was sent to announce that the Sun of righteousness was about to arise. "There was a man sent from God, whose name was John. The same came for a witness, to bear witness of the Light, that all men through him might believe. He was not that Light, but was sent to bear witness of that Light" (John 1. 6-8). All nations at that time lay in darkness. "Darkness covered the earth, and gross darkness the people." But when the Lord of life and glory was about to appear upon earth, when he had already taken the body which was prepared for him, the very flesh and blood of the children, which he was to offer as a propitiation for sin, "the dayspring from on high" had begun to dawn. God's mercy, in the face of his dear Son, was just visiting the benighted world.

But there is another, an experimental meaning, connected with these words. "The dayspring from on high" is not to be confined to the approach of the Son of God in the flesh; but it may be extended to signify the appearance of the Son of God in the heart. I cannot be benefited by the appearing of Jesus in the flesh eighteen hundred years ago, unless he come and dwell in my soul. "The dayspring from on high" which visited the benighted Jewish church will not profit us except that same dayspring visits our benighted heart. "The dayspring from on high" is the manifestation of God's mercy in the face of the Saviour. And when this "dayspring from on high" visits the soul, it is the first intimation, the dawning rays of the Sun of righteousness in the heart.

September 26

"To give light to them that sit in darkness and in the shadow of death, to guide our feet into the way of peace." – Luke 1. 79.

What was it that moved the divine Father to send his own Son into the world? Was it not the free mercy of God flowing forth from his bosom to his family? Then, what merit, what claim can his family ever have? Their misery is their claim. Their worthlessness, their sunken state, the depth of their fall – these things call forth God's compassion. It is not what I have done for the glory of God; not what I am doing, or trying to do; not my wisdom, my strength, my resolutions, my piety, my holiness. No; my misery, my helplessness, my worthlessness, my deeply sunken state, my fallen condition; which I feel only because of interest in the blood and love of the Lamb – this it is that makes me need God's mercy; and this it is that qualifies me to go to God through Jesus to receive mercy: for "he is able to save to the uttermost them that come unto God by him." Are you sitting in darkness and the shadow of death – far from the way of peace, troubled, perplexed, exercised, confused? You are the very characters for whom Jesus came. Are not unutterable mercies locked up in the bosom of God for you? What is to exclude you? Your sins? No; God has pardoned them. Your worthlessness? No; there is a robe of righteousness prepared for you. Your demerits? No; the merits of Jesus are upon your side. Your unholiness? No; "He of God is made to you sanctification." Your ignorance? No; "He of God is made to you wisdom." These are no barriers. I will tell you what is a barrier – self-righteousness, self-esteem, self-exaltation, pride, hypocrisy, presumption; a name to live, a form of godliness, being settled upon your lees, and at ease in Zion – these are barriers. But helplessness, hopelessness, worthless-ness, misery – these are not barriers; they are qualifications; they shew, when felt, that your name is in the book of life, that the Lord of life and glory appeared in this world for you; and sooner or later, you will have the sweet enjoyment of it in your heart; and then be enabled to adore him for his grace, and admire and bless his name for glorifying his love and mercy in your free and full salvation.

September 27

"But ye should say, Why persecute we him, seeing the root of the matter is found in me?" – Job 19. 28.

In almost every plant it is at the root that disease begins. If ever you see even a plant in a flowerpot unhealthy, depend upon it there is something wrong at the root. It is overwatered or underwatered, or from some other cause the root has become diseased, and what is called "root-action" is suspended or unhealthy. So it is in religion: if there is anything wrong with a man, it is almost sure to be something wrong at the root. "The root of the matter", Job said, "is found in me." Job could appeal unto God that the root of his religion was right. If "the root" had been wrong, "the matter" would not have been right; but as long as the root was sound, like the "teil tree" of which the prophet speaks, though "it cast its leaves, the substance would still be in it," to put forth in due time boughs like a plant (Isa. 6. 13). If a man's religion has no root, or if the root be injured by disease, it will be sure to discover itself in his profession. He cannot have a prosperous soul – prosperous inwardly and prosperous outwardly – unless the root be deep in the soil, and unless it be full of active fibres, drawing up secret nourishment from that river the streams whereof make glad the city of God. Then he shall be "as a tree planted by the waters, and that spreadeth out her roots by the river, and shall not see when heat cometh, but her leaf shall be green; and shall not be careful in the year of drought, neither shall cease from yielding fruit" (Jer. 17. 8).

September 28

"But now they desire a better country, that is, an heavenly: wherefore God is not ashamed to be called their God: for he hath prepared for them a city." – Hebrews 11. 16.

In desiring a better country these ancient pilgrims wanted something heavenly, something that tasted of God, savoured of God, smelt of God, and was given of God; a heavenly religion, a spiritual faith, a gracious hope, and a love shed abroad in the heart by the Holy Ghost; something which came from heaven and led to heaven; which gave heavenly feelings, heavenly sensations, heavenly delights, and heavenly joys, whereby the heart was purified from the love of sin, carnality, and worldliness by having something sweeter to taste, better to love, and more holy to enjoy. It is these heavenly visitations, droppings in of the favour, goodness, and mercy of God, which keep the soul alive in its many deaths, sweeten it amidst its many bitters, hold it up amidst its many sinkings, and keep it from being drowned while conflicting with many waters. A carnal mind has no taste for heavenly things, no sweet delight in the word of God; no delight in the Lord Jesus as revealing himself in the word; no delight in closet duties, secret meditation, searching the Scriptures, communion with God, or even in the company of God's dear family. There must be a heavenly element in the soul to understand, realise, enjoy, and delight in heavenly things. The Holy Ghost must have wrought in us a new heart, a new nature, capable of understanding, enjoying, and delighting in heavenly realities, as containing in them that which is sweet and precious to the soul. They desired, therefore, a better country, that is, a heavenly, a city which hath foundations, whose builder and maker is God; where pleasures are at God's right hand for evermore; where the pure river of the water of life ever flows; where the tree grows on which are found leaves for the healing of the nations; such a city as John describes in the book of Revelation, where all is happiness, harmony, and peace.

September 29

"Nevertheless when it shall turn to the Lord, the veil shall be taken away." – 2 Corinthians 3. 16.

The blessed Spirit, as a needful preparation for his own divine instruction, convinces us of our *ignorance,* of the veil of unbelief that is by nature spread over our heart, and of our utter inability to take it away. So great is this darkness, as a matter of personal inward experience, that like the darkness in Egypt, it may be "felt"; so deep this ignorance that all knowledge or capability of knowledge seems utterly gone; so strong, so desperate this unbelief that it seems as if thoroughly incurable. And yet amidst all this deep and dense cloud of ignorance, darkness and unbelief, rays and beams of light every now and then break through, which, though they seem at the time only to shew the darkness and make it deeper, yet really are a guiding light to the throne of God and the Lamb. There Jesus sits enthroned in glory, not only as an interceding High Priest to save, not only as an exalted King to rule, but as a most gracious Prophet to teach. Thus, in soul experience, as the veil is felt to be thick and strong over the heart, there is a turning to the Lord with prayer and supplication that he would take it away; and as he, in answer to prayer, is pleased to do this, light is seen in his light, his truth drops with savour and sweetness into the soul, and the word of his grace sways and regulates the heart, lip, and life.

September 30

"For we have not an high priest which cannot be touched with the feeling of our infirmities; but was in all points tempted like as we are, yet without sin. Let us therefore come boldly unto the throne of grace, that we may obtain mercy, and find grace to help in time of need." – Hebrews 4. 15, 16.

What heart can conceive or tongue recount the daily, hourly triumphs of the Lord Jesus Christ's all-conquering grace? We see scarcely a millionth part of what he, as a King on his throne, is daily doing; and yet we see enough to know that he ever lives at God's right hand, and lives to save and bless. What a crowd of needy petitioners every moment surrounds his throne! What urgent wants and woes to redress; what cutting griefs and sorrows to assuage; what broken hearts to bind up; what wounded consciences to heal; what countless prayers to hear; what earnest petitions to grant; what stubborn foes to subdue; what guilty fears to quell! What clemency, what kindness, what long-suffering, what compassion, what mercy, what love, and yet what power and authority does this Almighty Sovereign display! No circumstance is too trifling; no petitioner too insignificant; no case too hard; no difficulty too great; no suer too importunate; no beggar too ragged; no bankrupt too penniless; no debtor too insolvent, for him not to notice and not to relieve. Sitting on his throne of grace, his all-seeing eye views all, his almighty hand grasps all, and his loving heart embraces all whom the Father gave him by covenant, whom he himself redeemed by his blood, and whom the blessed Spirit has quickened into life by his invincible power. The hopeless, the helpless; the outcasts whom no man careth for; the tossed with tempest and not comforted; the ready to perish; the mourners in Zion; the bereaved widow; the wailing orphan; the sick in body, and still more sick in heart; the racked with hourly pain; the fevered consumptive; the wrestler with death's last struggle - O what crowds of pitiable objects surround his throne; and all needing a look from his eye, a word from his lips, a smile from his face, a touch from his hand! O could we but see what his grace is, what his grace has, what his grace does; and could we but feel more what it is doing in and for ourselves, we should have more exalted views of the reign of grace now exercised on high by Zion's enthroned King!

October 1

"Wherefore seeing we also are compassed about with so great a cloud of witnesses, let us lay aside every weight, and the sin which doth so easily beset us, and let us run with patience the race that is set before us." - Hebrews 12. 1.

Every fervent desire of your soul after the Lord Jesus Christ; every inward movement of faith, and hope, and love toward his blessed name; every sense of your misery and danger as a poor, guilty, lost, condemned sinner, whereby you flee from the wrath to come; every escaping out of the world and out of sin for your very life, with every breathing of your heart into the bosom of God, that he would have mercy upon you and bless you; all these inward acts of the believing heart in its striving after salvation as a felt, enjoyed reality, as the prize of our high calling, are pointed out by the emblem - "running the race set before us". The Christian sees and feels that there is a prize to be obtained, which is eternal life; a victory to be gained, which is victory over death and hell; and he sees the certain consequences if this prize is not obtained, this victory not won - an eternity of misery. He sees, therefore, let others think and say what they may, he must run if all stand still, he must fight if all are overcome. But to do this or any part of this a man must have the life of God in his soul. To begin to run is of divine grace and power; to keep on he must have continual supplies communicated out of the fulness of a covenant Head; and to be enabled to persevere to the end so as to win the prize, he must have the strength of Christ continually made perfect in his weakness. But he does win; he is made more than conqueror through Him who loved him. Jesus has engaged that he shall not be defeated; for the race is not to the swift nor the battle to the strong; but the lame take the prey; and not by might nor by power, but by my Spirit, saith the Lord of hosts.

October 2

"For thou, O God, hast proved us: thou hast tried us, as silver is tried." - Psalm 66. 10.

The Lord's dealings with his people in the wilderness are very much to this purpose and to this end - to prove them, and to know what is in their hearts. Has the Lord implanted life in your soul? Has he touched your conscience with his finger? Has he begun a work of grace upon your heart? If so, in your travels through this wilderness there will be things from time to time to prove the reality of this work upon your soul. You will have *temptations;* now, when temptation comes, it will prove whether you have the fear of God in your soul to stand against the temptation, or whether you fall under the temptation; or, if you fall under the temptation, whether you are ever recovered out of it. And if you are a living soul, the Lord will keep bringing circumstance upon circumstance, event upon event, one thing after another; and all these things, as they come upon you, shall be made to prove whether the fear of God be in your soul or not. Now, if the fear of God be not in a man's heart, he must decline, he must fall away. Satan will be more than a match for every one except God's own family; sin will overcome and destroy every one but those whose sins are pardoned through atoning blood and dying love; and the world, sooner or later, will overcome every one who has not the faith of God's elect whereby alone the world is overcome. Thus the Lord, in his mysterious dealings (and how mysterious his dealings are!) proves the reality of the work of grace in every heart where that work is begun, and proves the hypocrisy of all who have but a name to live while their soul is dead before God.

October 3

"But we all, with open face beholding as in a glass the glory of the Lord, are changed into the same image from glory to glory, even as by the Spirit of the Lord." – 2 Corinthians 3. 18.

When our desires and affections ascend to where the Lord Jesus Christ now is, when raised out of all the smoke and fog, din and strife, noise and bustle, cares and anxieties, pursuits and pleasures, sins and sorrows of this earthly scene, we can in faith and hope, in love and affection, live above and beyond all things here below, and beholding with unveiled face the glory of the Lord, "are changed into the same image from glory to glory, even as by the Spirit of the Lord" – this is being made to sit together in heavenly places in Christ Jesus.

When the Lord Jesus went up on high he entered into his glory. As then we behold him in his glory in faith and love, there is the reflection of his glory, and saints thus favoured enter into heaven when still upon earth, and have the foretaste of the glory which is to be revealed at the Lord's coming before they are for ever clothed with it. There are indeed comparatively few who are so highly favoured, and even they only at rare intervals, and for short moments; but that does not affect the truth and certainty of the fact. It is a most blessed truth that if we are members of the mystical body of Christ, the deficiency of our experience, though it deprives us of much of the enjoyment, does not deprive us of our interest in, or union with, our great covenant Head, and of the fruits which spring out of it.

October 4

"I will strengthen that which was sick." – Ezekiel 34. 16.

Peculiar maladies require peculiar remedies; but here is a general remedy, a family medicine. The Lord not only has strong remedies for desperate diseases; but in the divine medicine chest he has his restoratives and cordials. "Stay me with flagons; comfort me with apples," cries the Bride, "for I am sick of love." She was in a swoon, and needed a reviving cordial to restore her. So a poor fainting soul may come to hear the preached gospel, or may open his Bible, and say, "What is here for me? When I hear any deep experience described, that seems to cut me off as too deep; and when I hear great manifestations entered into, that cuts me off as too high. So I seem to be a strange being, a peculiar out-of-the-way creature, that can neither dive nor fly, sink nor rise." Well, you are sick; you are like one in a hospital, ill of a malady that puzzles all the doctors. At last, one more skilful than his brethren, says, "There is no peculiar disease. But the man, like many of our London patients, is suffering from want of nourishment, dying from sheer exhaustion. He wants better blood put into him. He must have some good meat and wine, and a nourishing diet to recruit his strength and put new life into his body." Thus acts the great Physician – Jehovah-rophi. "I will strengthen that which was sick." The blood and righteousness of Jesus – that flesh which is meat indeed, and that blood which is drink indeed, is given to the hunger-bitten wretch to revive him as with a heavenly cordial. There is balm in Gilead; there is a Physician there;

to that balm and to that physician sin-sick souls seek. If you have a real case, you may depend upon it, there is a remedy in the family chest. It is not found out yet, at least you may not have found it, but there is a drawer, and in that drawer there is a draught devised by infinite wisdom and compounded by everlasting love. It is indeed a remedy such as no learned physician of the school of the Pharisees ever prescribed, or an apothecary wise in his own conceit ever compounded; but yet the very thing, the very thing. And when that drawer is opened and the draught brought out, and you take it, you will be able to say with David in the joy of your heart, "Bless the Lord, O my soul, and all that is within me, bless his holy name."

October 5

"And this I pray, that your love may abound yet more and more in knowledge and in all judgment" (margin, sense). – Philippians 1. 9.

Love is especially the effect of knowledge; and love we know is a fruit of the blessed Spirit. As then the Lord the Spirit is pleased to open up the precious truth of God to the soul, love embraces what the Holy Ghost reveals. Thus there is a knowledge of the only true God by the teaching of the Spirit. But our love is to abound not only in knowledge, which is the foundation of it, because if there is no knowledge of the Lord there can be no love to the Lord or his people, but also in all feeling, in all sense, in all experience. Spiritual knowledge, therefore, and experimental feeling are the two feeders of Christian love; the two streams, as it were, that run side by side out of the very throne of the most High, and meet and melt into that boundless river, love. And it is by this union of knowledge and experience, of divine light and heavenly life, of the Spirit's teaching and the Spirit's testimony, of truth in the understanding and of feeling in the affections, that love is maintained in the soul, and flows out towards the Lord and his people. This spiritual knowledge differs very widely from carnal, intellectual, barren head knowledge. The one is a flowing river, the other a stagnant pool; the one fertilises the heart, and makes it fruitful in every good word and work; the other leaves it a barren swamp, in which creeps and crawls every hideous thing, and out of which ever rise miasma, disease, and death. Thus the union of knowledge and experience as sustaining love distinguishes the work of the Spirit from every imitation of it, and where there is the true work of the Spirit there will be gracious knowledge and experimental feeling.

This, then, is the peculiar blessedness of living experience that it goes hand in hand with gracious knowledge to sustain heavenly love; and that Christ is the end and object of both; the end and object of all saving knowledge, and the end and object of all true experience; for in this as in everything else he is the Alpha and the Omega, the beginning and the end, the first and the last.

October 6

"For thus saith the high and lofty One that inhabiteth eternity, whose name is Holy; I dwell in the high and holy place, with him also that is of a contrite and humble spirit, to revive the spirit of the humble, and to revive the heart of the contrite ones." – Isaiah 57. 15.

O what a mystery that God should have two dwelling-places! The "heaven of heavens" that "cannot contain him". and the humble, broken, and contrite heart! But in order that the Lord of heaven might have a place in which he could live and lodge, God gives to his people gifts and graces; for he cannot come and dwell in the carnal mind, in our rebellious nature, in a heart full of enmity and wickedness; he therefore makes a lodging-place for himself, a pavilion in which the King of glory dwells, the curtains of which are like the curtains of Solomon. His abode is that holy, divine nature which is communicated at regeneration – "the new man, which after God is created in righteousness and true holiness." Thus Christ dwells in the heart by faith; and is in his people, "the hope of glory". And this made Paul say, "I am crucified with Christ: nevertheless I live; yet not I, but Christ liveth in me: and the life which I now live in the flesh I live by the faith of the Son of God, who loved me, and gave himself for me." This is the object of God's dealings – that the Lord God might dwell in his people; that there might be a union between the Church and her covenant Head: "I in them, and thou in me, that they may be made perfect in one." This is the unfolding of the grand enigma, the solution of the incomprehensible mystery, "God manifest in the flesh" – that the Lord God might dwell in his people; "I will dwell in them, and walk in them; and I will be their God, and they shall be my people"; and thus glorify himself by filling their hearts with his grace and glory, as Solomon's temple was of old, and that they might enjoy him, and be with him when time shall be no more. This is the grand key to all the Lord's dealings with the soul, and all his mysterious leadings in providence, – that the Lord God might dwell in the hearts of his people here, and be eternally glorified in them in a brighter and a better world.

October 7

"Brethren, farewell." – 2 Corinthians 13. 11

To fare well, spiritually understood, is to have everything that God can make us happy in. All God's people will eventually fare well. They all stand complete in Christ: nothing can touch their eternal safety; for they are all complete in him, without spot, or blemish, or any such thing. In this point of view, they must all in the end and for ever *fare well.*

But when we come to the matter of experience, we often find that those very times when God's people think they are *faring ill,* are the seasons when they are really *faring well;* and again, at other times, when they think they are *faring well,* then they are really *faring ill.* For instance, when their souls are bowed down with trouble, it often seems to them that they are *faring ill.* God's hand appears to be gone out against them: he has hidden his face from them; they can find no access to the throne of grace; they have no sweet testimonies from the Lord that the path in which he is leading them is one of his choosing, and that all things will end well with them. This they think is indeed faring ill, and yet perhaps they never fare better than when under these circumstances of trouble, sorrow, and affliction. These things wean them from the world. If their heart and affections were going out after idols, they instrument-ally bring them back. If they were hewing out broken cisterns, they dash them all to pieces. If they were setting up, and bowing down to idols in the chambers of imagery, affliction and trouble smite them to pieces before their eyes, take away their gods, and leave them no refuge but the Lord God of hosts. If you can only look back, you will see that your greatest sweets have often sprung out of your greatest bitters, and the greatest blessings have flowed from the greatest miseries, and what at the time you thought your greatest sorrows: you will find that the brightest light has sprung up in the blackest darkness, and that the Lord never made himself so precious as at the time when you were sunk lowest, so as to be without human help, wisdom, or strength. So that when a child of God thinks he is *faring very ill,* because burdened with sorrows, temptations, and afflictions, he is never faring so well. The darkest clouds in due time will break, the most puzzling enigmas will sooner or later be unriddled by the blessed Spirit interpreting them, and the darkest providences cleared up; and we shall see that God is in them all, leading and guiding us "by the right way, that we may go to a city of habitation" (Psalm 107. 7).

October 8

"I have gone astray like a lost sheep; seek thy servant; for I do not forget thy commandments." – Psalm 119. 176.

If the Lord did not seek us, we should never seek the Lord. That is most certain. If you are one that seeks the Lord in prayer, in supplication, in secret desire, with many a heart-rending groan, and often by night and by day, be well assured, that you would never have sought the Lord, had not the Lord first sought you. He is now seeking you. It may be (as you fear), some time before he finds you; but he will find you at last. How sweetly the Lord has set this forth in the parable of the lost sheep! The poor sheep has gone astray; and having once left the fold, it is pretty sure to have got into some strange place or other. It has fallen down a rock, or has rolled into a ditch, or is hidden beneath a bush, or has crept into a cave, or is lying in some deep, distant ravine, where none but an experienced eye and hand can find it out. And so with the Lord's lost sheep: they get into strange places. They fall off rocks, slip into holes, hide among the bushes, and sometimes creep off to die in caverns. When the literal sheep has gone astray, the shepherd goes after it to find it. Here he sees a footmark, there a little lock of wool torn off by the thorns. Every nook he searches; into every corner he looks, until at last he finds the poor sheep wearied, torn, and half expiring, with scarce strength enough to groan forth its misery. Nor does he beat it home, nor thrust the goad into its back; but he gently takes it up, lays it upon his shoulder, and brings it home rejoicing. Similar in grace are the Lord's ways with his lost sheep. Men act otherwise. Let a Pharisee see a sheep *cast,* as it is called in the country, that is, lying helpless upon its back, he would soon kick it up and kick it home, beat its head with his crook, or drive the sharp nail into its flank.

David's was a wise prayer, "Let me fall into the hands of God, and not into the hands of man." O to fall into the hands of God; into the hands of a merciful and compassionate High Priest, who was tempted in all points, like as we are, and can therefore sympathise with his poor tempted people! These, these are the only hands for us safely to fall into; and he that falls into these hands will neither fall out of them, nor through them, for "underneath are the everlasting arms", and these can neither be sundered nor broken.

October 9

"Looking unto Jesus the author and finisher of our faith." – Hebrews 12. 2.

No one can ever run the race set before him, except by looking unto Jesus. He is at the head of the race; he stands at the goal, holding the crown of victory in his hand, which he puts upon the head of the successful runner. And we can only run on as we view Jesus by the eye of faith at the right hand of the Father opening his blessed arms to receive us into his own bosom at the end of the race. Nor indeed can anyone really look to him but by the special gift and grace of God. He must be revealed to the soul by the power of God; we must behold his glorious Godhead and his suffering manhood by the eye of faith; and we must view him as the incarnate God; the only Mediator between God and man. We must see the efficacy of his atoning blood to purge a guilty conscience; the blessedness of his obedience to justify a needy, naked soul; the sweetness of his dying love as an inward balm and cordial against all the thousand ills and sorrows of life. We must see his glory, as the only begotten of the Father, full of grace and truth; his suitability to every want and woe; his infinite compassion to the vilest and worst of sinners; his patient forbearance and wondrous long-suffering of our sins and backslidings; his unchanging love, stronger than death itself; his readiness to hear; his willingness to bless; and his ability to save to the uttermost all that come unto God by him. Thus the heavenly runner looks not to the course however long, nor to the ground however rough, not to his own exertions however multiplied, nor to his own strength whether much or little; nor to applauding friends or condemning foes; but wholly and solely to the incarnate Son of God. Jesus draws him onward with his invincible grace. Every glance of his beauteous Person renews the flame of holy love; every sight of his blood and righteousness kindles desires to experience more of their efficacy and blessedness; and every touch of his sacred finger melts the heart into conformity to his suffering image. This is the life of a Christian, - day by day, to be running a race for eternity; and as speeding onward to a heavenly goal, to manifest his sincerity and earnestness by continually breathing forth the yearnings of his soul after divine realities, and to be pressing forward more and more toward the Lord Jesus Christ, as giving him a heavenly crown when he has finished his course with joy.

October 10

"From the end of the earth will I cry unto thee, when my heart is overwhelmed: lead me to the rock that is higher than I." - Psalm 61. 2.

There is something in this expression in our text, *"rock"* which seems, to my mind, to throw a sweet and blessed light upon what Jesus is to the poor and needy. The rock must go down to the bottom of the deep waters, as well as rise out of them, to be a sufficient place of refuge for the shipwrecked mariner! If the rock did not go to the bottom of the deep, it would not be firm; it would be but a quicksand. Is not this agreeable to the Spirit's testimony concerning the humanity of Christ? How deep that went into all our sorrows, into all our sufferings, into all our sins, into all our shame! However deep the waters may be, the rock is deeper than all; however deep the sufferings, sins, and sorrows of the Church may be, the sufferings and sorrows of "Immanuel, God with us," were infinitely deeper. But the waves and billows beat in vain against the rock; they cannot move it from its place. So it is with the rock, Jesus. All the sins, temptations, sufferings, and sorrows of the elect, with the wrath of God, and the fury of hell, beat against that rock, but they never moved it from its place. But this rock is spoken of in our text as *"higher than I." There* we have the Godhead. For if Jesus were not God as well as man, the God-man, what support could he be to the sinking soul? what efficacy could there be in his atoning blood? what power and glory in his justifying righteousness? what suitability in him as a Saviour to the utterly lost? But being God as well as man, yea, the God-man, the great and glorious Immanuel, he could descend in his human nature into the very depths of the fall, and rise up in his divine nature to the throne of the most High; and thus, like Jacob's ladder, the bottom of it was upon the earth, but the top exalted to the clouds. Then will not, must not, this be ever, as the Lord is pleased to raise it up, the cry of our soul, "Lead me to the rock that is higher than I?" No salvation anywhere else; no peace anywhere else; no consolation anywhere else. Buffeted by the waves, and well-nigh drowned by the billows, away from that rock; but if led there, brought there, kept there by the blessed Spirit, finding it a safe and sure standing for eternity. And what else but such a rock can save our souls, or what else but such a Saviour and such a salvation, without money and without price, can suit such ruined wretches?

October 11

"We know that we have passed from death unto life, because we love the brethren." – 1 John 3. 14.

The Lord's people in their early days have a measure of heavenly love. Though perhaps they cannot say that Jesus is theirs; though they dare not declare they shall certainly go to heaven when they die; though they sometimes cannot even assert that the work of grace is really begun upon their souls; yet there is love manifested in them to God's word, God's people, God's servants, and God's truth. There is in them, in their weakest and tenderest days, a separation from the world, a casting-in of their lot amongst the people of God, a going-out in the tenderness of their heart and affection towards them. We see this in Ruth: though she was a poor heathen idolatress, no sooner was her heart touched by the finger of God, than she clave to Naomi.

Divine love can only spring from the teachings and operations of God upon the heart. Our "carnal mind is enmity against God" - nothing but implacable, irreconcilable enmity. But when the Lord is pleased to make himself, in some measure, known to the soul; when he is pleased, in some degree, to unveil his lovely face, and to give a discovery of his grace and glory - immediately love springs up. He is so lovely an Object! As the Bride says, He is "altogether lovely." His beauty is so surpassing, his grace so rich, his mercy so free – all that he is and has is so unspeakably glorious – that no sooner does he unveil his lovely face, than he wins over all the love of the heart, takes possession of the bosom, and draws every affection of the soul to centre wholly and solely in himself.

October 12

"But let us, who are of the day, be sober, putting on the breastplate of faith and love; and for an helmet, the hope of salvation" – 1 Thessalonians 5. 8.

Sobriety in religion is a blessed gift and grace. In our most holy faith there is no room for lightness. The things which concern our peace are solemn, weighty matters, and if they lie with any degree of weight and power on our spirit, they will subdue that levity which is the very breath of the carnal mind. But sobriety implies not merely the absence of all unbecoming levity in speech and conduct, but the absence also of all wild, visionary imaginations in the things of God. It denotes, therefore, that "spirit of a sound mind" which the Apostle says is the gift of God. Vital godliness, it is true, has its mysteries, its revelations and manifestations, its spiritual and supernatural discoveries and operations; but all these come through the word of truth, which is simple, weighty and solid, and as far removed from everything visionary or imaginative, wild or flighty, as light is from darkness; and therefore every act of faith, or of hope, or of love, will be as simple, solid, and weighty as the word of truth itself, through the medium of which, by the power of the Spirit, they are produced and called forth. If any doubt this, let them read in some solemn moment the last discourses of our blessed Lord with his disciples. How simple, how solid, how weighty are these discourses. Must not, then, the faith which receives, believes, and is mixed with these words of grace and truth, the hope which anchors in the promises there spoken, the love which embraces the gracious and glorious Person of him who spoke them, be simple and solid too? What room is there in such faith, hope, and love for visionary ideas, wild speculations, and false spiritualisations of Scripture, any more than there is in the words of the Lord himself?

October 13

"Who hath saved us, and called us with an holy calling, not according to our works, but according to his own purpose and grace, which was given us in Christ Jesus before the world began." – 2 Timothy 1. 9.

Have you any testimony that God has called you by his grace, quickened your soul into divine life, brought you under the curse of a condemning law, given you repentance for your sins, raised up a sigh and a cry in your breast for a sense of his pardoning love, brought you to the footstool of mercy, given you faith to believe in his dear Son, with any sweet hope that he has begun a gracious work upon your heart? Can you look back upon any never-to-be-forgotten period when the Lord, by his special and omnipotent grace, quickened your soul into divine life? for I do believe we never can forget the first sensations of the Spirit of God in his quickening movements upon the soul; when he, to use the figure of Moses, fluttereth over it as an eagle which stirreth up her nest, infusing and communicating a new and heavenly life, as when in creation he moved upon the face of the waters communicating life and energy to dead chaos. Surely if we ever felt the mighty hand of the Lord upon us, we can never forget the memorable time when he was first pleased to communicate divine light and life to our dead souls, to pour out upon us the spirit of grace and of supplications, to separate us from the world, to bring us to his feet with confessions and supplications, opening up and revealing eternal realities with a weight and a power that they entered into our deepest and most inward thoughts and feelings. Can you look back to such a time? Then God is for you; and if God is for you then you can, as he is pleased to strengthen your faith, look right through that blessed chain, with all its heavenly links, and see how he foreknew you before the foundation of the world, and wrote your name in the Book of Life.

October 14

"Wherefore we receiving a kingdom which cannot be moved, let us have (margin, let us hold fast) grace, whereby we may serve God acceptably with reverence and godly fear." – Hebrews 12. 28.

Grace is the very foundation of the kingdom which cannot moved. It is all of grace, from first to last. By grace we are saved; by grace we are called; by grace we are what we are. In order, therefore, to maintain our interest clear in the kingdom which cannot be shaken, we must hold grace fast; for directly we cease to do this, we lose our comfortable prospects of this kingdom, and of our own participation in it and its heavenly blessings. It is a kingdom of present grace and of future glory, therefore built wholly upon grace and not upon merit; wholly upon the favour of God and not upon the works of the creature. As long, then, as we hold fast grace, we hold the kingdom; for the kingdom stands in grace.

But why should this exhortation be needed? Is it not very easy to hold fast grace? Yes, very, when there is nothing to try it; and that is the way that most hold it – in the head, not in the heart. But the real partakers of the life of God are tempted on every hand to renounce their hold of grace, through the power of the world, the strength of sin, the subtlety of their unwearied adversary, the unbelief, infidelity, and despondency of their wretched heart. Thus sometimes we are tempted to look away from the kingdom which cannot be shaken, and descend to lower things; to stand either upon that earth which has been shaken under our feet, or that heaven, that

Pharisee's heaven which has been shaken over our heads, and thus get lost and bewildered among the wreck and ruin of those things which have been shaken and are removed. The Apostle therefore exhorts us to hold fast that grace whereby in the first instance we came to have an interest in the kingdom not to be shaken; whereby we were introduced into an experimental knowledge and possession of it; and whereby alone we can maintain a firm hold of it to the end. Whatever you do, then, however low you may sink and fall, never relinquish your firm hold of grace. It will never be more precious than when clasped by a dying hand, and clung to with expiring breath.

October 15

"That I may win Christ." – Philippians 3. 8.

What is it to "win Christ"? It is to have him sweetly embraced in the arms of our faith. It is to feel him manifesting his heavenly glory in our souls. It is to have the application of his atoning blood, in all its purging efficacy, to our conscience. It is to feel our heart melted and swooning with the sweet ravishments of his dying love, shed abroad even to overpowering. This is winning Christ. Now, before we can thus win Christ, we must have a view of Christ, we must behold his glory, "the glory as of the only begotten of the Father, full of grace and truth." We must see the matchless dignity of his glorious Person, the atoning efficacy of his propitiating blood, the length and breadth, the depth and height of his surpassing love. We must have our heart ready to burst with pantings, longings, and ardent desires that this blessed Immanuel would come down from the heaven of heavens in which he dwells beyond the vail, into our heart, and shed abroad his precious dying love there. Now, is not this your feeling, child of God? It has been mine over and over again. Is it not your feeling as you lie upon your bed, sometimes, with sweet and earnest pantings after the Lord of life and glory? As you walk by the way, as you are engaged in your daily business, as you are secretly musing and meditating, are there not often the goings forth of these longings and breathings into the very bosom of the Lord? But you cannot have this, unless you have seen him by the eye of an enlightened understanding, by the eye of faith, and had a taste of his beauty, a glimpse of his glory, and a discovery of his eternal preciousness. You must have had this gleaming upon your eyes, as the beams of light gleam through the windows. You must have had it dancing into your heart, as the rays of the sun dance upon the waves of the sea. You must have had a sweet incoming of the shinings of eternal light upon your soul, melting it, and breaking it down at his footstool, as the early dawn pierces through the clouds of night. When you have seen and felt this you break forth – 'O that I might win Christ!' Like the ardent lover who longs to win his bride, you long to enjoy his love and presence shed abroad in the heart by the Holy Ghost.

October 16

"Thy words were found, and I did eat them; and thy word was unto me the joy and rejoicing of mine heart: for I am called by thy name, O Lord God of hosts." – Jeremiah 15. 16.

There is a sweetness in the promises which captivates the heart; a beauty in Christ which wins the soul; a saving unction and power in the word of God, when applied, which draws forth toward it every secret and sacred affection. Can you not sometimes look up and say, "Blessed Jesus, I do love thee"? And when the word of God is opened up, applied, and made sweet and precious, have you not felt sometimes as if you could kiss the sacred page, as conveying such sweetness into your soul? This is embracing a promise in love – throwing our arms round it, drawing it near to our breast, kissing it again and again with kisses of love and affection, and taking that sweet delight in it with which the bridegroom rejoices over the bride, as now all his own – at times almost lost, but now wooed and won, no more to be parted. This is rejoicing in the word of God, delighting in a blessed Jesus and in the promises which testify of, and centre in him. Have you not felt these sweet embracements in your soul of the truth as it is in Jesus as so precious, so suitable, so encouraging, and so adapted to every want and woe? Then you are a believer; then you are a child of God; then there is a work of grace upon your heart; then you know the truth for yourself by divine teaching and divine testimony. You may still not have had that full deliverance, that blessed revelation, that overpowering manifestation whereby all your doubts and fears have been swept away, and your soul settled in a firm enjoyment of the liberty of the gospel. You may have had it or may have had it not. But if you have this character stamped upon you that you have seen the promises afar off and been persuaded of them, and embraced them in faith, hope, and love, you have a mark of being a partaker of the faith of God's elect.

October 17

"For ye have need of patience, that, after ye have done the will of God, ye might receive the promise." – Hebrews 10. 36.

Why is patience needed? Because if we are the Lord's people, we are sure to have many trials. The Lord sends us afflictions that he may give us the grace of patience to bear them. But O, what a rebellious heart do we carry in our bosom! What perverseness, peevishness, and self-will dwell in us! How soon our temper is stirred up, and our irritable minds roused in a moment by the veriest trifle! How little patience have we under the trials that God sees fit to lay upon us! We thus learn our need of patience, and that it is not a fruit of nature's soil. The want of it makes the soul follow after it; and when the Lord does give submission to his will, and enables his children to see how profitable these trials are for their souls, and how, but for this heavy ballast, they would certainly have been carried away into the world, they can see his merciful hand in their heavy afflictions. Thus sometimes by feeling peevish and rebellious, and thus knowing their need of patience; and sometimes by feeling submissive, and enjoying the sweetness of it, they see what a blessed grace patience is. Scarcely any grace do we more daily need. We need it toward God, when he crosses us in our schemes, thwarts us in our desires, and instead of showing why he afflicts us, hides himself behind a thick cloud that neither faith nor prayer can pierce through. We need patience with each other, with the world, with our relations in life, and with the Church of God. We need patience when anything is said or done to hurt our minds, wound our feelings, irritate our tempers, and stir us up to revenge. And what a mercy it is, under these sharp trials, to have patience, and thus follow the example of the blessed Lord, "who, when he was reviled, reviled not again; when he suffered, he threatened not but committed himself to Him that judgeth righteously."

October 18

"Can two walk together, except they be agreed?" – Amos 3. 3.

There was a time, child of God, when the world held in your heart the chief place. It was not so in God's heart. You and he were therefore at variance. But now, through grace, you are brought to make eternity your chief concern. You and God are agreed there; for in the mind of God eternity as much outweighs time as the stars in the midnight sky outweigh a grain of dust. There was a time when you loved the world and the things of time and sense; and earth and earthly things were your element and home. You and God disagreed upon that matter; because the Lord saw that the world was full of evil, whilst you saw it full of good. The Lord saw the world under his curse, and you loved its favour and its blessing – seeking madly and wickedly to enjoy that which God had denounced; therefore you could not agree. Thus you see that in order to be agreed with God, we must have God's thoughts in our heart, God's ways in our soul, and God's love in our affections. "For my thoughts are not your thoughts, neither are your ways my ways, saith the Lord." But they must become such; and when once God's thoughts become our thoughts and God's ways our ways; when once we have the mind of Christ and see with the eyes of God, then God and we become agreed, and being agreed, we can walk together. What is it to walk together? Why, it is to enjoy union, communion, fellowship, and friendship. Now as we are brought to agree with God, we walk with God. He has set up a mercy-seat on high, and when they thus agree, God and man may meet at the mercy-seat of the Redeemer. As the eyes are enlightened to see the truth of God; as the heart is touched to feel the power of God; and as the affections are drawn forth to love the things of God, we meet at the mercy-seat. It is sprinkled with blood; it contains and hides from view the broken tables of the law. There God meets man in gracious amity, and enables him to pour out his soul before him and to tell him his troubles, trials, and temptations. And every now and then he sweetly relieves by dropping in a gracious promise, applying some portion of his sacred truth, encouraging him to believe in his dear Son, and still to hope in his mercy.

October 19

"The sword of the Spirit, which is the word of God." – Ephesians 6. 17.

There is only one weapon whereby we can fight Satan to any purpose, and that is the word of God. But observe, that it must not be merely *the letter* of the word. It must be the "sword of *the Spirit,*" and there-fore a spiritual sword, which can only be taken in hand when the word of God is applied with a divine power to your heart, and you have a living faith in it as made "life and spirit" to your soul. It is of no use my bringing forward a text to resist a temptation of Satan, unless I can make that text my own; in other words, unless I can handle that sword as one who knows how to wield it. To take up a text and not know the sweetness and power of it, would be like a child taking up a warrior's sword without having the warrior's hand. He might play with the sword, but what is the sword of a giant in the hand of a child? The sword of Scanderbeg, a famous Albanian warrior against the Turks, used to be shown at Vienna. A man who once looked at and handled it said, "Is this the sword which won so many victories? I see nothing in it; it is but a common sword." The answer was, "you should have seen the hand that wielded it." So it is not merely taking a text, adopting scripture language, and quoting passages, which will beat back the fiery assaults of Satan. This is having Scanderbeg's sword without having Scanderbeg's arm. But it is having the word of truth brought into our heart by the power of God, faith raised up to believe that God himself speaks it to our heart, being thus enabled to wield it in the strength of the Spirit and by the power of faith in living exercise, to resist every hellish thrust. In this battle we must not give way. To flee is to be conquered, for, as Bunyan well says, there is no armour for the back. Thus even if in this conflict you should slip and fall, lie not still as a conquered captive, but get up again and fight. "Resist Satan, and he will flee from you." He is a conquered enemy; he cannot destroy you if you are the Lord's. The word of truth, therefore, is full of most gracious promises, and sweet encouragements "to endure hardness as good soldiers of Jesus Christ," and never in heart or hand submit to be conquered by sin or Satan.

October 20

"Therefore, behold, I will allure her, and bring her into the wilderness, and speak comfortably unto her." – Hosea 2. 14.

It is in the margin "to her heart"; and God speaks to the heart; that is the special characteristic of his voice. Men may speak to the ear, and they can do no more; but God speaks to the heart, for it is there that his voice alone is heard. All religion first and last lies in a man's heart. He may have his head well furnished with notions, yet a heart destitute of grace. But not so with the vessels of mercy, for they "believe with the heart unto righteousness;" and it is by the voice of God heard in the heart that a saving faith is raised up in the soul. There God must speak if there is to be any heart religion, any sound or saving experience, any knowledge of the truth so as to be blessed and saved thereby. But in the wilderness we learn the deep necessity there is that God should speak to our heart. We want the Lord himself to speak and the Lord alone; and to speak such words as shall reach our heart and enter with divine power into our conscience. When you are in the wilderness, you have no friend, no creature help, no worldly comfort: these have all abandoned you. God has led you into the wilderness to bereave you of these earthly ties, of these creature refuges and vain hopes, that he may himself speak to your soul. If, then, you are separated from the world by being brought into the wilderness; if you are passing through trials and afflictions; if you are exercised with a variety of temptations, and are brought into that spot where the creature yields neither help nor hope, then you are made to see and feel that nothing but God's voice speaking with power to your soul can give you any solid grounds of rest or peace. But is not this profitable? It may be painful; it *is* painful; but it is profitable, because by it we learn to look to the Lord and the Lord alone, and this must ever be a blessed lesson to learn for every child of God.

October 21

"Therefore let no man glory in men. For all things are yours; whether Paul, or Apollos, or Cephas, or the world, or life, or death, or things present, or things to come; all are yours; and ye are Christ's; and Christ is God's." – 1 Corinthians 3. 21-23.

Whatever there be in heaven, whatever there be in earth, that can be for your spiritual good, all is yours so far as you are an heir of God and a joint-heir with Christ. The silver and the gold and the cattle upon a thousand hills are all Christ's because all power is given to him in heaven and in earth. Whatever your temporal wants may be, he can supply them, because he is king on earth as well as in heaven. Whatever enemies you may have, he is able to defeat them; whatever evils may press upon you, he is able to subdue them; whatever sorrows surround you, he is able to console you under them. Everything in time, everything in eternity, in this world and in the world to come, are all on your side, that are heirs of God and joint-heirs with Christ.

October 22

"And ye shall seek me, and find me, when ye shall search for me with all your heart." – Jeremiah 29. 13.

After the Lord has quickened our souls, for a time we often go, shall I say, blundering on, not knowing there is a Jesus. We think that the way of life is to keep God's commandments, obey the law, cleanse ourselves from sin, reform our lives, and cultivate universal holiness in thought, word, and action; and so we go, blundering and stumbling on in darkness; and all the while never get a single step forward. But when the Lord has suffered us to weary ourselves to find the door, and let us sink lower and lower into the pit of guilt and ruin, so that all our attempts to extricate ourselves have only plunged us deeper and deeper, and the Spirit of God opens up to the understanding and brings into the soul some spiritual discovery of Jesus, and thus makes known that there is a Saviour, a Mediator, and a way of escape – this is the grand turning-point in our lives, the first opening in the valley of Achor of the door of hope. And when the soul has once seen that there is a Jesus, and once felt a measure of the power of his resurrection, it never goes to any other quarter for pardon, justification, and salvation. When the Spirit of God begins to open up with power in his conscience that there is a Jesus, that he is the only Mediator, that the Son of God has come down and taken a holy human nature into union with himself, and is now at the right hand of the Father, it is the first break of day, the first dawn of hope; and upon that bright spot does the shipwrecked soul fix his longing eyes till the Sun of righteousness arises upon it with healing in his wings. It is a great step in a man's experience to turn wholly and solely to the Lord, and renounce all creature righteousness, all forms and ceremonies as a way of salvation. It is a great mercy to turn away from them, as the shipwrecked mariner turns away from his sinking ship, and looks to the rising sun to show him some way of escape, and thus afford him some gleam of hope.

October 23

"O wretched man that I am!" – Romans 7. 24.

Now, these feelings which the Apostle groaned under are experienced by all the quickened family. Blessed then be the name of God most High, that he inspired him to trace out and leave upon record his experience, that we might derive comfort and relief from it. What should we otherwise have thought? We should have reasoned thus: 'Here is an apostle perfectly holy, perpetually heavenly-minded, having nothing but the image of Christ in him, continually living to the Lord's glory, and unceasingly enjoying communion with him!' We should have viewed him as a perfect saint, if he had not told us what he was; and then, having viewed him as a perfect saint, we should have turned our desponding eyes into our own bosom, and seen such an awful contrast, that we should despair of ever being saved at all! But seeing the soul conflict which the Apostle passed through, and feeling a measure of the same in our own bosom, it encourages, supports, and leads the soul on to believe that this is the way in which the saints are called to travel, however rough, rugged, and perplexing it may be to them.

Be assured, then, if you have never cried out from the depths of your soul, "O wretched man that I am!" you are dead in sin, or dead in a profession. If internal guilt, misery, and condemnation never forced that cry from your bosom, depend upon it, the life and power of God is not in your soul. But if there has been, and still is, from time to time, this cry in your breast, forced out of it by the pressure of sin and guilt, you have a testimony that the same Lord who taught Paul is teaching you.

October 24

"Who shall deliver me from the body of this death?" – Romans 7. 24.

If the Lord the Spirit has implanted that piteous cry in our soul, "O wretched man that I am!" this will follow as a necessary consequence – *"Who shall deliver me from the body of this death?"* Where shall I look for deliverance? From what quarter can it come? Shall I look to the law? O no! that curses and condemns me, because I am continually breaking it. Can I look to friends? They may pity and sympathise; but they cannot remove the body of sin and death; it is too fast linked on for them to remove. Shall I go to ministers of truth? I may hear what they say with approbation; but there is something more wanted to remove this chilling embrace of the body of sin and death. Shall I look to the Scriptures? They contain the remedy; but I want that remedy to be sweetly applied "Who then shall deliver me?" What refuge can I look to? Whither can I go, or whither shall I turn? From what quarter can help or deliverance come? See the embarrassment! view the perplexity of an exercised soul! – looking here, and looking there; turning to the right hand and turning to the left. Yet from one quarter only can the deliverance come. And thus, when the Apostle was brought here – when he was sunk down to a low spot, and anxiously turning his eyes to every quarter to see whence deliverance could come – God blessed his soul with a view of his precious Son. God the Spirit wrought in his heart that living faith whereby he saw Jesus, and whereby there was a communication of the blood and love of the Lamb to his conscience.

October 25

"For his eyes are upon the ways of man, and he seeth all his goings." – Job 34. 21.

The Christian has to prove that nothing escapes the eye of a just and holy God; that he lays bare every secret thought, searches every hidden purpose, and scrutinizes every desire and every movement of the mind. He thus discovers and brings to light all the secret sins of the heart. Men in general take no notice of heart sins; if they can keep from sins in life, from open acts of immorality, they are satisfied. What passes in the chambers of imagery they neither see nor feel. Not so with the child of grace; he knows the experience described in Psalm 139. He carries about with him the secret conviction that the eye of God reads every thought. Every inward movement of pride and self-righteousness, rebellion, discontent, peevishness, fretfulness, lust, and wantonness, he inwardly feels that the eye of God reads all, marks all, condemns by his righteous law all, and because he is so intrinsically pure, hates and abhors all. Thus he proves, amongst the "all things" which are weighed up and measured in the inward court of conscience by the unerring standard of the word of truth, the light of the Spirit's teaching, and the workings of godly fear, that he is a sinner before God, and that of a deeper dye and more crimson hue than any other transgressor, for he sees and knows his own heart, which nobody else can see or know. He is indeed aware that many may have sinned more deeply and grossly as regards outward acts; but he feels that no one can have sinned inwardly more foully and continually than he; and this makes him say with Job, "I have heard of thee by the hearing of the ear; but now mine eye seeth thee: Wherefore I abhor myself and repent in dust and ashes" (Job 42. 5, 6).

October 26

"Let us hold fast the profession of our faith without wavering; for he is faithful that promised." – Hebrews 10. 23.

Faith cannot rest upon fancy; it can only rest upon the solid truth of God, as revealed in the Scriptures. And when it comes into the truth of God, as Noah's dove came into the ark as its own nest and home, then it finds rest and peace. Many persons think we build our faith and hope, not on the Scriptures, but on some mental feelings, or fancies of our own, distinct from the word of God. I do not and cannot build my faith on anything but what is revealed in the Bible; and I must do it because I have no other foothold for it to stand upon. Do you not feel the same, you who know anything of the trial of faith? You have had many a tossing up and down, and have often wanted a foothold for your faith to stand upon. You have tried to believe this or that doctrine, or to get into this or that experience; but you kept still falling short, for you found that your faith wanted something stronger than the testimony of men; you needed a solid foundation on which to build for eternity; for the things to be believed were so invisible and so mysterious, that nothing but the word of God could suffice for your faith to stand upon and rest in. When, then, in this trial of faith, the truth of God as it stands revealed in the Scriptures was applied to your heart by a divine power, then you found that there was a foothold for belief, and that your faith could then rest upon the inspired word of God, as a rock on which to build, for life and death, time and eternity. It was so with Abraham. When Abraham was looking forward to the birth of the promised seed, many a doubt or fear might have arisen in his mind as to whether he should have a son by Sarah. But he rested upon the word of promise, and thus obtained a foothold for his faith. As the Apostle speaks, "Who against hope believed in hope, that he might become the father of many nations, according to that which was spoken, So shall thy seed be" (Romans 4. 18). Our faith must in the same way rest on the word of promise, that "by two immutable things, in which it was impossible for God to lie, we might have a strong consolation, who have fled for refuge to lay hold upon the hope set before us."

October 27

"Peace, peace to him that is far off." – Isaiah 57. 19.

Far off! What means that? It means that the soul passing through that experience is separated, in its feelings, and at an infinite distance from God. Now this inward sense of being "far off" is one of the most painful feelings that a quickened soul can experience. The ungodly, who are really afar off, know nothing experimentally of distance from God, for they have never been brought spiritually near. They have felt no "cords of love, no bands of a man" drawing them with sweet attraction to the throne of the most High; they have never sighed after the sweet manifestations of God's mercy and love; but they live gladly, and wallow wilfully in those things which separate the soul from its Maker. But those who are "afar off" in their feelings, are such as have seen something of the beauty of the Lord, and felt the evil of sin, who spiritually know Jehovah's purity and the creature's impurity, and have experienced the inward curse, bondage, and condemnation of a holy law. A spiritual discovery of his purity and holiness, making manifest their own vileness, has thrust them down from their self-righteous or presumptuous standing, and made them far off from him; not daring to draw near, nor able to approach; not feeling any spiritual access, but sighing and mourning over their evil hearts in the wilderness, in desolate places; and unable to move a single step forward, because the Lord does not draw them by his smile. A man must know something experimentally of this before he is brought near. How can we know a feeling of nearness if we have not known a feeling of distance? How can we know what it is to be brought "from the end of the earth" (Psalm 61. 2) by the manifestation of God's mercy and love, unless we have been driven there, in our feelings, by some manifestation of the wrath of God against sin? But to see the blessed Lord, and not be able to draw near to him; to view his atoning blood at an infinite distance from us, his glorious righteousness almost out of sight, and his lovely Person out of the reach of our spiritual view, so as not to enjoy any access to these glorious realities – to know this experimentally and feelingly, is to be "far off" from God. And I believe that God's people know very much of this feeling. There is not much nearness in our day; not much dandling upon the knees, not much smiling upon the soul, not many love visits, nor love tokens communicated. There is, indeed, a great deal of talking about them; and there are abundance of people who profess to have them; but I fear they are, for the most part, cheats and counterfeits. The real people of God, the true-hearted family are, for the most part, "afar off upon the sea," for it is a dark and cloudy day in which we live.

October 28

"Wherein shall it be known that I and thy people have found grace in thy sight?" – Exodus 33. 16.

Grace is always *"found."* It is not earned, nor merited, nor worked into; but it is *found;* and if a man never "found" it, he never had it. It is stumbled upon, so to speak, as the Lord sets forth in the parable of the man who found the treasure hid in a field (Matt. 13. 44). The man was not thinking about the treasure. He was, we may suppose, ploughing in the field. He had no idea that there was gold beneath the clods. But he finds it all on a sudden, in the most unexpected and unlooked-for manner, and for joy thereof "goeth and selleth all that he hath, and buyeth that field." So it is with the way in which grace is found. It comes so suddenly, so unexpectedly, and so sweetly into a man's soul, that when it comes he is like a man who has found something which he had no conception of till he found it. He had no idea what it was, nor how it was to be got, nor whence it was to be had; but when it came into his heart he found that he had a treasure there. The treasure which the man found in the field was much sweeter to him, because unexpectedly found, than if he had earned it penny by penny. Its coming in so peculiar a way, from the surprise and joy produced, doubled and trebled the value of the money. Thus, when grace visits the earth in an unexpected moment, and drops down like the dew of heaven into the soul, it is valued much more than if laboriously earned penny by penny. The sweetness of the gift is doubled by its unexpectedness, and by its coming in such a marvellous and miraculous manner.

October 29

"A little that a righteous man hath is better than the riches of many wicked." – Psalm 37. 16.

Hard may be your lot here below, ye suffering saints of the most High, as regards external matters; painful may be the exercises through which you almost daily pass, through the rebellion and desperate wickedness of your carnal mind; grievous temptations may be your continual portion; many a pricking thorn and sharp brier may lie in your path; and so rough and rugged may be the road, that at times you may feel yourself of all men to be the most miserable; and so indeed you would be but for the grace of God in your heart now and the glory prepared for you beyond the grave. Yet with it all, were your afflictions and sorrows a thousand times heavier, well may it be said of you – "Happy, thrice happy, art thou, O Israel!" Whom upon earth need you envy if you have the grace of God in your heart? With whom would you change, if ever the love of God has visited your soul? Look around you; fix your eyes upon the man or woman who seems surrounded with the greatest amount of earthly happiness, and then ask your own conscience – "Would I change with thee, thou butterfly of fashion, or with thee, thou gilded dragon-fly, that merely livest thy little day; sunning thyself for a few hours beneath the summer sun, and then sinking into the dark and dismal pool which awaits thee at eventide?" Then with all your cares at home and abroad – with all your woes and trials, sunk under which you feel yourself at times one of the most miserable beings that can crawl along in this vale of tears – would you change with anybody, however healthy, or rich, or favoured with the largest amount of family prosperity, if at the same time destitute of the grace of God?

October 30

"Wherefore in all things it behoved him to be made like unto his brethren, that he might be a merciful and faithful high priest in things pertaining to God, to make reconciliation for the sins of the people." – Hebrews 2. 17.

What heart can conceive or tongue express the infinite depths of the Redeemer's condescension in thus being made like unto his brethren – that the Son of God should assume a finite nature, subject to the sinless infirmities necessarily connected with a time-state and a dwelling on earth; that he should leave the bosom of his Father in which he had lain before all worlds, and should consent to become a denizen of this world of tears; to breathe earthly air; to be an eye-witness of, and himself share in human sorrows; to have before his eyes the daily spectacle of human sins; to be banished so long from his native home; to endure hunger, weariness, and thirst; to be subject to the persecutions of men, the flight of all his disciples, and the treachery of one among them whose hand had been with him on the table; not to hide his face from shame and spitting, but to be mocked, struck, buffeted, and scourged, and at last to die an agonizing death between two malefactors, amid scorn and infamy, and covered, as men thought, with everlasting confusion and disgrace! O what infinite condescension and mercy are displayed in these sufferings and sorrows of an incarnate God! The Lord give us faith to look to him as suffering them for our sake!

October 31

"Seek meekness." – Zephaniah 2. 3.

How are we to follow after this grace of meekness? By learning the contrary. How often have we mistaken false fire for the light and fire of God's Spirit! and have contended more for our own views, in our own spirit, with many rash and unbecoming words, rather than for the glory of God. But after a time we are led to see that strife and contention, in our own spirit, are contrary to the spirit and temper of the gospel, and are brought to see what a blessed grace the spirit of meekness is. Nay, the very want of it, the risings up of an excited temper, the anger, strife, envy, and jealousy that often work in our bosoms convince us how little we know of "the meekness and gentleness of Christ." We thus feel what a blessing it is to be made humble and submissive; and how impossible it is to enter into communion with a broken-hearted Jesus, till the soul is in some measure meekened by his Spirit. But it is by having a succession of things to try and provoke us, that we learn whether we have meekness or not. The husband can be very meek, while his wife and children are doing everything to please him; but where is his meekness when they thwart and provoke him? The master may be very meek, while the servant is obedient, obliging, and attentive, but how is he when things are different? Thus the knowledge of the disease makes us desire the remedy; and by the wretched sensations caused by wrath and evil temper, we are brought to desire an experience of those sweet feelings which gospel meekness produces in our consciences.

November 1

"Father, I will that they also, whom thou hast given me, be with me where I am; that they may behold my glory, which thou hast given me; for thou lovedst me before the foundation of the world." – John 17. 24.

Nothing short of the revelation and communication of this glory could satisfy the heart of God; and nothing short of the partaking of this glory can satisfy the heart of man. Heaven short of this would be no heaven to his soul. Not to see the glory of God in the face of Jesus Christ; to have no view of the glory of an incarnate God; not to be conformed to his glorious image, so as to be perfectly holy both in body and soul – were these things denied, there would be no heaven at all for the redeemed among the children of men. But God, in giving the saints heaven as their happy home, gave them with it an eternal weight of glory. He has designed that all whom he has chosen unto salvation should reach the heavenly shore; that none should suffer shipwreck by the way; that sin should not be their ruin; that Satan should not succeed in any of his devices against their eternal safety; but that every member of the mystical body of Christ should be for ever with their glorious Head in the realms of bliss, to behold and to be partakers of the glory which shall be revealed when he comes and all his saints with him. It is the prospect of this glory which animates the Christian in all his battles against sin, and encourages him never to quit the field until victory crown the strife. It nerves his heart in all the troubles and trials of this mortal state, still to press forward to win this immortal prize, that he may safely reach that land where tears are wiped from off all faces, and where the glory of God the Father, God the Son, and God the Holy Ghost will be seen and enjoyed through the glorified humanity of Jesus without a cloud to dim its rays, or intercept its eternal lustre.

November 2

"I will cry unto God most High; unto God that performeth all things for me." – Psalm 57. 2.

In the word "most High," there is something to my mind very expressive. It is to "God most High" that prayers go up from broken hearts, in all parts of the world where the Lord has a quickened people. "Unto God most High" every eye is pointed, every heart is fixed, and every breath of living prayer flows. Jesus sits in glory as "God most High," hearing the sighs and cries of his broken-hearted family, where they dwell in the utmost corners of the earth; and he is not only sitting on high to hear their cries, but also to bestow upon them the blessings which he sees suitable to their case and state. Now when shall we thus come "unto God most High?" When we are pleased and satisfied in self? when the world smiles? when all things are easy without and within? when we are in circumstances for which our own wisdom, strength, and righteousness are amply sufficient? We may, under such circumstances, appease our conscience by prayer, or rather its form; but there is no cry "unto God most High." Before there is a real, spiritual cry raised up, we must be brought to that spot, "Refuge failed me; no man cared for my soul" (Psalm 142. 4). Here all the saints of old were brought; Job upon his dunghill, Hezekiah upon his bed, Hannah by the temple gate. All were hopeless, helpless, houseless, refugeless, before they cried "unto God most High." And we must be equally refugeless and houseless before we can utter the same cry, or our prayers find entrance into the ears of the Lord of Sabaoth. "Unto God that performeth *all* things for me." If God did not perform something for us; nay more, if God did not perform *all* things for us, it would be a mockery, a delusion to pray to him at all. "The Hope of Israel" would then be to us a dumb idol, like Ashtaroth or Baal, who could not hear the cries of his lancet-cutting worshippers, because he was hunting or asleep, and needed to be awakened. But the God of Israel is not like these dumb idols, these dunghill gods, the work of men's hands, the figments of superstition and ignorance; but the eternal Jehovah, who ever lives to hear and answer the prayers that his people offer up.

November 3

"O Ephraim, what shall I do unto thee?" – Hosea 6. 4.

Most of the Lord's people have some peculiar thing that they want to have granted. Most living souls have some peculiar temptation from which they want to be delivered. If some of the Lord's family could sum up all their desires in one petition, it would be to *have the pardon of their sins sealed upon the conscience.* If others of God's people could crowd up in one sentence all the wants of their soul, it would be *to be brought into the enjoyment of gospel liberty.* If others could condense in one short prayer the chief desire of their heart, it would be *to be delivered from some powerful temptation, or be preserved from some peculiar besetment.* And if others could get into one request the longings that heave in their bosom, it would be *to be relieved from some special trial or trouble* that at times seems as though it would weigh them down to the dust. When the Lord, then, does but enable them to come before him and tell him what is working in their hearts, it is as though he said, 'Be not afraid to tell me: I know it already: I have the power to grant thy request: I have the will to bestow the desired answer. "What shall I do unto thee?" Tell me what it is!' The Lord encourages and enables every one that he thus draws near to himself to tell him what he most needs; and when he is enabled to lay it before his throne, it is half answered. The needed blessing is on its way: like Gabriel, it has left the palace, and is speeding its course to the soul.

November 4

"He raiseth up the poor out of the dust, and lifteth up the beggar from the dunghill, to set them among princes, and to make them inherit the throne of glory." – 1 Samuel 2. 8.

A man can never reach heaven unless he travel heavenwards, Zionwards, in the way that God has marked out for his people to walk in. It is a delusion to think that we are going to heaven unless we know something of divine teaching in the soul. But if we know anything of divine teaching, we know what it is to be poor and needy, we know what it is, more or less, to have our mouth in the dust. But many people do so mistake the way to heaven. The ordinary way is to set up a ladder to reach from earth to heaven, and progressively clambering up the different rounds, at last to climb up into the abode of God. But that is not the way of God's people. They have to go down, down, down, that they may be raised up. It is not with them first "up, up, up," to scale the battlements of heaven. Every such step upwards in self is in reality only a step downwards; but, on the other hand, every step downwards in self, downwards into the depths of poverty, downwards into felt misery, downwards into soul-trouble and the real groanings of a broken heart – every such step downwards in self is, in fact, a step upwards in Christ. Until we get to the very bottom there is no promise. "He raiseth up the poor *out of* the dust." But how? He does it in a moment. The Lord does not raise up his people round by round, enabling them to clamber and crawl with their hands and feet to him. But, when he lifts up the poor out of the dust, he gives them a smile which reaches, so to speak, to the very bottom of their hearts; and that smile has such a miraculous power, such a drawing efficacy, that it lifts them in a moment out of the dust into the very bosom of God. When, therefore, the Lord raises up the poor out of the dust, he does not lift them up by a gradual process, step by step as they went down. They were, perhaps, many years going down; but they are raised up in a moment. The God of all grace, by one word, or by one smile, lifts them up in a moment out of the lowest depths of felt degradation, "sets them among princes, and makes them inherit the throne of glory."

November 5

"Jesus answered and said unto him, If a man love me, he will keep my words: and my Father will love him, and we will come unto him, and make our abode with him." – John 14. 23.

There are two grand vital points that every Christian should seek to be established in. The first is, – Is he a believer in Christ? Has the blessed Spirit made Christ known to his soul? Has he embraced Jesus in the arms of living faith? The second point which he should seek to have established in his soul is, – Does he abide in Christ? This he may know by having some testimony that Christ abides in him, and produces the fruits that flow out of this inward abiding. If Christ abide in him, his heart will not be like the nether millstone. He cannot rush greedily into sin; he will not love the world, and the things of time and sense; he cannot happily love idols, or do those things which ungodly professors do without one check or pang. Jesus in the soul is a guest that will make himself known; yea, abiding there, he is King therein. He is Ruler in Zion, and when he comes into the heart, he comes as King. Being, therefore, its rightful Sovereign, he sways the faculties of the soul, and makes it obedient to his sceptre; for "thy people shall be willing in the day of thy power" (Psalm 110. 3). "O Lord our God, other lords beside thee have had dominion over us: but by thee only will we make mention of thy name" (Isaiah 26. 13).

November 6

"Who is a God like unto thee, that pardoneth iniquity, and passeth by the transgression of the remnant of his heritage? he retaineth not his anger for ever, because he delighteth in mercy." – Micah 7. 18.

God delighteth in mercy. It is not drawn from him unwillingly; it is not forced out of him even by importunity; it is not dragged out of his heart by the cries of his family; but he delights in it as being his darling attribute, the very pleasure of God being in showing mercy to the miserable. How hard it is for us to believe this until mercy visits the soul and a sweet sense of it is felt in the conscience. How we represent to ourselves God in his anger, in his justice, in his terrible displeasure against sin and sinners; how unable to believe that there is mercy for us, and that he delights in manifesting mercy to poor miserable, penitent sinners. Whoever would have thought of mercy unless it had first been in the bosom of God? Who could have ventured to entertain or suggest such a thought, that there is forgiveness with God; that he can pardon iniquity, and transgression, and sin; that he can cast all our sins behind his back, and blot them out as a cloud, yea, as a thick cloud? This is what God has revealed of himself in his word, but it is only as mercy visits the troubled breast, and God displays his goodness and love in the revelation of his dear Son, that we can rise up into any sweet apprehension of what his mercy really is, and rejoice in it not only as suitable but as saving.

November 7

"For this purpose the Son of God was manifested, that he might destroy the works of the devil." – 1 John 3. 8.

There will be no thorough destruction of sin within until the body drops into the grave, and the soul mounts aloft to be with the Lord; nor a full destruction of its effects in the body until the resurrection morn, when the body shall be raised from the sleeping dust and changed into the glorious image of the body of the Son of God, meet companion for the immortal soul. Then will the victory be complete; then will Christ appear, shining forth with the lustre of a million suns; then will be the glorious manifestation of the Son of God, and the works of the devil thoroughly destroyed. The burden of heaven's anthem, the grand theme of eternal adoration, will be the manifestation of the Son of God to destroy the works of the devil. The redeemed will look down from the battlements of heaven and see what works have been executed by the devil; they will see millions of fellow-beings consigned to eternal misery, weltering in hell, whilst they view themselves safe in the arms of eternal love. They will see the Son of God, without a veil between, manifested to their eyes in such heart-ravishing glory as the three disciples had but a feeble, dim view of on the Mount of Transfiguration. It will be their joy to see him as he is. He will always wear his human nature; he will never lay that aside. That will always shine resplendent with all the glory of Godhead; that will be the object of eternal admiration and love; and to that glory of the God-man all the saints in bliss will be for ever looking and for ever adoring, for sin will no longer have a being in them, but they will be conformed to the glorified image of the Son of God, and be celebrating for ever the grand triumph of the cross.

November 8

"Judgment also will I lay to the line, and righteousness to the plummet: and the hail shall sweep away the refuge of lies, and the waters shall overflow the hiding place." – Isaiah 28. 17.

Wherever God the Holy Ghost begins and carries on a work of grace in the heart, he will weigh up, and mete out, from time to time, all a man's religion and try every inch of the way whether it lies straight and level with the word and will of God. Depend upon it the Lord who "weigheth the spirits" (Prov. 16. 2), and by whom "actions are weighed" (1 Sam. 2. 3), will put into his righteous and unerring scales both nature and grace, both human and divine teaching, and make us know which is full weight in heaven's court. The religion of the present day is too much to confuse everything of an experimental nature; to cover and obscure the work of grace in the heart. But there can be no question that God will never suffer our religion, if, indeed, he has mercifully taken us in hand, to be huddled up in this confused way; but he will measure it all by his standard, and refine it in his crucible. It is in this way that we learn the reality and genuineness of his work. Thus, if he give faith, he will bring that faith to the touchstone, and prove it with heavy trials. It is in grace as in nature. When we would ascertain the exact weight of a thing, we put it into one scale, and a standard weight into the other, till the scales are even. So when the Lord puts faith in one scale, he puts a burden in the other to try whether it is standard weight. And the greater the faith the heavier the trial. The father of the faithful had to slay his own son. If he communicate a measure of hope, there will be many things that cause despondency to be put into the opposite scale, that despondency and hope may be well balanced. If the love of God be shed abroad in the soul, there will be trials and temptations to prove it. Thus the child of God learns the meaning of the words – "The work of faith, and labour of love, and patience of hope" (1 Thess. 1. 3). Every token for good, every sip of mercy, every manifestation of love is examined and searched into, weighed up and balanced in the court of conscience, to know whether it is full weight or not. And in this nice and accurate scrutiny not only is religion weighed up, but also that which is *not* religion. Sins, open and secret, backslidings, idolatrous affections, covetous desires, presumptuous confidences, rotten hopes, and vain props – all are weighed up in the balances of the sanctuary. And as that which is received from God, when put into the balances, will be found sterling and genuine; so all that did not come from God, all that sprang from nature and the flesh, all vain confidence, bold claims, and presumptuous notions, when put into the scales, will have *tekel* stamped upon them – "Weighed in the balances, and found wanting."

November 9

"Accepted in the beloved." – Ephesians 1. 6.

We are ever looking for something in self to make ourselves acceptable to God, and are often sadly cast down and discouraged when we cannot find that holiness, that obedience, that calm submission to the will of God, that serenity of soul, that spirituality and heavenly-mindedness which we believe to be acceptable in his sight. Our crooked tempers, fretful, peevish minds, rebellious thoughts, coldness, barrenness and death, our alienation from good, and headlong proneness to ill, with the daily feeling that we get no better but rather worse, make us think that God views us just as we view ourselves. And this brings on great darkness of mind and bondage of spirit, till we seem to lose sight of our acceptance in Christ, and get into the miserable dregs of self, almost ready to quarrel with God because we are so vile, and only get worse as we get older. Now the more we get into these dregs of self, and the more we keep looking at the dreadful scenes of wreck and ruin which our heart presents to daily view, the farther do we get from the grace of the gospel, and the more do we lose sight of the only ground of our acceptance with God. It is "in the Beloved" that we are accepted, and not for any good words, or good works, good thoughts, good hearts, or good intentions of our own. And a saving knowledge of our acceptance "in the Beloved," independent of everything in us good or bad, is a firm foundation for our faith and hope, and will keep us from sinking altogether into despair.

November 10

"Ye also, as lively stones, are built up a spiritual house, an holy priesthood, to offer up spiritual sacrifices, acceptable to God by Jesus Christ." – 1 Peter 2. 5.

God's people require many severe afflictions, harassing temptations, and many powerful exercises to hew them into anything like shape, to chisel them into any conformity to Christ's image. For they are not like the passive marble under the hands of the sculptor, which will submit without murmuring, and indeed without feeling, to have this corner chipped off, and that projecting angle rounded by the chisel; but God's people are living stones, and, therefore, feel every stroke. We are so tender-skinned that we cannot bear a thread of trouble to lie upon us, we shrink from even the touch of the probe. To be hewed, then, and squared, and chiselled by the hand of God into such shapes and forms as please him, O what painful work it is! But could the pillar know, could it tell what the sculptor was doing, would it not see that not a single stroke was made in vain? The sculptor, we know, must not make a single hair's breadth too little or too much in some parts of the marble, or he will spoil the statue. He knows perfectly well where to place the chisel, and in what direction, and with what force to strike it with the mallet. And does not God, who fixes the spiritual pillars each in its destined spot, that they may be "as corner stones, polished after the similitude of a palace" (Ps. 144. 12), know where to inflict the stroke, what carnal projection to chip off, and how to chisel the whole column, from the base to the capital, so that it shall wear the very shape and the very same proportion which he designs that it should wear? If the Lord, then, is at work upon our souls, we have not had, we are not now having, we shall never have, one stroke too much, one stroke too little, one stroke in the wrong direction, but there shall be just sufficient to work in us that which is pleasing in God's sight, and to make us that which he would have us to be. What a great deal of trouble should we be spared if we could only patiently submit to the Lord's afflicting stroke and know no will but his.

November 11

"Except a man be born again, he cannot see the kingdom of God." – John 3. 3.

True religion begins with an entrance into the soul of supernatural light and supernatural life. How or why it comes the soul knows not; for "the wind bloweth where it listeth, and thou hearest the sound thereof, but canst not tell whence it cometh, or whither it goeth, so is every one that is born of the Spirit." The wind itself is not seen, but its effects are felt. The sound of a going is heard in the tops of the mulberry trees, where God himself is not seen. The voice of the Lord, powerful and full of majesty, was heard by those who saw no similitude (Deut. 4. 12). Thus effects are felt, though causes are unknown. Streams flow into the heart from a hidden source; rays of light beam into the soul from an unrisen sun; and kindlings of life awake in us a new existence out of an unseen fountain. The new-born babe feels life in all its limbs, though it knows not yet the earthly father whence that natural life sprang. And thus new-born souls are conscious of feelings hitherto unpossessed, and are sensible of a tide of life, mysterious and incomprehensible, ebbing and flowing in their heart, though "Abba, Father," has not yet burst from their lips. A man's body is alive to every feeling, from a pin's scratch to a mortal wound, from a passing ache to an incurable disease. The heart cannot flutter or intermit for a single second its wonted stroke, without a peculiar sensation that accompanies it, notices it, and registers it. Shall feelings, then, be the mark and evidence of natural life, and not of spiritual? Shall our ignoble part, the creature of a day, our perishing body, our dust of dust, have sensations to register every pain and every pleasure, and be tremblingly alive to every change without and every change within; and shall not our immortal souls be equally endowed with a similar barometer to fluctuate up and down the scale of spiritual life? We must lay it down, then, at the very threshold of vital godliness, that if a man has not been conscious of new feelings, and cannot point out, with more or less precision, some particular period, some never-to-be-forgotten season, when these feelings came unbidden into his heart, he has not yet passed from death unto life. He is not in Christ, if he is not a new creature (2 Cor. 5. 17).

November 12

"He that spared not his own Son, but delivered him up for us all, how shall he not with him also freely give us all things?" – Romans 8. 32.

I have thought sometimes of the sweet figure of Solomon, as a type of Christ, in his royal munificence to the queen of Sheba. We read of him that he "gave unto the queen of Sheba all her desire, whatsoever she asked, beside that which Solomon gave her of his royal bounty." (1 Kin. 10. 13) So our Royal Benefactor gives more to the sons of men than is in their heart to ask for. And what he gives, he gives freely, out of his royal bounty. As freely as the rain drops from the sky; as freely as the sun casts forth his glorious beams and ripens the fruits of the field; as freely as the wind courses over the earth; as freely as the dew drops upon the morning grass; so free are the gifts of God to his Church and people. Indeed, in giving Christ, God gave everything. The Apostle declares, he "hath blessed us with *all* spiritual blessings in heavenly places in Christ." We must never look upon spiritual blessings as broken fragments of the love of God, mere shreds and patches, scattered crumbs, waifs and strays, like floating pieces of some shipwrecked vessel; but we must look on the blessings of the gospel as all stored up in Christ our covenant Head. Whatever is given, is given out of Christ, in whom it hath pleased the Father that all fulness should dwell; and it is by virtue of union to him, and out of his fulness, that all these blessings are received. How can we lift up our thoughts – how raise up our hearts – adequately to conceive of the gift of God's only-begotten Son – his eternal Son – the Son of the Father in truth and love – given out of the bosom of God that he might become incarnate, suffer, bleed, and die; and by a suffering life and meritorious death offer a sacrifice acceptable to God, a sacrifice whereby the sins of God's people were for ever put away? The grand source of all the admiration and adoration and the eternal blessedness of the saints, will be the holy enjoyment of the mystery of an incarnate God. The incarnation of the second Person in the glorious Trinity – the eternal Son of the eternal Father – his taking human nature into union with his own divine Person – will be the mystery that will ravish the hearts and fill the lips of God's saints with an endless theme of admiration and joy through the countless ages of eternity.

November 13

"Unto thee lift I up mine eyes, O thou that dwellest in the heavens." – Psalm 123. 1.

O how simple, suitable, complete, and blessed a remedy is this for all our distresses, when the Lord is pleased to open our eyes, and fix them on himself. He must do it all. If the eyes are to be upon him, he must first give us eyes; if lifted upon him, he must raise them upwards; if kept upon him, he must hold them waking. It is good to be in this spot. There are times and seasons, perhaps, when we seem to have no religion whatever; when we look, and look, and look, and cannot find a grain. Where is our spirituality? where our heavenly affections? where our prayerfulness of spirit? where our tenderness of conscience? where our godly fear? where our meditations upon God's word? We look, and look, and look – they seem gone. Now, perhaps, in the midst of this uncertainty we are brought into some painful exercise, some affliction, some temptation, some apprehension, something that lies with weight and power upon the soul. Now is the time we want our religion. But it is gone, it is gone, leaving us empty, needy, naked, and bare; religion, as regards its blessedness and comfort, we seem to have none. This is emptying work; this is stripping the soul as it were to the very bone. But what a preparation to receive the religion which is from above!

How the vessel must be emptied of the dirty water of creature religion, well rinsed, and washed out, to have the pure water of heavenly religion communicated from the divine fountain. God never mingles the pure stream of heavenly religion with the dirty, filthy water of our own creature religion. We must be emptied of every drop, so to speak, of our natural religion, to have the holy and spiritual religion, which is from above, poured into the soul. But to look, and look, and look, and find nothing but emptiness, nakedness, barrenness, and destitution – to have a "great company" of enemies all coming against us, and we as weak as water – what an emptying for divine filling, what a stripping for divine clothing, and what a bringing down of self for the raising up of Christ. True religion consists mainly in two points – to be emptied, stripped, made naked and bare; and then to be clothed and filled out of Christ's fulness.

November 14

"And he said unto them, Unto you it is given to know the mystery of the kingdom of God; but unto them that are without, all these things are done in parables." – Mark 4. 11.

By "the kingdom of God" is meant the same thing as "the kingdom of heaven," that is, the internal kingdom set up in the heart by the power of the Spirit – that kingdom which shall stand for ever and ever, and last when time shall be no more. This the Lord calls a mystery. And if it is a mystery, it will have these three marks; it will be beyond nature, sense, and reason, will be hidden from the wise and prudent, and will be revealed unto babes. Let us see if we can find these marks belonging to the kingdom of heaven set up in the heart. It certainly is above nature, sense, and reason, that God should dwell in a man's heart, as the Apostle says, "Christ in you, the hope of glory" and again, "Ye are the temple of the living God; as God hath said, I will dwell in them, and walk in them" (2 Cor. 6. 16). That God should take up his abode in a man's heart; that Christ should be in a man; and the Holy Ghost should make the body of his saints his temple; how can nature, sense, and reason understand such a mystery as this? When one of the ancient martyrs, I think it was Polycarp, was brought before Trajan, when the Emperor asked him his name, he answered, "I am Polycarp, the God-bearer, for I carry God in me!" At this answer the Emperor laughed, and said, "Let him be thrown to the wild beasts." That was the only answer a persecuting tyrant could give. That a man frail and feeble, whom a lion could tear to pieces in a few moments, carried God in his bosom! – how could the wise and prudent Trajan believe a thing so unheard of? Yet it is a mystery revealed to babes; for they receive it in the love of it under divine teaching, as one of the mysteries that God the Spirit makes known in the heart.

November 15

"But the dove found no rest for the sole of her foot, and she returned unto him into the ark." – Genesis 8. 9.

What a restless being is a tempted child of God! How unable he often is even to rest locally, to take his chair, and sit quietly by his fireside! Like Noah's dove, he can find no rest for the sole of his foot on the floating carcases of a ruined world.

It is recorded of the prisoners, who in the first French revolution were awaiting in their dungeons the summons to the dread tribunal of blood, that some passed nearly the whole of their time in walking up and down their cells. So sometimes under trials and temptations, we pace up and down the room as if we sought to dissipate the exercise of our minds by the exercise of our bodies; or rush into the streets and fields to pour out the heart in sighs and groans, the restless mind acting and reacting upon the body. And as an exercised child of God often cannot rest locally, so cannot he rest spiritually. He cannot rest in his own righteousness, nor in a sound creed, nor in a form of godliness, nor in the opinions of men, nor in anything that springs from or centres in the creature. There is always something uneasy, either in himself or in the ground on which he would repose. Sometimes it is strewed with thorns and briers; sometimes beset with sharp and rugged rocks. And yet, but for these restless, uneasy feelings, how many even of the Lord's own family would settle down short of gospel rest! Some would settle down in false religion; others in the world; some would make a god of their own righteousness; and others, like the foolish virgins, would securely sleep whilst their lamp was burning out. But there is that restless, painful exercise where the life and grace of God are, that the soul cannot, if it would, settle down in any rest but that of God's own providing. "There remaineth therefore a rest to the people of God." That rest is Christ; the blood, righteousness, love, and grace of the Lamb of God.

November 16

"They wandered in the wilderness in a solitary way; they found no city to dwell in." – Psalm 107. 4.

They wandered in the wilderness *in a solitary way;* – a way not tracked; a path in which each has to walk alone; a road where no company cheers him, and without landmarks to direct his course. This is a mark peculiar to the child of God – that the path by which he travels is, in his own feelings, a solitary way. This much increases his exercises, that they appear peculiar to himself. His perplexities are such as he cannot believe any living soul is exercised with; the fiery darts which are cast into his mind by the wicked one are such as he thinks no child of God has ever experienced; the darkness of his soul, the unbelief and infidelity of his heart, and the workings of his powerful corruptions, are such as he supposes none ever knew but himself. To be without any comfort except what God gives, without any guidance but what the Lord affords, without any support but what springs from the everlasting arms laid underneath; in a word, to be in that state where the Lord alone must appear, and where he alone can deliver, is very painful. But it is the very painful nature of the path that makes it so profitable. We need to be cut off from resting upon an arm of flesh; to be completely divorced from all props to support our souls, except that Almighty prop which cannot fail. And the Lord will take care that his people shall deal only with himself; that they shall have no real comfort but that which springs from his presence, and no solid testimonies but those which are breathed into their conscience from his own lips. His object is to draw us away from the creature; to take us off from leaning on human pity and compassion; and to bring us to trust implicitly on himself, "whose compassions fail not," – to lean wholly and solely upon him, who is "very pitiful, and of tender mercy."

November 17

"Hungry and thirsty, their soul fainted in them. Then they cried unto the Lord in their trouble, and he delivered them out of their distresses." – Psalm 107. 5, 6.

Until they wandered in the wilderness – until they felt it to be a solitary way, until they found no city to dwell in, until hungry and thirsty their soul fainted in them – there was no cry. There might have been prayer, a desire, a feeble wish, and now and then a sigh or a groan. But this was not enough. Something more was wanted to draw forth lovingkindness out of the bosom of the compassionate Head of the Church. A cry was wanted, – a cry of distress, a cry of soul trouble, a cry forced out of their hearts by heavy burdens. And a *cry* implies necessity, urgent want, a perishing without an answer to the cry. It is the breath of a soul bent upon having eternal realities brought into the conscience, or perishing without them. It is this solemn feeling in the heart that there is no other refuge but God. The Lord brings all his people here – to have no other refuge but himself. Friends, counsellors, acquaintance – these may sympathise, but they cannot afford relief. There is no refuge, nor shelter, nor harbour, nor home into which they can fly, except the Lord. Thus troubles bring us to deal with God in a personal manner. They chase away that half-hearted religion of which we have so much; and they drive out that notional experience and dry profession that we are so often satisfied with. They chase them away as a strong north wind chases away the mists; and they bring a man to this solemn spot that he must have communications from God to support him under, and bring him out of his trouble; and if a man is not brought to this point by his troubles, they have done him no good. But what a mercy it is when there is a cry! and when the Lord sends a cry in the trouble, he is sure in his own time and way to send deliverance out of it.

November 18

"And he led them forth by the right way, that they might go to a city of habitation." – Psalm 107. 7.

He *led them forth.* Forth out of the world – forth out of sin – forth out of a profession – forth out of a name to live – forth out of everything hateful to his holy and pure eyes.

"To go to a city of habitation." They had no city to dwell in here below; but they were journeying to a city of habitation above, whose walls and bulwarks are

salvation, and whose gates are praise; where there are eternal realities to be enjoyed by the soul; where there is something stable and eternal; something to satisfy all the wants of a capacious and immortal spirit, and give it that rest which it never could find while wandering here below. If we have a city here, we want no city above; and if we have a city above, we want no city here.

This then must be our state and case; either to be pilgrims, journeying onwards, through troubles, to things above, or taking up our abode below; seeking heaven here, or heaven hereafter; resting upon the world, or resting upon the Lord; panting after the things of time, or panting after the things of eternity; satisfied in self, or satisfied only in Christ. One of the two must be our state and case. The Lord decide it clearly in the hearts of his people that they are on his side; and give us to know and feel that our very restlessness and inability to find food and shelter in the things of time and sense, are leading us more earnestly and believingly to seek after the things that have reality in them; that finding no city to dwell in here below, we may press forward to be manifestly enjoying testimonies of being citizens of that city which is above, "which hath foundations, whose builder and maker is God!"

November 19

"Underneath are the everlasting arms." – Deuteronomy 33. 27.

The "everlasting arms" of the Father, Son, and Holy Ghost, the divine Jehovah, are "underneath" every one of his people, and, being underneath them, they can neither fall through them nor out of them; but they are borne, and supported, and carried along by them until they are brought to the eternal enjoyment of a Three-One God. Now, if these "everlasting arms" were not underneath a man, so deceitful is his heart, so desperately wicked is his corrupt nature, such awful stratagems does Satan lay for his feet, and such numerous perils encompass every step, that he must infallibly perish. But what we want to *feel* is, that these arms *are* underneath us. What good will the doctrine do us? The doctrine of the "everlasting arms" being underneath us will not satisfy our souls, if we feel that we are sinking fathoms. If we keep sinking, sinking, sinking, and are afraid, at times, that we shall sink at last into hell, the bare doctrine that the "everlasting arms" are underneath God's people will not satisfy us; but we want to *feel them under us,* so that we can rest upon them, and enjoy a blessed support in them and coming out of them. How secure the babe lies in its mother's arms as long as it *can feel* the arms touching and supporting its body; but let the mother withdraw the arm, the babe is in fear; it cries out in alarm; but so long as it feels the pressure of the mother's arms, it sleeps on calm and secure. So with living souls; if they cannot find the "everlasting arms" underneath them, they cannot rest in the mere doctrine of God's upholding the Church; but when they can feel a support given; when in trouble, in affliction, in sorrow, in temptation, there is a sensible leaning upon the everlasting arms, and a sensible support communicated by them, then they can rest calmly and contentedly upon them.

November 20

"The Lord knoweth how to deliver the godly out of temptations." – 2 Peter 2. 9.

Few will sincerely and spiritually go to the Lord, and cry from their hearts to be delivered from the power of a temptation, until it presses so weightily upon their conscience, and lies so heavy a burden upon their soul, that none but God can remove it. But when we really feel the burden of a temptation; when, though our flesh may love it, our spirit hates it; when, though there may be in our carnal mind a cleaving to it, our conscience bleeds under it, and we are brought spiritually to loathe it and to loathe ourselves for it; when we are enabled to go to the Lord in real sincerity of soul and honesty of heart, beseeching him to deliver us from it, I believe, that the Lord will, sooner or later, either remove that temptation entirely in his providence or by his grace, or so weaken its power that it shall cease to be what it was before, drawing our feet into paths of darkness and evil. As long, however, as we are in that state of which the prophet speaks, "Their heart is divided; now shall they be found faulty" (Hosea 10. 2); as long as we are in that carnal, wavering mind, which James describes, "A double-minded man is unstable in all his ways"; as long as we are hankering after the temptation, casting longing, lingering side glances after it, rolling it as a sweet morsel under our tongue, and though conscience may testify against it, yet not willing to have it taken away, there is no hearty cry, nor sigh, nor spiritual breathing of our soul, that God would remove it from us. But when we are brought, as in the presence of a heart-searching God, to hate the evil to which we are tempted, and cry to him that he would, for his honour and for our soul's good, take the temptation away, or dull and deaden its power; sooner or later the Lord will hear the cry of those who groan to be delivered from those temptations, which are so powerfully pressing them down to the dust.

November 21

"That he would grant unto us, that we being delivered out of the hand of our enemies might serve him without fear, in holiness and righteousness before him, all the days of our life." – Luke 1. 74, 75.

Holiness consists mainly of two points: 1. being made a partaker of the spirit of holiness whereby, as born of God, we are made meet to be partakers of the inheritance of the saints in light; set our affections on things above, where Christ sitteth on the right hand of God; have our conversation in heaven; put on the new man which is renewed in knowledge after the image of him which created him; live a life of faith in the Son of God, and beholding, as in a glass, the glory of the Lord, are changed into the same image from glory to glory, even as by the Spirit of the Lord. To be thus spiritually-minded, to be thus brought near unto God through his dear Son, to walk before him in the light of his countenance, and to know something of spiritual communion with the Lord of life and glory as sitting on his mercy-seat in the fulness of his risen power, and in the heights, depths, lengths, and breadths of his dying love – this to taste, to handle, to experience, and to enjoy is to be made a partaker of true holiness, and to be sanctified by the Spirit of God as an indwelling Teacher, Guide, Advocate, and Comforter. And if we know nothing of these things, at least in some small measure, or are not looking after and longing for them to be brought into our heart by a divine power, we give but little evidence that the grace of God has reached our heart and renewed us in the spirit of our mind.

2. The second branch of holiness is a life, conduct, and conversation agreeable to the precepts of the gospel; and the one springs out of the other. "Make the tree good," said our blessed Lord, "and his fruit good, for the tree is known by his fruit." Gospel fruit must grow upon a

gospel tree, and thus the fruits of a holy and godly life must spring out of those divine operations of the Holy Ghost upon the heart of which we have just spoken. Thus to speak, live, and act is to be "holy in all manner of conversation," that is in our daily walk; and is a fulfilling of the precept which God gave of old to his typical people Israel, and quoted in the New Testament to show that it is spiritually fulfilled in that peculiar people whom he calls by his distinguishing grace under the gospel.

November 22

"By his knowledge the depths are broken up, and the clouds drop down the dew." – Proverbs 3. 20.

When the Lord said, "Let there be light", instantly there was light. So when the Lord says, "Let the earth open", (Isa. 45. 8) the heart immediately opens, the conscience is made tender, and the soul hears and receives what God speaks. And what follows this opening? The heart receives the dews and showers of God's grace that fall into it; and these dews and showers of God's grace communicate to it softness, fertility, and productiveness. O how we have to learn this by painful experience! Is not our heart as hard sometimes as the nether millstone; and to our feelings, utterly destitute of light, life and power, without one grain of brokenness, contrition, godly sorrow, spiritual desire, or fervent breathing after the Lord? This painful experience the Lord's people have to pass through perpetually, that they may know that "in them, that is, in their flesh dwelleth no good thing" and that "power belongeth unto God." Could I make my own heart soft, should I want the Lord to do it for me? Could I communicate fertility to my own soul, should I ever pant after the dews and showers of the Holy Ghost? Could I bring pardon and peace into my own con-science, should I need the Lord himself to speak with power? Could I believe, hope, rejoice, and have at my own command every gracious and blessed feeling that I desire to experience, there would be no pleading the Lord's own promises, no wrestling in importunate prayer, no taking the kingdom of God by violence, no longing and panting for the Lord to appear in our souls. The Lord therefore sees fit that we should walk in these paths, that we may know, "it is not of him that willeth, nor of him that runneth, but of God that sheweth mercy."

November 23

"Blessed is the man whom thou chastenest, O Lord, and teachest him out of thy law." – Psalm 94. 12.

We may observe in the words before us, that the Lord puts *chastening* before *teaching*. Is there not something remarkable in this? Why should chastening precede teaching? For this reason. We have no ear to hear except so far as we are chastened. It was so with the prodigal. Until he was brought to his right mind by strokes of hunger, he did not think of his father's house; he had no heart to return; but a mighty famine sent him home. So it is with God's children; as long as they are allowed to wander in their backslidings, they have no heart to return. But let the rod come; let them be driven home by stripes; then they have an ear to listen, while God teaches them to profit, instructs them by his blessed Spirit, and speaks into their heart those lessons which are for their eternal good.

"And teachest him out of thy law." "The law" in the Scriptures has a very wide signification; it means, in the original, *instruction*. The word is *Torah,* which signifies "teaching," or "direction." Thus the word "law" is not confined to the law of Moses given in thunder and lightning upon Mount Sinai; but it includes also the gospel of the Lord Jesus Christ – "the perfect law of liberty"; "the law of the spirit of life in Christ Jesus"; that law which was in the heart of the Redeemer, when he said, "I come to do thy will, O God; yea, thy law is within my heart."

Now, as the Lord teaches his children "out of the law", strictly so called, so he teaches them "out of" the gospel; and to my mind, there is something exceedingly sweet and expressive in the words *"out of* the law." It seems to convey, not only that the law is a treasure-house of wrath, but that the gospel also is a treasure-house of mercy. And as those who know most of the law are only taught "out of the law", and not the whole of the law, only a few drops, as it were, out of the inexhaustible wrath of God; so out of the heavenly treasure-house of the gospel, "the perfect law of liberty", it is but a little of grace and mercy that in this life can be known. As Christ said to his disciples in promising the Spirit: "He shall take *of mine,* and shall shew it unto you." He cannot take "all", and show it unto them; for none could live under the sight. The Spirit, therefore, takes *of* the things of Christ, and shows here a little, and there a little; some little blessedness here, and some little blessedness there; a suitable promise, a gracious testimony, a comforting text, an encouraging word, a sight of atoning blood, a smile of his countenance, a view of his Person, a discovery of his righteousness, or a glimpse of his love. This is taking of the things of Christ, and revealing them to the soul. And thus, the man whom the Lord takes in hand, he teaches "out of" the gospel by making Christ experimentally known, and revealing his dying love. And thus he teaches each and all "out of his law" - both the law from Sinai, and the law from Zion.

November 24

"And he said unto them, I beheld Satan as lightning fall from heaven." – Luke 10. 18.

It deserves our utmost attention and prayerful consideration to see, by the eye of faith, the display of wisdom and power shining forth in the way in which the all-wise God sent his dear Son "to destroy" or, as the word is in the original, to unloose "the works of the devil" (1 John 3. 8). Satan had, so to speak, spun a ravelled knot when he cast the cords of sin round man's heart. This tangled and tight-drawn knot could not be cut through as by a sword of omnipotent power; but had by infinite wisdom and patience to be unravelled through its whole length. The work which Satan had done was to be undone. Disobedience had to be repaired by obedience – the voluntary obedience of the Son of God, and therefore of infinite value. Sin had to be atoned for by sacrifice – the sacrifice of the nature which had sinned, in union with the Person of the Son of God, and therefore deriving from it unspeakable efficacy. Death had to be destroyed by the ever-living Son of God submitting to die. The law must be magnified by being obeyed by him who by his divine Person is above law. The Law-giver must be the Law-fulfiller. He who is the ever-blessed One must be made a curse; and the holy One of Israel, who knew no sin, must be "made sin, that we might be made the righteousness of God in him." "Who would set the briers and thorns against me in battle?" asked the Lord: "I would go through them," is his answer (Isa. 27. 4). So our blessed Lord went through these thorns and briers set against him in battle. He thoroughly went through all that he undertook; and by going through unravelled the work of Satan.

November 25

"Let us therefore follow after the things which make for peace." – Romans 14. 19.

What a sweetness is contained in the word "peace". Bunyan well represents this in his Pilgrim's Progress, where he speaks of Christian, after having been entertained in the "house Beautiful", going to sleep in the chamber called "Peace." And what blessed sensations are couched in that word "peace"! It was the legacy that Jesus left to his Church. "Peace I leave with you, my peace I give unto you; not as the world giveth, give I unto you"; and the Apostle says of it that it "passeth all understanding". Now many even of the Lord's people seem as if they wanted and were expecting raptures. There is, I believe, a vast deal of enthusiasm in the natural mind of man, as is evident from what I may call its religious history in all ages; and this leads many who, in other points, seem rightly taught to look for wonderful visions, ecstasies, and raptures, things which nature can imitate, or Satan, as an "angel of light", counterfeit to delude souls. But I believe Satan cannot speak gospel peace to the conscience; he cannot bring a holy calm into the soul. He could lash the waters of Gennesareth into a storm; but there was only One who could say to them, "Peace, be still." Satan may raise up a storm in our carnal mind, but he cannot allay it; he cannot pour oil upon the waves; nor calm the troubled breast, and enable it to rest upon God. Of all spiritual blessings, none seem preferable to peace; and I believe that it is what a child of God covets more than anything. For, O how much is implied in the word "peace"! Is not man by nature an enemy to God? Then to be saved he must be reconciled; and that implies peace. Is not his heart often troubled, as the Lord said, "Let not your heart be troubled?" Then he wants peace. And is not his mind often agitated and tossed up and down by conflicting emotions? Then he wants peace to calm it. And when he has to lie upon his dying bed, O, if he can but lie there in peace, peace with God through Jesus Christ, and a holy calm comes over his soul, flowing out of manifested mercy and felt reconciliation, it will beat all the raptures in the world! To be blessed with peace, through the blood of sprinkling, before the soul glides out of its earthly tabernacle to enter into the haven of peace above - this indeed will make a deathbed happy, this will extract every thorn from the dying pillow, and enable the departing believer to say, with holy Simeon, "Lord, now lettest thou thy servant depart in peace, for mine eyes have seen thy salvation."

November 26

"And they shall spring up as among the grass." - Isaiah 44. 4.

The Lord's people are spoken of here as at once "springing up" under the influence of the water poured and of the floods given. We cannot mistake the spiritual meaning of the figure, as it is so clear and certain. In those burning regions where rain does not fall at all seasons from the skies, as in our dripping clime, the effect of copious showers falling upon the parched vegetation is almost miraculous. A few days completely reverse the scene, and on every side vegetation springs up as if it started with gigantic growth out of the bosom of the heated soil. To this the figure in the text alludes, "They shall spring up", that is, Zion's children, "as among the grass," with all that young and active growth which so clearly manifests the power and the blessing of God.

But what may we understand by the expression *"grass?"* May we not interpret it as emblematic of the flesh, according to the words of the prophet, "All flesh is grass!" (Isa. 40. 6.) All the pride, pomp, and beauty of the flesh are but as grass, for "all the glory of man is as the flower of grass" (1 Peter 1. 24), which, when cut down by the scythe, soon withers, is gathered into heaps, and swept away out of the field. From this point of view we may consider the children of God to spring up amongst the sons of men as flowers among the grass, bedecking it with beauty - the only beautiful objects among the green blades. O how blessed it is to see children of God springing up here and there amongst the grass which everywhere so thickly covers the mead! Time may have been when you were hidden beneath the grass - when, though a flower in God's sight, your root was in the dust, and you lay undistinguished amidst the thick herbage. But being a flower, one of the Redeemer's own lilies, among whom he feeds (S. of S. 6. 3), when the rain of heaven dropped upon you, you sprang up amid the crowded blades which before hid you from view.

November 27

"As willows by the water courses." - Isaiah 44. 4.

The willow, we know, cannot exist without water; it must be near the brook or river, or it withers and dies. Take a young willow and plant it upon a mountain top or in the sandy desert, and it soon droops and perishes. But take the barest twig off the willow, and plant it near a stream, so that the water may reach it, and it will soon shoot downwards and push a vigorous stem upwards. So it is with the child of grace: he must live by the river side; he must dip his roots into that "river, the streams whereof make glad the city of God," and by it he must be continually bathed, or he droops and dies. He cannot live in the world, away from Jesus, his word, ordinances, house, people, presence, Spirit, and grace, any more than a willow can live upon the mountain top;

he cannot live among carnal men, cut off from union and communion with his great and glorious Head, any more than the willow can thrive and grow in the wilderness. How beautifully is this set forth by the prophet Jeremiah – "Blessed is the man that trusteth in the Lord, and whose hope the Lord is. For he shall be as a tree planted by the waters, and that spreadeth out her roots by the river, and shall not see when heat cometh, but her leaf shall be green; and shall not be careful in the year of drought, neither shall cease from yielding fruit" (Jer. 17. 7, 8). The saints of God, then, grow like "willows by the water courses."

How enduring, too, is the willow. What life in every branch! and even when pollarded, or cut down low, still reviving "through the scent of water" (Job 14. 9), and shooting out its branches afresh. May we not see in this a fitting emblem of the child of God, and admire how, like the willow, he preserves life and vigour when the nobler trees of the forest are blown down by the storm or are cut down for fuel?

November 28

"So then after the Lord had spoken unto them, he was received up into heaven, and sat on the right hand of God." – Mark 16. 19.

The right hand of God means the right hand of power, of dominion, of authority and of acceptance. When our blessed Lord went back to the courts of bliss, and the gates of heaven lifted up their heads, and the everlasting doors were lifted up, and the King of glory went in, he sat down at once at the right hand of the Majesty on high. But what did this place of pre-eminence imply? It certified to principalities and powers, and the whole bright and glorious throng of angelic hosts, that God had accepted his work and given him for his reward that exalted place of power, of honour, and of dignity. For remember this, that our gracious Lord went up to heaven and sat down at the right hand of God in his human nature. He did not go up to heaven as he came down from heaven only as the Son of God. He went up to heaven as the Son of man as well as the Son of God. He went up to heaven in a human nature united to the divine, and therefore entered the courts of bliss as the God-man, Immanuel, God with us. It is a point of great importance, and to be ever borne in mind by every spiritual worshipper, and by every true believer in the Son of God, that our blessed Lord sat down at the right hand of the Majesty on high in the same human body which he wore upon earth - glorified indeed beyond all thought or utterance, but the same pure, spotless, holy, and immortal humanity which he assumed in the womb of the Virgin, and which he offered as a sacrifice upon the cross. To this point the Apostle would specially direct our thoughts, and bring it before us as the object and food of our faith (Rom. 8. 34). And what an object of faith it is, for, as viewing Jesus at the right hand of God, we see there a mediator between God and men, the man Christ Jesus; we see an advocate with the Father, Jesus Christ the righteous; we see a brother, a friend, a husband enthroned in glory, there ever living, ever reigning, ever ruling, until God shall have put all enemies under his feet.

November 29

"O my dove, that art in the clefts of the rock." - Song of Solomon 2. 14.

Jesus is the hiding-place, the only hiding place from sin and self. "Thou art my hiding place," said David of old. This was shown to Moses, in figure, when the Lord put him into the cleft of a rock, which Toplady has so beautifully versified, to paint the longing desires of his soul:

> "Rock of Ages, cleft for me,
> Let me hide myself in thee!"

It is on this "Rock of Ages" that God has built his Church. As a rock, he is deep as well as high - so deep as to have under-bottomed the depths of the fall, so high as to be God's fellow, seated at his right hand. As a rock, too, he is broad as well as long - broad enough to bear millions of living stones built on him, and long enough to reach from eternity to eternity. The Apostle, therefore, prays that the Church at Ephesus may comprehend with all saints, "what is the breadth, and length, and depth, and height; and to know the love of Christ which passeth knowledge."

November 30

"Wherefore he is able also to save them to the uttermost that come unto God by him, seeing he ever liveth to make intercession for them." - Hebrews 7. 25.

If the gracious Lord did not live to make intercession for us, he could hardly be said to save us to the uttermost. But as he ever lives at God's right hand and is ever interceding, ever presenting the perfume of his acceptable mediation, this gives us a certain pledge of his love, his pity, and his power. Is not this very encouraging to all who come unto God by him? and may we not say, "Such are we, O Lord; we do come, we daily come to thee by Jesus Christ"? And do we not need all the encouragement that God may give us out of it? for we often sink very low through temptation and trial and the manifold afflictions of the way. How blessed, then, it is if you can only trace this mark of grace in your soul when others seem almost lost out of sight. If you know anything of internal work, you know this - whether you have come, whether you are coming to God by Jesus Christ. It is very simple, yet very expressive. Have you come as an outcast? Have you come as ready to perish? for these are expressly spoken of as coming in that day when the great trumpet is blown, the great and glorious trumpet of the gospel, for its jubilee notes are sounded specially for them. Have you come in faith? have you come in hope? have you come in love? and have you found any measure of acceptance and approbation in your own bosom? "Yes," say some, "with all my doubts, fears, and questioning, I can answer your question with an honest heart and a firm front, that I have come to God by Jesus Christ, and have felt the blessedness of so doing." Then you have known something or will know something about the uttermost; and the more you know about the uttermost, the more you will prize salvation by grace, the more you will cleave to the Son of God, the more you will hang upon his finished work, and the more you will look unto him who has so kindly said, "Look unto me, and be ye saved, all the ends of the earth; for I am God, and there is none else."

December 1

"Praise waiteth for thee, O God, in Sion: and unto thee shall the vow be performed." – Psalm 65. 1.

What a sweet thing it is to bless and praise God! There is no feeling upon earth equal to it. But how often are we in that state when we can neither pray nor praise, when sullenness, frowardness, and peevishness seem to take such complete possession, that, so far from praising God, there is no power even to seek his face; and so far from blessing him, there are even dreadful things working up in the heart against him, which awfully manifest the enmity of the carnal mind. Those who are painfully exercised with such feelings are certain, therefore, that it is God's work to enable them to praise and bless his holy name. And does not the heaven-taught soul come sometimes into this spot, "O that the Lord would give me something to praise him for, would bring me out of this trial, break this wretched snare, remove this awful temptation, lift me out of this providential difficulty, bless and water my soul, comfort my heart, strengthen my spirit, give me some sweet testimony of his covenant love!" "O," says the soul, "how I would then bless and praise him! I would spend all my breath in exalting his holy name." But when the Lord withholds from the soul the blessings it so eagerly covets, it can only look at them at a great distance, view them wishfully, and long to experience them. But it says, "Until they come with power, until they are brought in with sweetness, until they are sealed upon my very heart, so as to take full possession of my breast, I cannot, I dare not, bless and praise God's holy name." O what a dependent creature a heaven-taught soul is! How it hangs upon the Spirit of God to work in it that which is well-pleasing in his sight; how convinced it is that it cannot feel sin nor confess it, that it cannot breathe forth prayer nor praise unless the "God of all grace" create by his own powerful hand these blessed fruits of the lips (Isa. 57. 19). Are you so helpless in your feelings as this? Are you such complete dependents upon sovereign grace? Then you are spiritually taught of God; for it is God's teaching in the soul which brings a man to an experimental knowledge of his own complete helplessness before him.

December 2

"Look unto the rock whence ye are hewn, and to the hole of the pit whence ye are digged." – Isaiah 51. 1.

It is as though the Lord would here by the pen of his prophet turn our eyes to our native origin. And what is that? The same quarry out of which the other stones come. If you and I, by God's grace, are "living stones", we come out of the same quarry with the dead, unbelieving, unregenerate world; there is no difference in that respect. Nay, we are perhaps sunk lower in the quarry than some of those in whom God never has and never will put his grace. It is not the upper stratum, what is called "the capstone," of the quarry, which is to be taken to be hewn into a pillar; they go down deep into the pit to get at the marble which is to be chiselled into the ornamental column. So with God's saints. They do not lie at the top of the quarry; but the Lord has to go down very low, that he may bring up these stones out of the depths of the fall, and lift them, as it were, out of deeper degradation than those which lie nearer the surface. I remember reading once an expression which a Portland quarryman used when he was asked a question with respect to the hard labour of getting out the stone. He said, "It is enough to heave our hearts out." The stone lay so deep, and required such severe bodily exertion, that the labourer was forced to throw not only all his weight, sinews, and muscles into the work, but his very heart also. So it is with the elect of God. They are sunk so low, in such awful depths of degradation, at such an infinite distance from God, so hidden and buried from everything good and godlike, that, so to speak, it required all the strength and power of Jehovah to lift them out of the pit. In raising them out of the quarry of nature, he spent, as it were, upon them all his heart; for wherein was the heart of God so manifested as in the incarnation of his only-begotten Son, and in the work, righteousness, sufferings, blood, and death of the Lord Jesus Christ?

December 3

"The eternal God is thy refuge." – Deuteronomy 33. 27.

There is, to my mind, much sweetness in the contrast between the eternal God being the refuge of his people, and the lying refuges that most hide their heads in. God's people want *an eternal* refuge. They have a never-dying soul; and unless they have a never-dying refuge, it is not sufficient for a never-dying soul. Works! these are for time; the never-dying soul wants something to stand when works and wonders cease. Doctrines, opinions, sentiments, ordinances, the good opinion of men, the applause and flattery of the creature – these are of the earth, earthy; they fail when a man gives up the ghost. But a child of God wants a refuge, not merely that his soul may anchor in it in time, but that when time is ended, when the angel proclaims, "There shall be time no longer", and his liberated soul escapes its prison-house, and is wafted into the presence of the eternal God, it may find in Him at that solemn moment a refuge. Nay, all through eternity, in the rolling circle of its never-ending ages, the soul will still want a refuge. For could it even in eternity exist for a moment out of Christ – in a word, were the refuge of the elect anything but eternal, the moment the limited time of their shelter closed, the frowns of God would hurl them into perdition; so that nothing but an eternal God can ever be a refuge for a never-dying soul. It does not say, "His grace is thy refuge", No; because grace will end in glory. Nor does it say, "His mercy is thy refuge", for his mercy will end in blessing and praise. Nor does it say, "His attributes or his perfections are a refuge." It drops the gifts and leads the soul up to the Giver, as though God's own gifts and mercies were not sufficient, but that the immortal soul must have the immortal God, and the never-dying spirit is only safe in the bosom of an eternal Jehovah.

December 4

"It is written, Man shall not live by bread alone, but by every word that proceedeth out of the mouth of God." – Matthew 4. 4.

Man shall not live by bread alone. There is heavenly food to support his soul, as well as natural food to support his body. If a man is supported spiritually by every word that proceedeth out of the mouth of God, if this be the only food the Lord's people enjoy, how little they have! If you and I have no more religion than that which comes from what God has spoken into our soul; if that be the bread we are to live upon; if that be the strength of our heart; if that be our living portion and our dying sufficiency; - how it narrows up our religion into so small a compass, that sometimes we seem to require a microscope to see whether we have any or not. But thus we learn this lesson, "that man liveth not by bread alone". He cannot live by doctrines in the head. He cannot live by bodily gestures. He cannot live by rites and forms and ceremonies. He cannot live by anything that springs from the creature. His life is first given by God, and his life is maintained by every word that proceedeth out of the mouth of God. What the Lord teaches, he knows; what the Lord works, he feels; what the Lord gives, he possesses; what the Lord speaks to his heart, he has in his soul, as from the lips of the sovereign Majesty himself. But what a narrow path is this! How it cuts up all creature righteousness! How it lays the creature low in the dust of abasement! With all your religion, you have none but what God gives, nor can you procure a grain; for you have to live, not by bread alone, as in your natural life, but on every word that proceedeth out of the mouth of God. How then are you spiritually to live, except from time to time the Lord speak a word to your soul?

December 5

"What will ye see in the Shulamite? As it were the company of two armies." – Song of Solomon 6. 13.

Are you not often a mystery to yourself? Warm one moment, cold the next; abasing yourself one half-hour, exalting yourself the following; loving the world, full of it, steeped up to your lips in it to-day; crying, groaning, and sighing for a sweet manifestation of the love of God tomorrow; brought down to nothingness, covered with shame and confusion, on your knees before you leave your room; filled with pride and self-importance before you have got down stairs; despising the world, and willing to give it all up for one taste of the love of Jesus when in solitude; trying to grasp it with both hands when in business. What a mystery are you! Touched by love, and stung with enmity; possessing a little wisdom, and a great deal of folly; earthly-minded, and yet having the affections in heaven; pressing forward, and lagging behind; full of sloth, and yet taking the kingdom with violence! And thus the Spirit, by a process which we may feel but cannot adequately describe, leads us into the mystery of the two natures, that "company of two armies," perpetually struggling and striving against each other in the same bosom. So that one man cannot more differ from another than the same man differs from himself. But do not nature, sense, and reason contradict this? Do not the wise and prudent deny this? "There must be a progressive advance", they say, "in holiness; there must be a gradual amendment of our nature until at length all sin is rooted out, and we become as perfect as Christ." But the mystery of the kingdom of heaven is this, that our carnal mind undergoes no alteration, but maintains a perpetual war with grace: and thus, the deeper we sink in self-abasement under a sense of our vileness, the higher we rise in a knowledge of Christ; and the blacker we are in our own view, the more comely does Jesus appear.

December 6

"That the trial of your faith, being much more precious than of gold that perisheth, though it be tried with fire, might be found unto praise and honour and glory at the appearing of Jesus Christ" – 1 Peter 1. 7.

Trials and temptations are the means which God employs to manifest to the soul the reality and strength of the faith which he bestows upon it; for there is in every trial and temptation opposition made to the faith that is in the heart; and every trial and temptation, so to speak, threaten the life of faith. And they threaten it in this way. Under the trial God for the most part hides himself. He puts forth, indeed, a secret power whereby the soul is held up, or otherwise it would sink into utter despair, and be overcome and swallowed up by the power of unbelief. Hence comes the conflict between the trial that fights against the faith and the faith which fights against or rather under the trial. Now, when in this trial, in this sharp conflict, in this hot furnace, faith does not give way, is not burned up, is not destroyed, but keeps its firm hold upon the promise and the faithfulness of him who has given it, this trial of faith becomes very precious. It is precious to the soul when God again smiles upon it, and becomes thus manifest as genuine. It is precious in the sight of God's people, who see it and derive strength and comfort from what they witness in the experience of a saint thus tried and blessed; and it is precious also in the sight of God himself, who crowns it with his own manifest approbation, and puts upon it the attesting seal of his own approving smile. But above all things, it will be found precious at the appearing of Jesus Christ, and that not only in his various appearings in grace, but in his final appearance in glory, for of that the Apostle mainly speaks when he says that "it may be found unto praise and honour and glory at the appearing of Jesus Christ."

December 7

"But the God of all grace, who hath called us unto his eternal glory by Christ Jesus, after that ye have suffered a while, make you perfect, stablish, strengthen, settle you." – 1 Peter 5. 10.

If "the God of all grace" has indeed "called you unto his eternal glory", – if he has indeed touched your heart with his blessed finger, – remember you will have to walk, from beginning to end, in a path of suffering; for the whole path, more or less, is a path of tribulation. And, while walking in this path, and suffering from sin, Satan, the world, and the evil of your own heart, it is only to lead you up more unto "the God of all grace"; it is only that God may, in his own time, "make you perfect, stablish, strengthen, and settle you." And when your soul has passed through these trials, you will see God's hand in all, praise him for all, and will perceive how good it was for you to have been afflicted, and to have walked in this painful path; that having suffered with Christ Jesus, you might sit down with him in his eternal glory!

December 8

"But where sin abounded, grace did much more abound." – Romans 5. 20.

In order to know what grace is in its reign over sin, and in its superaboundings over the aboundings of iniquity, we must be led experimentally into the depths of the fall. We must be led by God himself into the secrets of our own heart; we must be brought down into distress of mind on account of our sin and the idolatry of our fallen nature. And when, do what we will, sin will still work, reign, and abound, and we are brought to soul poverty, helplessness, destitution, and misery, and cast ourselves down at the footstool of his mercy - then we begin to see and feel the reign of grace, in quickening our souls, in delivering us from the wrath to come, and in preserving us from the dominion of evil. We begin to see then that grace superabounds over all the aboundings of sin in our evil hearts, and as it flows through the channel of the Saviour's sufferings, that it will never leave its favoured objects till it brings them into the enjoyment of eternal life! And if this does not melt and move the soul, and make a man praise and bless God, nothing will, nothing can! But until we have entered into the depths of our own iniquities, until we are led into the chambers of imagery, and brought to sigh, groan, grieve, and cry under the burden of guilt on the conscience and the workings of secret sin in the heart - it cannot be really known. And to learn it thus, is a very different thing from learning it from books, or ministers. To learn it in the depths of a troubled heart, by God's own teaching, is a very different thing from learning it from the words of a minister, or even from the word of God itself. We can never know these things savingly and effectually, till God himself is pleased to apply them with his own blessed power, and communicate an unctuous savour of them to our hearts, that we may know the truth, and find to our soul's consolation, that the truth makes us free!

December 9

"When thou passest through the waters, I will be with thee." - Isaiah 43. 2.

How many of the dear saints of God, when they have been brought into tribulation and sorrow, have found the fulfilment of this most gracious promise! And is there not one of these waters through which all must go - that deep and rapid Jordan which every one must pass through? How dark and gloomy those waters have appeared to the eyes of many a child of God, in whom is continually fulfilled the experience of the words, "Who through fear of death were all their lifetime subject to bondage." But how often have these waters only been terrible in prospect, in anticipation. How different has been the reality. When he comes down to the river's bank and his feet dip in these waters, and it appears as though they would rise higher and higher, the Lord suddenly appears in his power and presence, and then the water sinks. He speaks a word of peace to his soul upon a dying bed - reveals Christ in his love and grace and blood - removes those doubts, fears, and disturbing thoughts which have perplexed him for years, and brings into his heart a holy calm, a sweet peace, assuring him that all is well with him, both for time and eternity. Has he not then the fulfilment of the promise, "When thou passest through the waters, I will be with thee"?

December 10

"That they all may be one; as thou, Father, art in me, and I in thee, that they also may be one in us: that the world may believe that thou hast sent me." – John 17. 21.

The Apostle declares, "He that is joined unto the Lord is one spirit" (1 Cor. 6. 17). If, then, we are joined to the Lord, in other words, have a union with him, this is the closest of all unions. A man and his wife are one flesh, but Jesus and the saint are one spirit. If possessed of this we are one spirit with him; we understand what he says; we have the mind of Christ; we love what he loves, and hate what he hates. But out of this spiritual union flows communion with him, intercourse with him, communications from him, and the whole of that divine work upon the heart whereby the two spirits become one. The Spirit of Christ in his glorious Person and the Spirit of Christ in a believing heart meet together, and meeting together as two drops of rain running down a pane of glass, or two drops of oil, kiss into each other, and are no longer two but one. Now if you have been ever blest with a manifestation of Christ, your spirit has melted into his, and you have felt that sweet union and communion with him that you saw as with his eyes, heard as with his ears, felt as with his heart, and spoke as with his tongue.

December 11

"Come unto me, all ye that labour and are heavy laden, and I will give you rest." - Matthew 11. 28.

When we rest, we find relief to our weary limbs. So spiritually. When the soul comes to Jesus, he gives it rest and relief from its burdens; as well as deliverance from anxiety, and cessation from the labour that distresses and distracts it. He promises to give this - "Come unto me, and I" - who else can do it? None, either in heaven or earth - "Come unto me, all ye that labour and are heavy laden, and I will give you rest." How? By communicating to the soul out of his infinite fulness, by sprinkling upon the conscience his atoning blood, by shedding abroad in the heart his dying love, and enabling the soul to believe on his name, and cling to his Person. In this there is rest - nothing else will do it - nothing else will give it. Other remedies will leave us at last under the wrath of God. But he that comes to and leans upon Jesus, his finished work, his dying love, will have rest here and heaven hereafter. Are not our poor minds often restless, often anxious and pensive, because of a thousand doubts, perplexities, painful trials, and grievous afflictions - do they not all make your spirit weary and restless within you? There never can be anything but restlessness while we move round this circle of sin and self. But when by precious faith we come out of our own righteousness, our own strength, our own wisdom, our own worthiness; come to, believe in, hang upon, and cleave unto the

Person, blood, and work of the only-begotten Son of God, so as to feel a measure of his preciousness in our hearts – then there is rest. This is solid, this is abiding, this is not delusive; this will never leave the soul deceived with false hopes. No, it will end in eternal bliss and glory – in the open vision of eternal love – in seeing him face to face whom the soul has known, looked to, believed in, and loved upon earth.

December 12

"Likewise the Spirit also helpeth our infirmities: for we know not what we should pray for as we ought: but the Spirit itself maketh intercession for us with groanings which cannot be uttered." – Romans 8. 26.

In all our prayers, in all our approaches to the throne, our mercy and wisdom will be to seek to possess the mind of the Spirit; to desire to know the will of God, and do it; to look up more believingly and continually to the Lord Jesus, that he himself would teach and guide us; that he would by his Spirit and grace conform us more inwardly and outwardly to his suffering image; that he would grant unto us to know him more, and serve him better; that our prayers may day by day be more and more fervent, earnest, and sincere, more spiritual, more in accordance with the will of God; that thus they may be more and more manifested as the interceding breath of the Spirit of God in our hearts, and as such may bring more clear and evident answers down. Pray for the manifestation of Christ to your soul, for a revelation of the Person, blood, righteousness, and love of Jesus; seek to have your signs and evidences of divine life more cleared up; your Ebenezers and tokens for good more brightly shone upon; your doubts and fears more plainly dispelled, and a fuller and sweeter assurance of personal interest given in the finished work of Christ. Desire also to have the promises applied to your heart, the word of God brought with divine power into your conscience, and a living faith raised up and drawn forth to mix with the truth which you read or hear. Beg, as the Lord may enable, for submission, patience, resignation, brokenness, contrition, humility, godly sorrow for sin, heavenly affections, and that sweet spirituality of mind which is life and peace. Above all, seek an inward assurance that your prayers are heard and accepted, and then watch for the answer. This will give you the surest and best of all evidences that the blessed Spirit is himself interceding for you with groanings which cannot be uttered.

December 13

"And being made perfect, he became the author of eternal salvation unto all them that obey him." – Hebrews 5. 9.

By his sufferings in the garden and upon the cross the Lord Jesus was made perfect. But what perfection was this? It clearly does not mean that by these sufferings in the garden and upon the cross our Lord was made perfect as the Son of God, nor perfect as the Son of man, for he was perfect before as possessing infinite perfection in his eternal Godhead, and was endued also with every possible perfection of which his sacred humanity was capable. He needed no perfection to be added to his Godhead; it was not susceptible of it; no perfection to be added to his manhood, for it was "a holy thing" in union with eternal Deity. But he needed to be made perfect as a High Priest. It was through his sufferings that he was *consecrated* or dedicated in an especial manner to the priesthood, for this corresponds with his own words: "And for their sakes I sanctify myself" (John 17. 19); that is, I consecrate or dedicate myself to be their High Priest. The two main offices of the high priest were to offer sacrifice and make intercession. Sacrifice came first; and the sufferings of our Lord in the garden and upon the cross were a part of this sacrifice. He was therefore "made perfect through suffering," that is, through his sufferings, blood-shedding, and death he was consecrated to perform that other branch of the priestly office which he now executes. Thus as Aaron was consecrated by the sacrifice of a bullock and a ram, of which the blood was not only poured out at the bottom of the altar and sprinkled upon it, but put also on his right ear and hand and foot, so was his great and glorious Antitype consecrated through his own sacrifice and blood-shedding on the cross; and thus being made perfect, or rather, as the word literally means, being perfected, he became the author of eternal salvation unto all them that obey him.

December 14

"Thus saith the Lord, Let not the wise man glory in his wisdom, neither let the mighty man glory in his might, let not the rich man glory in his riches; but let him that glorieth glory in this, that he understandeth and knoweth me." – Jeremiah 9. 23, 24.

So we are allowed to glory. But in what and in whom? Not in ourselves; *that* is for ever disannulled. The Lord has purposed to pour contempt upon all human glory, that none should glory in himself, whatever he be or whatever he have. But when a man has a view of the Son of God in his beauty, in his suitability, in his heavenly grace and divine glory, then he can and may glory in the Lord. He can say, "O what a Lord there is above! How glorious is he in his excellency, in his suitability, and in his blessedness; how glorious his wisdom, his righteousness, his sanctification, and his redemption. Let my whole glory be there; let me not take to myself a single atom of it. If I am wise, let me give him the glory of being my wisdom; if righteous, let me give him the glory of being my righteousness; if I have any fruit of the Spirit, let me give him the glory of being my sanctification; if I am redeemed from death and hell, let the glory of my redemption be his." This is doing as God would have us to do, glorying in his dear Son. And the Lord will bring all his people to this spot sooner or later. He will give them such views of the effects of the fall, of the misery of sin, and of their own helplessness; and will give them such gracious views of his dear Son, as shall wean them from glorying in the creature and make them glory in the Lord as all their salvation and all their desire. It may be by a long course of severe discipline, but the Lord will eventually bring all his people there; for he has determined to glorify his dear Son, and when we can thus glorify him, then we have the mind of Christ, and are doing the will of God.

December 15

"Surely, shall one say, in the Lord have I righteousness and strength." – Isaiah 45. 24.

The same blessed Spirit who shines as with a ray of light and life into the conscience, to make it feel the guilt of sin, the curse of the law, and its own miserable state as a transgressor, leads it also into this secret, that it has no strength. Have you never felt that you were utterly powerless – that you would believe, but could not; would hope, but could not; would love, but could not; would keep God's word, but could not; would obey his commandments, but were not able? Has a sense of your own miserable impotency and thorough helplessness never pressed you down almost to despair? You felt sure that there was a faith, a hope, a love, a blessing, and a blessedness in the truth of God; a pardon, a peace, a heavenly joy; an assurance of salvation, a union and communion with the Lord Jesus, which you saw, but could not reach. You felt that if you could believe, all would be well, but believe you could not. Thus you learnt you had no strength, and as we learn our weakness in this way, we begin to learn also in whom is our strength; and as we get access to Christ by a living faith, we receive strength out of him for a supply of our spiritual necessities. Despairing of all strength in self, we look to the Lord Jesus Christ, at the right hand of the Father, to give us his; we lift up our prayers and supplications to the great High Priest over the house of God, to strengthen us with strength in our soul; and when he is pleased, in answer to prayer, to send down his Spirit and grace, we are "strengthened with all might, according to his glorious power, unto all patience and long-suffering with joyfulness." This is being "strong in the Lord and in the power of his might"; and a being "strengthened with might by his Spirit in the inner man."

December 16

"Beloved of God, called to be saints." – Romans 1. 7.

The very word *"saint"* has become, through man's perverseness and wickedness, a word of reproach and contempt. But God will honour it, let men dishonour it as they please. God has put a crown of glory upon it, let men despise it as they may. There is no privilege or blessing that God can confer so great and glorious as to crown you with the crown of saint. He might have given you titles without number; he might have showered riches upon your head in the greatest profusion; rank, fame, talent, beauty, health, all might have been poured at your feet; but what would all these be compared to making you a saint of God? But what is it to be a saint? It is to be sanctified by God the Father, set apart for himself, to show forth his praise. It is to be washed in the atoning blood and clothed in the justifying righteousness of the Son, and to be regenerated by the Spirit of God. It is to be introduced into a new world by being delivered from the power of darkness and translated into the kingdom of God's dear Son. What heart can conceive or tongue express the state of blessedness to which the despised saints of God are advanced even in this time state! They are sons and daughters of the Lord Almighty; jewels in Jesus' mediatorial crown; members of his mystical body, and as such united to him by indissoluble ties; pillars in the temple of God which shall go no more out; sheep redeemed by precious blood; virgin souls espoused to the Lord the Lamb. They are heirs of God and joint-heirs with Christ, and mansions of glory are prepared for them beyond the skies. There they shall sit as overcomers with Christ on his throne, and there they shall sing upon harps of gold the praises of a Three-One God to all eternity.

December 17

"Ho, every one that thirsteth, come ye to the waters, and he that hath no money; come ye, buy, and eat; yea, come, buy wine and milk without money and without price." – Isaiah 55. 1.

How many a poor sensible sinner has, upon the strength of these words, looked unto Jesus and been lightened (Psalm 34. 5), come to him and met with a kind reception. By the power which attends such invitations the heart is opened, as was the heart of Lydia, to attend unto the things spoken in the gospel. It is not put away as too holy for a poor polluted sinner to touch, nor is the Lord Jesus viewed as an angry Judge; but in these invitations his clemency, tenderness, and compassion are seen and felt, and beams and rays of his mercy and grace both enlighten the understanding and soften and melt the heart. Thence spring confession of sin, self-loathing, renunciation of one's own righteousness, earnest desires and breathings after the Lord, and an embracing of the love of the truth so far as made known. And as all these effects, so different from the old dead pharisaic religion, are produced by the power of the word upon the heart, the Bible becomes a new book, and is read and studied with attention and delight. The ears, too, being unstopped, as well as the eyes opened, if there be the opportunity of hearing the preached gospel, with what eagerness is it embraced, and what a sweetness there is found in it. All who have passed through these things will agree with us that there are no such hearing days as what Job calls "the days of our youth, when the secret of God is upon our tabernacle" (Job 29. 4).

December 18

"That I may be found in him." – Philippians 3. 9.

The Apostle knew a time was coming when God would search Jerusalem as with candles. He knew a day was hastening on when the secrets of all hearts would be revealed. He knew an hour was approaching when the eyes of the Lord would try, and the eyelids of the righteous Judge would weigh the words and actions of men. And he knew in his own soul's experience, that all who, in that awful day, were not found in Christ, would be consigned to the eternal pit of woe. He knew that when the Judge took his seat upon the great white throne, and heaven and earth fled away from his presence, no one could stand before his look of infinite justice and eternal purity, but those who had a vital standing in the Son of God. And therefore, looking to that awful time, and the solemnities of that day of judgment, that day of wonders, this was the desire of his soul – and towards that he pressed forward, as an active runner presses towards the goal – "that he might be found in him"; that when the Lord comes a second time to judgment, and his eyes run over the assembled myriads, he might be found in the Man who is "a refuge from the storm, and the shadow of a great rock in a weary land", the only Saviour from the wrath to come, which will one day burst upon the world.

December 19

"That your faith should not stand in the wisdom of men, but in the power of God." – 1 Corinthians 2. 5.

It is true that real grace can suffer neither loss nor diminution, but its manifestations and its actings may. Who that possesses faith is not conscious that it ebbs and flows, rises and sinks, is strong and weak, and varies from day to day and from hour to hour? Thus when a sharp trial comes, its immediate effect is to depress faith. It falls upon it like a weight, and bends it down to the ground. Faith may be compared to the quicksilver in a weather-glass, or in a thermometer. The quantity of mercury in the *bulb* never varies; but it rises or falls in the *tube,* according to the weight of the air, or the heat of the day. Thus faith, though it abides in the heart without loss or diminution, yet rises or sinks in the feelings, as the weather is fair or foul, or as the sun shows or hides himself. Did Job's faith, for instance, mount equally high when "in the days of his youth" – the spring of his soul – "the secret of God was upon his tabernacle", and when "he cursed his day", and cried, "O that I knew where I might find him?" Was Peter's faith as strong when he quailed before a servant girl as when he was ready to go to prison and to death? Or Abraham's when he denied Sarah to be his wife, and when with but three hundred and eighteen men he pursued and smote the army of four mighty kings? If faith never fluctuates, never sinks and never rises, then we have at once the dead assurance of a professor; then faith is in our own keeping; then it does not hang on the smile or frown of God; then we are no more beggars and bankrupts, living on supplies given or withholden, but independent and self-sufficient; then we "have no changes, and so fear not God." But if faith ebb and flow, what is the cause? Is it in self? Can we add to its stature one cubit, or make one hair of it black or white? If not, then must its ebbings and flowings come from God.

December 20

"And I will give her her vineyards from thence, and the valley of Achor for a door of hope: and she shall sing there, as in the days of her youth, and as in the day when she came up out of the land of Egypt." – Hosea 2. 15.

Now the "valley of Achor" signifies the "valley of trouble." It was the valley in which Achan was stoned. And why stoned? Because he had taken the accursed thing; because his eye had been captivated by the Babylonish garment and golden wedge, and he had buried them in the tent. This may throw a light on what the "valley of Achor" is spiritually. Perhaps you have been guilty of Achan's sin; you have been taking the accursed thing; have been too deeply connected with the world; have done things which God's displeasure is against. Let conscience speak in the bosom of each. The consequence has been, that you have got into the "valley of Achor"! Trouble, sorrow, and confusion are your lot, and you do not know whether the lot of Achan may not await you there.

Now it is in this "valley of Achor", or sorrow, confusion, and fear, that the "door of hope" is opened. But why "in the valley of Achor"? That we may cease to hope in self; that a sound and true gospel hope may enter within the veil as an anchor sure and steadfast, and there be no hope but in the precious blood of the Lamb, and in a sweet manifestation of that blood to the conscience. This is the "door of hope" through which the soul looks into the very presence of God; sees Jesus on the throne of grace, the sprinkled mercy-seat, and the great High Priest "able and willing to save to the uttermost." Through this "door of hope," by which Christ is seen, the soul goes forth in desires, breathings, hungerings, and thirstings after him; and through this "door of hope" descend visits, smiles, tokens, testimonies, mercies, and favours. And thus, there is "a door of hope", no longer barred, closed, and shut back, but thrown wide open in the bleeding side of an incarnate God. Here is a renewing of visits almost despaired of; of joys that seemed never to return; of hopes almost extinct; of consolations remembered, but remembered almost with fear, lest they should have been delusive. "She shall sing there, as in the days of her youth, and as in the day when she came up out of the land of Egypt."

December 21

"Whom having not seen, ye love." – 1 Peter 1. 8.

How this speaks to our hearts; and cannot some, if not many of us say too, "Whom having not seen, we love"? Do we not love him, dear readers? Is not his name precious to us as the ointment poured forth? But we have not seen him. No, not by the eye of sense and nature; but we have seen him by the eye of faith; for he has manifested himself to us, or to some of us, and we have seen his glory, the glory as of the only-begotten of the Father, full of grace and truth. It is, then, by faith that we see Jesus. We read of Moses that, "by faith he forsook Egypt, not fearing the wrath of the king: for he endured, as seeing him who is invisible." So by faith we see Jesus who is invisible; for as faith is "the substance of things hoped for", so is it "the evidence of things not seen." Thus we see that it is by Jesus coming to the soul and manifesting himself unto it that we see him. And as he always comes with his love, and in manifesting himself manifests himself in his love, that manifested love kindles, raises, and draws up a corresponding love in the believer's heart. It is the express, the special work of the Holy Ghost to testify of Christ, to glorify him, to receive of the things which are Christ's and to show them unto the soul; and thus in the light of Christ's own manifestations of himself and the blessed Spirit's work and witness of him, what faith believes of the Person and work of Christ love embraces and enjoys.

December 22

"In whom, though now ye see him not, yet believing, ye rejoice with joy unspeakable and full of glory." – 1 Peter 1. 8.

Here we have linked together faith, love, joy, and glory. The word translated "rejoice" means a high degree of joy, and signifies literally, to leap with joy. Spiritual joy, holy joy, is therefore distinguished from earthly joy, natural joy, not only in nature, but in degree. Natural joy can never rise very high, nor last very long. It is of the earth, earthy, and therefore can never rise high nor long endure. It is always marred by some check, damp or disappointment; and, as in the bitterest cup of the righteous "There's something secret sweetens all", so in the sweetest cup of the ungodly there is something secret embitters all. All their mirth is madness; for "in laughter the heart is sorrowful, and the end of that mirth is heaviness." God frowns upon all the worldling's pleasure, conscience condemns it, and the weary heart is often sick of it, even unto death. It cannot bear inspection or reflection, has perpetual disappointment stamped upon it here and eternal sorrow hereafter. But how different is the joy of faith and love. It is *unspeakable,* for it is one of the things which eye hath not seen, nor ear heard, neither have entered into the heart of man; and therefore human language, which can only express human thoughts and feelings, has no words for this. Those who have experienced it understand it when spoken of by others, but not from the words themselves, but because those words are as if broken hints, dim and feeble shadows, imperfect and insufficient utterances, but interpreted by their own experience. *"And full of glory"* It is literally "glorified", that is, the joy is a joy which God especially honours by stamping upon it a divine glory. It is, therefore, a blessed preparation for, and foretaste of the glory that shall be revealed.

December 23

"And he that searcheth the hearts knoweth what is the mind of the Spirit, because he maketh intercession for the saints according to the will of God." – Romans 8. 27.

God's will must ever stand, it is as unchanging and as unchangeable as God himself. Our wills are ever fluctuating; God's will fluctuates not. And as that will must ever live and rule, it will be our highest wisdom and richest mercy to submit to, and be conformed unto it. Now the will of God to you who desire to fear his name is not your destruction, but your salvation; your profit now, your happiness hereafter; your present grace, and eternal glory. And the Spirit is making intercession for you according to the will of God; for is it not your earnest desire and prayer that your soul should be saved and blessed, that you should serve God and live to his glory, and when you die be with him for ever? Lie, then, at his feet. Be the clay, and let him be your heavenly Potter. Think not of saving yourself, or of putting your own hand to God's gracious work. Be content to be nothing. Sink even lower than that; be willing to be less than nothing, that Christ may be all in all. Covet above all things the Spirit's interceding breath; for in possessing that you will have a sure pledge that he will guide you in life, support you in death, and land you in glory. With his guidance we can never err; with his supporting arms we can never fall; taught by him we shall see the path of life plainly; upheld by his strength we shall walk in it without fear. Without his light we are dark; without his life we are dead; without his teaching we are but a mass of ignorance and folly. We cannot find the way except he guide; but if he do guide, we cannot but find it. The more we confide in his teaching and guidance the better it will be for us; and the more that under this teaching we can lie submissively at the Lord's feet, looking up to him for his will to be made known in us and perfected in us, the more it will be for our present peace, and the more it will redound to his eternal praise.

December 24

"It is good for me that I have been afflicted; that I might learn thy statutes." – Psalm 119. 71.

We may have everything naturally that the carnal heart desires, and only be hardened thereby into worldliness and ungodliness. But to be brought down in body and soul, to be weaned and separated from an ungodly world by affliction sanctified and made spiritually profitable, to be brought to feel our need of Christ, and that without an interest in his precious blood our soul must be for ever lost – how much better it is really and truly, to be laid on a bed of affliction, with a hope in God's mercy, than to be left to our own carnality and thoughtlessness. Affliction of any kind is very hard to bear, and especially so when we begin to murmur and fret under the weight of the cross; but when the Lord afflicts it is in good earnest; he means to make us feel. Strong measures are required to bring us down; and affliction would not be affliction, unless it were full of grief and sorrow. But when affliction makes us seek the Lord with a deep feeling in the soul that none but himself can save or bless, and we are enabled to look up unto him, with sincerity and earnestness, that he would manifest his love and mercy to our heart, he will appear sooner or later. The Lord, who searcheth the heart, knoweth all the real desire of the soul, and can and does listen to a sigh, a desire, a breath of supplication within. He knows our state, both of body and soul, and is not a hard taskmaster to require what we cannot give, or lay upon us more than we can bear, but can and does give all that he desires from us. But very often he delays to appear, that he may teach us thereby we have no claim upon him, and that anything granted is of his pure compassion and grace.

December 25

"Great is the mystery of godliness: God was manifest in the flesh." – 1 Timothy 3. 16.

A mystery indeed it is, a great, a deep, an unfathomable mystery; for who can rightly understand how the divine Word, the eternal Son of God, was made flesh, and dwelt among us? "Who shall declare his generation?" (Isa. 53. 8); either that eternal generation whereby he is the only-begotten Son of God, or the generation of his sacred humanity in the womb of the Virgin, when the Holy Ghost came upon her, and the power of the Highest overshadowed her? These are the things "which the angels desire to look into"; which they cannot understand, but reverently adore. And well may we imitate their adoring admiration, not attempting to understand, but believe, love, and revere; for well has it been said,

> "Where reason fails, with all her powers,
> There faith believes, and love adores."

Nor, if rightly taught and spiritually led, shall we find this a barren, dry, or unprofitable subject. It is "the great mystery of godliness"; therefore all godliness is contained in it, and flows out of it. The whole of God's grace, mercy, and truth is laid up in, is revealed through, is manifested by, the Son of his love; for "it pleased the Father that in him should all fulness dwell"; and this as Immanuel, God with us. Thus his sacred humanity, in union with his divine Person, is the channel of communication through which all the love and mercy of God flow down to poor guilty, miserable sinners, who believe in the name of the only-begotten Son of God. If blessed, then, with faith in living exercise, we may draw near and behold the great mystery of godliness. To tread by faith upon this holy ground is to come "unto Mount Sion, and unto the city of the living God, the heavenly Jerusalem, and to an innumerable company of angels, to the general assembly and church of the firstborn, which are written in heaven, and to God the Judge of all, and to the spirits of just men made perfect, and to Jesus the mediator of the new covenant, and to the blood of sprinkling, that speaketh better things than that of Abel" (Heb. 12. 22-24); for every blessing of the new covenant, if we are but favoured with a living faith in an incarnate God, is then experimentally as well as eternally ours.

December 26

"The Lord thy God in the midst of thee is mighty." – Zephaniah 3. 17.

What a mighty God we have to deal with! And what would suit our case but a mighty God? Have we not mighty sins? Have we not mighty trials? Have we not mighty temptations? Have we not mighty foes and mighty fears? And who is to deliver us from all this mighty host except the mighty God? It is not a little God (if I may use the expression) that will do for God's people. They need a mighty God because they are in circumstances where none but a mighty God can interfere in their behalf. Why, if you did not know feelingly and experimentally your mighty sins, your mighty trials, your mighty temptations, and your mighty fears, you would not want a mighty God. This sense of our weakness and his power, of our misery and his mercy, of our ruin and his recovery, of the aboundings of our sin and the superaboundings of his grace - a feeling sense, I say, of these opposite yet harmonious things brings us to have personal, experimental dealings with God; and it is in these personal dealings with God that the life of all religion consists. O what a poor, dead, useless religion is that in which there are no personal dealings with God - no calling upon his holy name out of a sincere heart; no seeking of his face, or imploring of his favour; no lying at his feet and begging of him to appear; no pitiable, lamentable case for him to have compassion upon; no wounds or sores for him to heal, no leprosy to cleanse, no enemies to put to the rout, no fears to dispel, and, I may almost say, no soul to save! And yet such is the religion of thousands. They draw near to God with their lips, but their hearts are far from him, and whilst they outwardly say, "Lord, Lord," they inwardly say, "This man shall not have dominion over us." If you differ from them, and want a God near at hand and not afar off, a mighty God in the very midst of your soul, of your thoughts, desires, and affections, you may well bless him for the grace which has made you to differ, and thankfully bow your neck to sufferings and trials, as means in his hand to bring you and him together.

December 27

"For we walk by faith, not by sight." - 2 Corinthians 5. 7.

The nature of faith is to trust in the dark, when all appearances are against it; to trust that a calm will come, though the storm be overhead; to trust that God will appear, though nothing but evil be felt. It is tender, child-like, and therefore is an implicit confidence, a yielding submission, a looking unto the Lord. There is something filial in this; something heavenly and spiritual; not the bold presumption of the daring, nor the despairing fears of the desponding; but something beyond both the one and the other - equally remote from the rashness of presumption, and from the horror of despair. There is a mingling of holy affection connected with this trust, springing out of a reception of past favours, ensuring favours to come; and all linked with a simple hanging and depending of the soul upon the Lord, because He is what He is. There is a looking to, and relying upon the Lord, because we have felt him to be the Lord; and because we have no other refuge.

And why have we no other refuge? Because poverty has driven us out of false refuges. It is a safe spot, though not a comfortable one, to be where David was, "Refuge failed me; no man cared for my soul" (Ps. 142. 4). And until refuge fails us in man, in self, in the world, in the church, there is no looking to Christ as a divine refuge. But when we come to this spot, "Thou art my refuge and my portion in the land of the living" (Ps. 142. 5) - "if I perish I will perish at thy feet - my faith centres in thee - all I have and all I expect to have, flows from thy bounty, I have nothing but what thou freely givest to me, the vilest of the vile" - *this is trust.* And where this trust is, there will be a whole army of desires at times pouring themselves into the bosom of the Lord; there will be a whole array of pantings and longings venting themselves into the bosom of "Immanuel, God with us."

December 28

"For unto you it is given in the behalf of Christ, not only to believe on him, but also to suffer for his sake." - Philippians 1. 29.

After the Lord, by his special work on the conscience, has called us to repentance and confession of sin, as well as to faith in Jesus; after he has called us to godly sorrow; to live according to the precepts of the gospel; and to walk in the ordinances of his Church; he then calls us to *suffer* for and with Christ. But we cannot "suffer according to the will of God," that is, in a gospel sense and from gospel motives, till the Lord enables us in some measure to look to him. The same Spirit, who calls the believer to walk in a path of suffering, strengthens and enables him to do so. To suffer aright, we must walk in the steps of the great Captain of our salvation, who "though a Son, yet learned obedience by the things which he suffered." The Father in this sense spared not his only-begotten Son, but led him into the path of tribulation. If the Lord of the house, then, had to travel in this dark and gloomy path of suffering, can his disciples escape? If the Captain of our salvation was "a man of sorrows and acquainted with grief", must not the common soldiers, who occupy the ranks of the spiritual army, be baptized into the same sufferings, and taste in their measure of that cup which he drank to the very dregs? Thus, every child of God is called, sooner or later, to "suffer with Christ"; and he that suffers not with Christ, will not reign with him (2 Timothy 2. 12). But the Lord, who sees what we are, as well as what we need, apportions out suffering to our several states and necessities. And however the suffering may differ, all have to pass through the furnace; for the Lord bringeth "the third part through the fire." All have to walk in the footsteps of a self-denying and crucified Jesus; all have painfully to feel what it is to be at times under the rod, and experience those chastisements of God, whereby they are proved to be sons, and not bastards.

December 29

"I am the vine, ye are the branches. He that abideth in me, and I in him, the same bringeth forth much fruit: for without me ye can do nothing." – John 15. 5.

The great secret in religion – that secret which is only with those who fear the Lord and to whom he shews his covenant – is first to get sensible union with the Lord, and then to maintain it. But this union cannot be got except by some manifestation of his Person and work to our heart, joining us to him as by one Spirit. This is the espousal of the soul, whereby it is espoused to one husband as a chaste virgin to Christ. From this espousal comes fellowship, or communion with Christ; and from this communion flows all fruitfulness, for it is not a barren marriage. But this union and communion cannot be maintained except by abiding in Christ; and this can only be by his abiding in us. "Abide in me, and I in you." But how do we abide in him? Mainly by faith, hope, and love, for these are the three chief graces of the Spirit which are exercised upon the Person and work of the Son of God. But as a matter of faith and experience, we have also to learn that to abide in Christ needs prayer and watchfulness, patience and self-denial, separation from the world and things worldly, study of the Scriptures and secret meditation, attendance on the means of grace, and, though last, not least, much inward exercise of soul. The Lord is, so to speak, very chary of his presence. Any indulged sin; any forbidden gratification; any bosom idol; any lightness or carnality; any abuse of the comforts of house and home, wife and children, food and raiment; any snare of business or occupation; any negligence in prayer, reading, watching the heart and mouth; any conformity to the world and worldly professors; in a word, anything contrary to his mind and will, offensive to the eyes of his holiness and purity, inconsistent with godly fear in a tender conscience, or unbecoming our holy profession, it matters not whether little or much, whether seen or unseen by human eye - all provoke the Lord to deny the soul the enjoyment of his presence. And yet with all his purity and holiness and severity against sin, he is full of pity and compassion to those who fear and love his great and glorious name. When these sins are felt, and these backslidings confessed, he will turn again and not retain his anger for ever. When repenting Israel returns unto the Lord his God, with the words in his heart and mouth: "Take away all iniquity, and receive us graciously"; then the Lord answers, "I will heal their backsliding, I will love them freely: for mine anger is turned away from him. I will be as the dew unto Israel: he shall grow as the lily, and cast forth his roots as Lebanon." Then, under the influence of his love, Israel cries aloud: "Who is a God like unto thee, that pardoneth iniquity, and passeth by the transgression of the remnant of his heritage? he retaineth not his anger for ever, because he delighteth in mercy. He will turn again, he will have compassion upon us; he will subdue our iniquities; and thou wilt cast all their sins into the depths of the sea."

December 30

"Better is the end of a thing than the beginning thereof." – Ecclesiastes 7. 8.

Thus saith the wise man, and it is often true in natural things, but invariably so in divine. Rarely at first can we foresee what will be the issue of any matter which we take in hand. We may begin it with much hope, and find in the end those hopes sadly disappointed. We may begin it with much fear, and find from the event those fears utterly groundless. Whatever we take in hand it is very rare that our expectations are fully carried out, for we have again and again to learn that "man's heart deviseth his way, but the Lord directeth his steps," and that there are many devices in a man's heart, nevertheless the counsel of the Lord, that and that only, shall stand. But so far as we are amongst the family of God, and as such are under especial guidance and divine teaching and leading, whether our first expectations are accomplished or not, the end stamps wisdom and goodness upon all the dealings of God with us both in providence and in grace. However chequered his path has been; however, as Job speaks, his purposes have been broken off, even the thoughts of his heart; however when he looked for good, then evil came unto him, and when he waited for light there came darkness; whatever bitter things God seemed to write against him when he made him to possess the sins of his youth, yet sooner or later every child of God will be able to say, "O how great is thy goodness which thou hast laid up for them that fear thee!" and this will embolden him to add, "Surely goodness and mercy shall follow me, as they have already followed me, all the days of my life, and I shall dwell in the house of the Lord for ever."

December 31

"All flesh is as grass, and all the glory of man as the flower of grass. The grass withereth, and the flower thereof falleth away: but the word of the Lord endureth for ever. And this is the word which by the gospel is preached unto you." – 1 Peter 1. 24, 25.

All flesh, and everything that springs from the flesh, and is connected with the flesh, is as grass, which, for a time, looks green and flourishing, but touched with the mower's scythe, or scorched by the midday sun, soon withers and fades away. Such is all flesh, without exception, from the highest to the lowest. As in nature, some grass grows thicker and longer than other, and makes, for a while, a brighter show, yet the scythe makes no distinction between the light crop and the heavy, so the scythe of death mows down with equal sweep the rich and the poor, and lays in one common grave all the children of men. You have seen sometimes in the early spring the grass in flower, and you have noticed those little yellowish "anthers", as they are termed, which tremble at every breeze. This is "the flower of grass"; and though so inconspicuous as almost to escape observation, yet as much its flower as the tulip or the rose is the flower of the plant which bears each. Now, as the grass withereth, so the flower thereof falleth away. It never had, at its best state, much permanency or strength of endurance, for it hung as by a thread, and it required but a little gust of wind to blow it away, and make it as though it never had been. Such is all the pride of the flesh, and all the glory of man.

But is there nothing that endures amidst all that thus withers and falls away? Yes, the word of the Lord. "And this is the word which by the gospel is preached unto you." Now, the same gospel which was preached by the Apostles is preached unto us in the word of truth which we have in our hands; and if we have received that gospel into a believing heart, we have received for ourselves that word of the Lord which endureth for ever. And thus, though all our own flesh is as grass, and all in which we might naturally glory is but as the flower of grass, and though this grass must wither in death, and the flower thereof shall fall away, when the place which now knoweth us shall know us no more, yet we have an enduring substance in the gospel of the grace of God, and, so far as we have received that gospel, and known it to be the power of God unto salvation, when our earthly house of this tabernacle is dissolved, we have a building of God, a house not made with hands, eternal in the heavens.

Index of Scripture References

Habakkuk

Hebrews

Hosea

Isaiah

James

Jeremiah

Job

John

Revelation

Romans